W9-AVQ-009

Mastering The Spring Creeks

A Fly Angler's Guide

BY JOHN SHEWEY

Mastering The Spring Creeks

A Fly Angler's Guide

BY JOHN SHEWEY

Frank Amato
PORTLAND

Dedication

To Tim Blount, Dewey Weddington and Forrest Maxwell and to the various collection of Shewey's who have shared my angling world: Good Fishing Partners are a Rare Breed.

Acknowledgements

I wish to thank McKenzie Flies, Umpqua Feather Merchants, Mike Lawson and Brant Oswald for their generosity and support in providing me with many of the flies photographed for this book— tying all the flies myself would have been a monumental and time-consuming task.

Many people offered ideas, suggestions and support for this project. I wish to thank all of them and hope I haven't forgotten anyone: Bill Stanley for his enthusiasm about the idea; Tim Blount, Dave McNeese, Brent Snow, Nelson Ishiyama, and Lou Lunte (The Nature Conservancy) for their valuable suggestions on format and content of the book; Chuck Kline (The Fly Shop in Redding), Mike Lawson (Henry's Fork Angler's Inc.), Brant Oswald and George Anderson (The Yellowstone Angler), Peter Crow (Silver Creek Outfitters) for helping in the compilation of hatch charts, and Frank Amato for believing in the project.

Also, I offer a special thanks to Tim Blount, who has put up with me on many a spring creek outing and who has helped in testing many theories and concepts on flatwater fly angling. I also wish to thank DeAnn for quietly accepting the heap of furs and feathers that littered my tying desk and surrounding area for weeks on end during the fly-photography phase of this project and for tolerating my continual absences while I am off partaking in "field research."

Finally, I offer a thanks from afar to Doug Swisher and Carl Richards, whose book *Selective Trout* I read cover to cover at the age of 12: In those days, growing up in Idaho, I spent nearly every summer day on the stream and I learned quickly the value of many of the observations discussed in *Selective Trout*. The book is as valuable today as it was then.

PHOTO CREDITS:
All photos by John Shewey except the following:
Pages 46, 48B, 61, 76-77, 80, 84, 95, 102-103, 124, 134, 136, 138, 139: by Jim Schollmeyer.
Pages 48A, 48C, 48D, 69, 70B, 73, 98, 109: by Dave McNeese.
Pages 130, 132: by Mike Mercer.

Illustrations by Bill Herzog

JOHN SHEWEY
First Edition, 1994

Frank Amato Publications
P.O. Box 82112 • Portland, Oregon 97282

Copyright, 1994, by John Shewey
Book Design by Kristi Workman

Printed in Hong Kong
Softbound ISBN: 1-57188-000-3 • Hardbound ISBN: 1-57188-001-1

CONTENTS

Introduction

The spring creeks of the West—those silky smooth meandering streams whose waters emanate from springs, rather than directly from snowmelt—offer perhaps the ultimate challenge for trout anglers. Waters like the Henry's Fork, Silver Creek and Fall River are famed for their immense hatches and big, difficult trout. Such streams carry with them a reputation for humbling the most experienced of anglers. This they can do. But much of that reputation is suspect: A fly fishing writer visits one of the famous spring creeks and doesn't do particularly well. He goes home to his freestone waters, regains some confidence and then writes an article telling just how rudely those spring creeks can treat the inexperienced angler.

Spring sources like Big Springs and the springs that feed Idaho's Silver Creek assure that such streams remain comparatively stable in both water volume and temperature.

That article appears in a national publication. Fly anglers read the article and some of them ask themselves how they could possibly hope to have any success if the popular literature says the Western spring creeks are not for the inexperienced and the uninitiated.

I'm not picking on any writers in particular here. Rather I am offering a theory on why the Western spring creeks have gained reputations that far exceed their respective realities. How many times have we read about the Henry's Fork and Silver Creek and Fall River? The articles have appeared for years, many of them similar in scope. They harp on the incredible wisdom of these spring creek trout and sometimes they seem to suggest that, in order to expect success on these waters, anglers must first become world-class magicians with a rod and experts in entomology and Latin.

The truth is this: First, the Western spring creeks are phenomenally rich in insect life. In such an environment, trout tend to feed selectively simply because such a feeding strategy makes the most sense. Second, these fish live under clear, smooth waters where they can detect danger at a greater distance than can their brethren living in the freestone rivers. Third, the trout inhabiting the Western spring creeks see a lot of anglers and a lot of artificial flies.

Lastly, spring creek veterans are rarely concerned with how many fish they catch each day because they understand that each good fish takes time and that each situation is challenging for different reasons. Spring creek anglers are hunters as much as fly fishers. Would you expect to bag 20 deer in a day afield? Then why set yourself up for failure by defining a successful day astream by the number of trout you bring to the net? By the very nature of the streams themselves, the trout that inhabit them, and the hatches that grace them, spring creeks are not meant for the counters amongst our ranks.

So first and foremost, understand that most spring creek regulars define their success one fish at a time, whether that means spending an hour, or a day on one trout. Once you appreciate that way of thinking, you need only concern yourself with the aforementioned peculiar characteristics of our Western spring creeks. To deal effectively with these characteristics—smooth water, selective trout, with trout that see a lot of people—fly anglers must simply learn and apply a few new techniques, most of which are not all that different from the fly fishing strategies and tactics we all grew up with.

That is the point of this book. I hope to offer an in-depth look at the techniques and strategies that will, with just a little practice, help you enjoy fly fishing at its aesthetic finest on the glassy waters of the Western spring creeks.

The real beauty of the strategies and tactics employed on the Western spring creeks and explored in this book is that they are applicable, for the most part, to any other trout stream. Learning the techniques used to effectively fish the spring creeks cannot help but improve your success on other waters.

So go to the spring creeks. Fish these waters as every fly angler deserves to. Don't let the hype—the reputations—frighten you away from what might be the most intriguing of angling experiences. But first learn the basic techniques for spring-creek angling so you can go afield with the right tools for the job and with the confidence to use them. Then ask questions: visit the fly shops that specialize in particular streams—Mike Lawson's Henry's Fork Angler, Silver Creek Outfitters, The Fly Shop in Redding, California, Craig Mathew's Blue Ribbon Fly Shop in West Yellowstone and several others (listed in the chapters on particular waters). The people who operate these shops know their home waters and are only too happy to give you the scoop on what's going on and what flies will produce at any given time of year.

Above all, go fishing. Visit the spring creeks. Experience them. Enjoy them for all their splendor. The wonderful hatches, the beautiful trout, the moose and her calf at mid-river on the Henry's Fork, the deer contently chewing willow greens on Silver Creek, the summer thunderstorm that casts the most angelic of hues over the valleys—all these things contribute to the spring-creek experience.

When frustration rears its head on the stream, understand that not all trout are always catchable. Just look for those that you can catch and enjoy everything the spring creeks have to offer. Pull up a streamside rock and just watch for a time. A friend of mine, Forrest Maxwell, says that the very best fly angler is the one who enjoys him or herself the most when astream. That is the best measurement of angling prowess I have ever heard and by that definition, Forrest is certainly one of the best anglers I know: His days and hours astream are perpetual enjoyment for himself and for those around him.

That is what the spring creeks mean to me: perpetual enjoyment, whether it be a day filled with dense hatches and numerous hook-ups or a frustrating day of fishing contrasted by the shear, intense beauty of our Western landscapes.

Preface:
The Spring Creek Defined

What, exactly, comprises a spring creek? First and foremost, a spring creek must emanate from an underground source—a spring. But beyond that, what characteristics of these streams make them such wonderful fisheries?

Indeed, if we examine all the spring creeks of the West, we find a collage of different images. But these images share common elements. Their waters are, for the most part, flat and smooth, owing to the gentle gradient of most spring creeks. Conversely, the riffles and rapids of our freestone streams belie their comparatively steep gradients. Naturally, some freestone rivers do indeed feature relatively gentle slope, and can look very much like a spring creek.

But spring creeks, being a product of underground sources, produce comparatively constant flows. Where a freestone river might explode with rage at the onset of the spring thaw and shrink to a mere trickle by late August, a spring creek ambles along at about the same level from season to season. Lou Lunte, Silver Creek Area Manager for the Nature Conservancy in Idaho, offers a comparison of relative stream flows: The Big Wood River, a freestone stream near Silver Creek, might vary from 200 cubic feet per second (cfs) between late summer and late winter, to as much as 2,000 cfs during the height of spring run-off (e.g. May-June). Nearby, Silver Creek runs as high as 200+ cfs or as low as 100 cfs or slightly less—a minimal change in flow when compared to the drastic seasonal flow changes experienced on the Big Wood. (During 1992, Silver Creek flows measured near the Nature Conservancy Visitor's Center ran between about 80 cfs and 118 cfs.)

This pattern is typical. Spring creeks remain at a fairly constant level throughout the year while the freestone rivers, inundated by snowmelt, swell to unruly levels during spring and early summer only to shrink to mere fractions of that size by late summer or early fall. The freestone rivers, swollen by snowmelt, experience thorough "scouring" each spring. Scouring, as the term suggests, refers to the way swollen spring flows sweep away debris from the river bed, at times so powerfully as to alter the channels themselves. While this scouring process has its benefits (e.g. cleaning sediment from spawning gravel) it also eliminates the opportunity for rooted aquatic plants to grow in any density.

These rooted plants are another characteristic of the spring creeks and their lush growth in our Western spring creeks is, in part, testimony to the lack of severe streambed scouring. While some rather flat freestone rivers may develop extensive algae growth, few (except some tailwaters) are able to grow extensive rooted aquatic weeds.

These rooted plants, which provide ample habitat for the phenomenal insect densities found in the spring creeks, also owe their existence to the relative alkalinity of the West-ern spring creeks. Due in part to features of the geography, the Western springs creeks tend to be slightly alkaline as opposed to the freestone rivers, which are generally more acidic than alkaline. (Silver Creek has a PH level between 7 and 8, while the Big Wood River is slightly acidic with a PH level of less than 7).

Finally, water temperature plays a vital role in the spring-creek habitat. At its source—at the springs themselves—the water that creates our Western spring creeks is usually in the low 50's (Fahrenheit). From these sources, as the water follows its meander, the temperature increases or decreases gradually, sometimes becoming frigid during the coldest part of winter, but rarely exceeding the mid-60's during the summer. Conversely, freestone rivers often experience dramatic and quite sudden temperature changes.

In most spring creeks, trout can take refuge from ocassional temperature extremes simply by seeking proximity to the springs themselves, where the water temperature is constant. Moreover, since the coldest water (during the height of winter) and the warmest water (which, again, rarely exceeds the mid-60's) reach their respective peaks very gradually, trout have ample time to acclimate.

The combination of these factors—spring sources that create stable water temperatures and stable water levels; comparatively alkaline water; gentle gradiant—allow for tremendous aquatic weed growth and thus abundant insect habitat in the spring creeks. In turn, the tremendous insect densities produce fast-growing trout. It is these things that define the spring creek both in the geographic sense and in the angling sense.

Big Springs is called the "birth place" of the Henry's Fork.

Prologue:
A Day On a Spring Creek

Normally I wouldn't be on the water until 9:30 or so during September, but I wanted to shoot photos in the early morning light. I was up at dawn to do just that, but was greeted by ominous, low-slung, soggy-looking clouds that cloaked the entire plain through which flows the Harriman section of the Henry's Fork.

What the hell. I was up; I might as well have a look at the river. I couldn't don my neoprenes fast enough in the 40-degree morning chill and was soon trudging along the north bank upstream from Osborn Bridge.

A lot of anglers pass by that first flat pool a few hundred yards above Osborn Bridge: It is deep and swift; difficult to wade and tough to fish. I love that pool. It has been good to me over the years. My friend Tim Blount got spooled there by a trout the size of a steelhead.

The rain held off so far and I could scarcely believe what I was seeing: Trout rising to little olive mayflies before 8 a.m. Too early in the morning for me to grapple with a No. 20 imitation, so I tied on a No. 16 chocolate-colored pattern—easy to see on the water and I assumed the trout had seen enough of the mahogany dun mayflies, which hatch during early autumn, to recognize them as both edible and worthy of pursuit. Besides, the little olive mayflies didn't seem numerous enough to trigger ultra-selective feeding.

I needed several casts to figure out the currents, but in short order my mahogany dun pattern had landed one rainbow, hooked and lost two others, and risen a fourth. I tried to rise that last fish again, but gave up after a few casts figuring that pool had given me more than I deserved anyway. They were nice rainbows, all around 16 inches, but only a warm-up for things to come that day.

Following the trail on the river's northeast bank, I rounded the corner to the first really large pool. Surely I was living an angler's dream: At least two dozen large rainbows were rhythmically devouring mayflies with methodical, gulping rises. The tail of that pool is deep and I came within two inches of a thorough soaking. Still, after some half dozen drifts, my mahogany dun pattern had fooled a rainbow that ran about 20 inches.

Having released that fish, I waded back through the channel and into position a mere 10 feet from the nearest trout. Lush underwater weed growth covered my approach perfectly. I made a conscious effort to pick out the largest trout, but this proved a difficult task considering not a fish in the group was less than 18 inches.

Almost immediately another trout gulped my fly. After two or three minutes I was sure I would beach that one, but he pulled free. I hooked two more of those pigs before they lost interest in the mahogany dun pattern. (I had yet to see a real mahogany dun, incidentally).

I switched to a little Griffith's gnat simply because it would be easy to see on the water. On the first cast the gnat took a 20-inch 'bow that showed scarring from a close call with an osprey. The Griffith's gnat seemed sure to be a winner, but some 30 casts later it had not fooled another trout.

Still reluctant to switch to a tiny olive mayfly imitation (too hard to see on the water, plus the fish hadn't acted too fussy up till then), I tried an admittedly oversized olive comparadun, a #18 I believe. The comparadun hooked another 20-inch 'bow, but the hook bent out on the initial run.

For the time being, I bent the point back into position and cast again—bad hook or not, the fly had drawn a confident rise. It did so again, but I bumbled the chance by leaving too much slack on the water.

Two hours passed as I worked that pod of trout. They just kept feeding and feeding all morning. A mother pelican, escorting a single youth that was a 3/4-size exact duplicate of the parent, glided past me some 40 feet away—so close I thought I read a look of bemusement in the mother's eye at the sight of a lone angler up to his armpits in her river.

About 10 a.m. the mahogany dun hatch began for real.

A beautiful little mayfly, these mahogany duns rarely hatch in dense numbers, but instead emerge rather sporadically over a period of several hours. This situation is generally to the angler's advantage because trout get used to seeing the mayflies for much of the day.

I switched back to the No. 16 mahogany dun pattern that had scored earlier. The fly's success began anew and I stood in that deep water until noon, by which time my feet were frozen despite 5mm neoprenes. During that span, a half dozen trout had taken the mahogany dun pattern. Several more fish continued to feed, but I couldn't fool them.

By then the low cloud cover had partially burned off, yielding to huge, dark thunderheads and the typical accompanying wind. Occasionally, sporadic bursts of sunshine quelled the breeze long enough to allow for reasonably easy casting.

I sat on a rock, thawing my extremities and hoping to rest those trout for a while. Countless ducks, some of them still re-growing their plummage after the late summer molt, fed and preened at mid-river, sitting in the middle of huge moss-beds. Mallards, pintails, widgeon, shoveler, blue-wing teal, ringnecks, goldeneye, cinnamon teal, ruddy ducks, gadwall—the variety was astonishing, and add to that a fair smattering of geese and a few majestic trumpeter swans.

When I could finally feel my thawing toes, I decided to head up river. Why I would leave a pod of trout like that I can't really explain except to say that I've always been a wanderer: I like to see the far bank or the upper end or around the next corner. I just like to wander.

So I started up the bank. Three anglers were fishing the big pool just below the old ranch buildings. Between us lay a huge, sprawling, weed-choked expanse of classic spring creek, the east bank of which offered a shallow, 20-foot-wide channel separated from the main river by a narrow, dense weed bed that ran parallel to shore for some 200 yards.

A lot of people walk right by this channel. If you fish the Henry's Fork, don't make that mistake. You can almost always find a bank feeder or two there, usually in the vicinity of one of the fallen logs protruding from the three-foot-high bank. I found three such trout that day.

The first required a very quiet approach, but then proved a sucker for a red ant. A fat hen rainbow, she went four pounds with ease. The second trout made amends for her sister: I couldn't touch that fish. In the process of being humbled, however, I noticed a riseform about 40 yards below and tight against the bank.

In approaching the first two trout, I had snuck into the water under cover of three lodgepole pines. But no such cover was available downstream. I walked back into the woods, giving the trout a wide berth. Certain I was well downstream from the trout's position, I approached the water's edge to await further rises that would help me pin down the rainbow's precise location. Having accomplished that, I again cut a wide loop, well back from the bank until I figured I was directly in line with the fish.

From there I bent low, stalking toward the bank. Then I dropped to all fours and crawled quietly through the hip-high grass until just a few dense tufts of grass shielded me from the trout. Ever so carefully I peered over the top of the weeds. He was huge. A rainbow of at least five pounds.

I eased into a sitting position, Indian-style, with my legs crossed. The grass concealed me quite perfectly. I stripped line off the reel, coiling it into my lap. A simple flip cast would do. I pulled all 13 feet of leader outside the last guide, followed by about five feet of line, all the while keeping the rod pointed to the rear, well out of the trout's vision.

The grass that had so nicely concealed my approach now exacted some form of twisted revenge. The densely packed little seed pods atop the stems snagged my tippet and leader in several places and freeing the monofilament proved frustrating at best. All I needed was a simple flip cast, but the grass seemed intent on foiling my efforts. For once the wind came to my rescue. Usually the bane of fly anglers, this particular wind began blowing gently from across the river, just strong enough to balloon my leader into an airborn arc to the rear, completely free of the weeds.

I still held the fly in one hand, but released it as I immediately flipped the line streamward. The ant pattern landed some six feet ahead of the trout, who was quietly investigating everything passing overhead. The fish, under a mere 10 inches of water, would gently rise toward the surface to examine and perhaps intercept whatever hapless trout food drifted in the silent currents.

Such was the case with my ant. My cast sailed a bit too far into the river, so I immediately skated the fly shoreward. Then I lowered the rod tip and watched breathlessly as the ant drifted at a nerve-racking deliberate pace toward the big rainbow.

With utter confidence; without a hint of hesitation, the trout glided effortlessly and gracefully upward, head slightly elevated, and stuck its massive nose into the terrestrial world just long enough to slurp in my ant with a deep "gulp."

I struck way too soon. I should have let the fish turn downward before I raised the rod tip, but everything seemed to be moving in slow motion. I thought my slight raising of the rod tip would happen in the same slow motion, but such was not the case. I felt the fly hang ever so briefly in the front of the trout's mouth. He felt the pressure, thrashed wildly, and was gone.

I anticipated and hurried when I should have just reacted. But I'll never forget that trout—he was awesome. The situation was thrilling. The opportunity was rare. It was a hell of a good day whether I beached that fish or not.

Early afternoon sunshine squelched most of the mayfly activity, but I rose a couple fish to ants along the grassy banks of the islands between the ranch buildings and the old wooden bridge. Then, for 20 minutes, a severe thundershower squelched my activity. I took shelter under a dense stand of young lodgepoles while a very black cloud bank descended on the valley.

A bit later, on the way back downstream, I noticed a large trout rising steadily just past midriver in the big pool just around the corner from the last of those islands. The red ant pattern, despite the fact that it was dragging ever so slightly when the fish rose to it, fooled what turned out to be one of the biggest trout I've ever hooked on the Railroad Ranch. He shot straight up in the air like a missile on the first leap, ran downstream, then upstream, then leaped straight up again. He looked and acted like a steelhead and spanned a good 26 or 27 inches. But my tippet was no match for that kind of power.

Another thundershower rolled through, the lightning piercing the steel-gray clouds with dazzling brilliance. This one ended quickly and behind it came the golden glow of filtered late-afternoon sunshine. The wind offered its final, faltering gusts and then all was quiet for the rest of this autumn afternoon.

It had been quite a day so far. Around 4 p.m. the hatch of those little olive mayflies (called blue-winged olives) began with renewed fervor, this time comprised of two species. One of these species was the tiny western olive, which usually runs along the lines of a No. 22 or 24 and whose emergence I have cursed vehemently on numerous occasions.

Luckily, however, the trout decided to eat any and all mayflies, not just the tiny ones.

That big pod of trout was back at it, rising profusely as they had been several hours earlier. Moreover, just upriver, in the channel between two dense matts of lush aquatic moss, another school of big trout was working. I tried these trout first. Using the massive, wavering underwater weeds for cover, I snuck to within 15 feet of several big rainbows.

A No. 20 olive dun did the trick, but only after some 30 or 40 drifts: The hatch was dense enough that one simply had to hope that the fly arrived in the trout's feeding lane at the exact moment the fish was ready to rise. Any other arrangement was made futile by the sheer number of naturals.

In any event I was into a nice trout, probably 19 or 20 inches and a leaper to boot. We remained attached through four jumps, after which I figured this trout was as good as on the beach. So I waded shoreward intent on photographing the colorful fish. Perhaps I was too eager or maybe the hook had just worked loose. I lost the trout and couldn't fool another from that suddenly suspicious school of rainbows.

Only when I quit working that school of trout did I notice the cow moose resting in the lodgepoles well up from the bank. Perhaps she had a calf with her, but I couldn't tell from that distance and I wasn't going to walk up there to find out: A mother moose is not to be trifled with.

The menacing thunderheads of earlier had retreated to the northeastern sky, while big, puffy cumulus clouds, lined in the silver of early evening and perforated by shafts of golden sunlight, reclaimed the western horizon. Due east, the Teton range gleamed ivory and overhead a few harmless stray storm clouds glowed vibrantly in an autumn shade of pastel orange.

A harvest moon clung quietly alone to the cloudless southern vastness, awaiting its moment of glory to come later. But now the sun was setting and the Island Park country caught fire in an ensemble of blazing fall colors.

I was alone, except for the birds: swans and pelicans; hundreds of ducks, including a huge flight of widgeon that had returned to the midriver moss beds after my departure. A brace of bluewing teal whistled overhead, the brilliant white crescent on the drake's deep gray face clearly discernable.

I sat on a rock and watched. Enjoyed. Appreciated. All of the evening brilliance reflected with redoubled magnificence in the glassy surface of Henry's Fork.

It was a great day.

A trout's position in the water, both vertically and horizantally, will in part determine your approach.

Approach & Positioning:
The First Steps in Effective Spring Creek Presentation

Selective, wary spring creek trout demand well-conceived presentation. I've seen many large trout taken on the "wrong" fly simply because the angler took the time to make the right approach.

The approach begins with the big picture. Consider all the variables: the position of the trout; the type of cover available to conceal your approach; the angle of the sun in relation to your position; direction and intensity of the wind in relation to casting strategy; potential casting obstructions; potential drift obstructions, such as mini-currents and swirls, weed growth, and current seams; the presence and position of other anglers or of wildlife; the actual feeding pattern of the trout in question and the anticipated duration of that feeding pattern or of the hatch in progress; your personal preferences in terms of how much time you are willing to devote to a single fish.

All of these factors (and perhaps others unique to particular waters) must be considered and accounted for before you ever uncork your fly. The sight of a large steadily feeding spring creek trout excites even the most experienced of anglers, no matter how many such trout they have cast to before. And certainly we should get excited about these most challenging of trout.

Controlling and channeling this excitement, however, is critical to consistent success on large, selective trout: Controlling the excitement assures that you will consider every element of the big picture; channeling nervous energy allows for steady concentration and, with experience, assures that correct approach and positioning will become second nature to you.

Like most dedicated trout anglers, my heart revs up considerably when I close in on a big spring creek trout. Many is the time, in fact, that I have cast with shaking hands. Despite such nervous energy, I try to concentrate on each step of the task at hand. Ideally, such concentration allows me to be at my best as a spring creek angler. I've talked to many experienced spring creek anglers who describe this level of concentration in similar terms: Calm assurance and confidence transcend the initial heart-racing excitement of locating and stalking a big trout that is sipping dry flies on glass-smooth water.

None of this is to suggest that experienced spring creek anglers don't make mistakes. I've blown more chances at big fish than I care to talk about—a missed cast, a dragging fly, a sloppy pick up, and so on. Still, I would rather put a fish down with a casting mistake than spook the trout be-fore ever having a chance to make the cast. That's where approach and positioning play a pivotal role: Careful approach and correct positioning allow you the opportunity to take your best shot at a good fish. With that in mind, let's examine the elements that comprise the "big picture."

Position of the Trout

Trout, of course, face upstream— a fact which is paramount to the very way in which we fish moving water. In a freestone river or tumbling creek, an angler can approach trout from the side or from below (downstream) and get quite close without the fish ever being the wiser.

Selective spring creek trout, however, are often best approached from above or from directly downstream so that you can avoid casting line over or near them (the specifics of which will be discussed in following chapters). Naturally, if you stalk a trout from above or from abreast, the trout stands a greater chance of detecting your presence than if approached from below.

Therefore, before approaching a rising trout, make every effort to determine its exact location, both vertically and horizontally, in the water column and in relation to structural elements that might help conceal your approach, such as weed beds, rocks and shoreline vegetation.

Over the years, a number of authors have suggested that vertical position of the trout is of concern because it determines, in part, the extent of the fish's vision above the water. The idea is that trout hovering just below the surface, sipping insects at leisure, has a much smaller "window" through which to view the terrestrial world than does a trout laying well below the surface.

Thus, during a heavy hatch, when trout are content to remain just under the surface, you can often approach quite close. This is frequently the case during dense emergences of mayflies, caddis pupa and chironomids and when trout are feeding heavily on spent caddis, swarming flying ants or beetles.

Conversely, you might locate a trout laying a foot or two below the surface, perhaps in the shadow of a cut bank or under overhanging vegetation. When trout occupy such stations on a spring creek, they often feed opportunistically, alternating between subsurface foods and the occasional ant, beetle, hopper, egg-laying caddis or other morsel floating above. The "window" theory suggests that such fish,

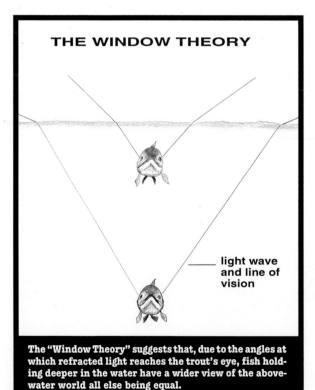

THE WINDOW THEORY

light wave and line of vision

The "Window Theory" suggests that, due to the angles at which refracted light reaches the trout's eye, fish holding deeper in the water have a wider view of the above-water world all else being equal.

holding close to the bottom in clear water, can see a wider view of the above-water world and should thus be approached even more carefully.

Indeed, my own experience suggests that trout hovering at the surface are more approachable than those holding on the bottom in two feet of water, but I cannot claim to be certain that the "window theory," which is based on the way refracted light reaches the trout's eye at different angles, is entirely responsible. After all, the extent of a trout's above-water vision certainly must also be affected by the depth, relative clarity and

from side to side, you can be sure the fish is content to hold just below the surface. In addition, these trout tend to sip insects quite deliberately.

On the other hand, trout rising from well below the surface often exhibit a less subtle rise, making a loud gulping noise or even throwing a splash. Such rises will seem quicker than rises from trout hovering at the surface. The difference can be subtle at times, but watch long enough and you can almost always determine how the trout is holding in the water column.

surface configuration of the water; light conditions; and significantly, the acuity of the trout's vision itself.

Another explanation about relative "approachability" makes a lot of sense too: When hovering right at the surface and sipping insects from a very narrow feeding lane during a dense hatch, a trout might simply be locked onto those bugs to such an extent that it more or less ignores all but a narrow swath of the surface.

Often, trout will feed during a more sparse hatch by rising through a foot or more of water each time they take a floating insect. These fish wait for an insect to float through their feeding window, ascend to take the bug, and then return to the depth at which they feel comfortable. By holding deeper, such trout can scan a wider surface area for food. Although unnecessary during dense emergences, this tactic allows trout to feed effectively on sparse hatches. According to the window-theory, trout exhibiting this feeding behavior have a wider view of the above-water area than trout holding just below the surface.

Trout holding and feeding right at the surface typically reveal their position by frequently breaking or "bulging" the water with their noses, tails, dorsal fins, and backs. Just watch a rising trout carefully. If you continually see fins and tail protruding from the water during the rise or while the fish works

Feeding Lanes

A trout's position in the horizontal water column plays a vital role in your approach as well. During heavy insect emergences or drifts, trout need only move a limited distance from side to side to find enough to eat. The horizontal extent to which a trout feeds during a hatch or insect drift is referred to as its "feeding lane."

A feeding lane might span only an inch or two during a "blanket hatch" of blue-winged olive mayflies; perhaps three feet or more during a drift of terrestrials or a sparse emergence of green drakes or *Callibaetis* mayflies. In other words, the width of a trout's feeding lane can vary widely depending on the density of insects on or under the surface.

Feeding lanes also vary from fish to fish. Older, larger trout tend to conserve energy during hatches by moving only as far as required to consume an ample supply of food. Younger trout, however, often travel further to feed. Several causes probably account for such actions. For starters, young trout are obviously less experienced at feeding in an energy-conserving mode. More importantly, though, the larger and more dominant trout tend to occupy the best feeding areas, where insect densities are greatest and where prey is harvested most efficiently.

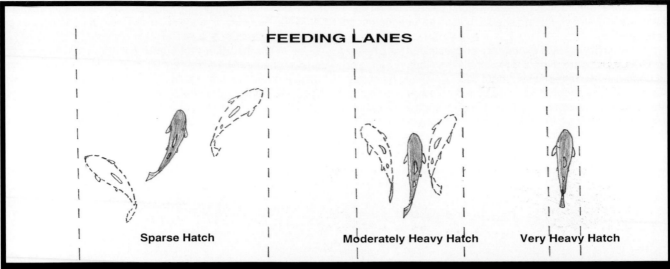

FEEDING LANES

Sparse Hatch

Moderately Heavy Hatch

Very Heavy Hatch

During a sparse hatch, trout must traverse a comparatively wide feeding lane to consume the same amount of food that they could eat while patrolling a very narrow feeding lane during a heavy hatch. Thus the width of a particular trout's feeding lane is largely a function of the relative density of food.

Both of these factors (density of food and the relative ease with which it can be eaten by trout) play critical roles in determining which lie will hold the best fish. Bear in mind that just because one place offers high food densities does not automatically mean that trout can feed most efficiently there.

Every year I fish a funnelling channel on the Henry's Fork that offers tremendous insect densities during the pale morning dun and *Baetis* emergences. The highest densities of the duns occur in the throat of the current, above which the nymphs are clustered in and around a large weed bed, which grows to the surface. Upon emergence, most of the duns are swept into the fastest part of the chute, which is about six feet wide.

After drifting through the throat of this channel, the duns (along with plenty of emergers and stillborns) are dispersed by a shifting array of slower currents and seams, resulting in less insects per square foot than are available in the somewhat faster water above.

Despite the high density of insects in the throat of this small run, I have never taken a trout of more than 14 inches there. However, in the slower currents some 10 feet below, I can usually count on finding two or three large trout feeding consistently on the mayflies.

These large, more dominant trout expend less energy feeding in the slower water than they would in the faster water above. Their feeding lanes are wider in the slow water than they might be in the fast water, but the tradeoff between energy expended patrolling a wider feeding lane and energy that would be required to hold in the faster water is quite apparently worth the effort. In other words, the trout would prefer to swim a little more from side to side to feed than to fight a faster current upstream.

Until I figured out why the big trout fed in the lower end of the aforementioned pool, I spooked a number of them by hooking and fighting small fish in the faster water. In an area of drastically different current speeds you will recognize such situations easily. But that channel on the Henry's Fork, like countless places on any spring creek, features current speeds that vary only slightly. Nonetheless, a slight difference in current

speed may be all that is required to move the largest trout out of an area of relatively higher food density.

In most cases, the opposite scenario occurs: The largest, most dominant trout occupy positions where they can feed from the narrowest feeding lanes. Just be aware of particular places on any given spring creek where such positioning is not the norm.

Obviously, the density of food available will determine the width of a trout's feeding lane. Areas where trout can feed on the highest number of organisms with the least amount of energy expended are aptly called prime feeding lies. When the dominant trout occupy these prime feeding lies, smaller, less aggressive fish are forced to reside in the less-than-ideal areas, where insect density may not be quite as high and where more energy is required to feed.

Naturally, the narrower the feeding lane, the more precise must be your presentation. If a trout is feeding in a three-inch-wide lane, your chances of hitting that target increase a great deal if you can get within 20 or 30 feet of the trout. In other words, don't try throwing a 60-foot cast to a narrow feeding lane unless you have no other choice. Most everybody I know can cast more accurately at 20 feet than at 50 or 60 feet.

One other thing about feeding lanes: Trout that traverse a two- or three-foot-wide feeding lane, rising here, then a few feet across current, then over here again but two feet downstream, etc., often patrol these lanes from deeper in the water column than if they were feeding in a narrow lane. So, as previously discussed, these trout may have a wider window through which to see above the surface.

In short, you should study the trout's position, both its horizontal position and its vertical position, before approaching. Study the trout's position in relation to its feeding lane as well as in relation to potential casting positions and stalking routes that you might use. Also account for currents, seams, swirls, weedbeds and various other obstacles related to the trout's position.

Choosing an Approach and a Position

Having determined the trout's position in the water

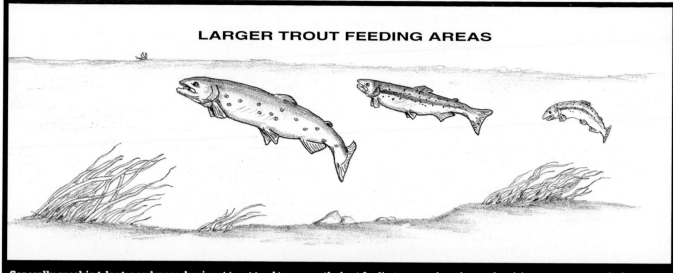

LARGER TROUT FEEDING AREAS

Generally speaking, larger and more dominant trout tend to occupy the best feeding areas, where insect densities are greatest and where prey is harvested most efficiently.

column and in relation to its surroundings, you can decide upon the best possible place from which to cast to that particular fish. Visualize your approach and your chosen casting position and then get there with all due stealth.

If a down-and-across presentation is possible with a particular fish, choose that angle first. If you must opt for an upstream presentation, choose one of two positions: 1. a position from which you can maximize your chances of drifting the fly ahead of the leader and line (through reach casts and/or curve casts) or 2. a position directly downstream from the fish, allowing you to cast the tippet directly over the trout's back with only the last two feet of tippet extending beyond his nose. Most large spring-creek trout—at least those that have been cast over countless times—will be easier duped if they never see the line or leader. A fly-first drift accomplished from the side and employing a reach-cast or a dead upstream cast directly over the trout's back can both accomplish this (these techniques are further discussed in following chapters).

Once you have located the ideal casting position, survey the surroundings for potential hazards to casting and drifting the fly. Plenty of room for a backcast? Enough casting room so you can avoid false casting right over the fish? Is the river between you and the fish clear of obstructions that could hinder the drift of your fly?

A few years ago I was walking along the bank after a morning's fishing on a small spring creek when I spotted the largest fish I'd seen all day. The big rainbow was sipping bugs just inches away from the shoreline. Intent on getting back to the car, I had walked up behind the fish, closing to within 15 feet before I saw the rise. I froze in my tracks, certain that I'd spooked the fish. But the trout rose twice more in quick succession and I knew he hadn't detected my presence.

"This should be an easy cast," I thought, figuring I could drop a No. 14 ant almost on top of the trout while purposely casting the line and most of the leader onto the bank. With no wasted motion I uncorked the fly, stripped a little line from the reel, made a carefully controlled backcast and immediately hung the fly in a tall willow behind me. In my haste and in my excitement I had simply not bothered to check my backcast

area. The trout took another natural while I stood there with my fly up a tree.

I gave a couple delicate pulls trying to free the fly—to no avail. I kneeled slowly, turned, pointed the rod at the fly, and pulled on the line to break the tippet. Sometimes 6X tippet seems amazingly strong. The leader finally broke, however, shaking the top of the willow vigorously. The trout quit rising and disappeared. I was out of his window; the top of that willow was not.

That same year I hooked the largest trout I've ever encountered on the Harriman Ranch on the Henry's Fork. In the process, I overcame plenty of adversity. Big black flying ants and a smattering of *Callibaetis* were on the menu that day. I located two large trout feeding vigorously in a slick on the far side of the river and just upstream from one of the deepest parts of the Harriman section.

I would have preferred to cross the river and approach from that side, but I couldn't risk doing so with several other anglers in the area, any one of whom might wade in on those fish before I could position myself. Besides, I would have had to go well out of my way to find a suitable crossing.

Knowing the river deepened over there and knowing I would be in for a tough wade, I started well upstream from the trout. I waded 40 or 50 yards before getting anywhere close to effective range. By that time, I was up to the bottom of my shorty vest and the river bed steepened exponentially from there.

Twenty five feet away, the trout continued feeding rapaciously on the ants, patrolling feeding lanes about 18 inches wide. Between me and the fish sprouted a large weed bed. Normally that weed bed would have been a blessing, providing me enough cover to sneak up on the fish, which occupied a rather fast slick comprised of myriad swirls and seams.

That was my intention—to use the wall of aquatic weeds as cover and to sneak within 12 feet or so of those trout. Child's play. The next two steps put an end to that strategy, however, with the first taking me to wader-top depth and the second step plunging me to my collar-bone in cold spring creek water.

Thoroughly soaked now, I had to back off a step

In planning your approach to a particular trout, you should account for the presence and attitude of wildlife because spooked birds or mammals can in turn frighten trout. Amongst the myriad types of animals found along some spring creeks are white pelicans, merganzers and moose.

because the current nearly swept me down river. So the weed bed now became a problem. My line would land on top of the mat of weeds when I cast to those fish, leaving me with only a couple feet of drag-free drift.

I was only slightly upstream of the trout and I knew that a steep downstream presentation would eliminate the weed bed as an obstacle, but would leave me with a 45 or 50 foot cast. No matter, though—unless I wanted to start the whole wade over again—because I could barely budge upstream in the deep, fast water. I had no intention of wading back toward shore and painstakingly beginning my approach anew, especially since I knew those good flying ant hatches could be rather fleeting affairs.

So I decided on a big-time pile cast with an upstream reach mend. First I added five more feet of tippet, freshly coiled from its spool. Then dug my feet into the gravel and carefully false cast well away from the fish to measure the amount of line I would need. I drew a deep breath then shot a wide loop across and slightly upstream, aiming the cast skyward to bring the leader and line down in something of a heap. As the line settled, I reached as far upstream and out as I could and then threw a second upstream mend after the line hit the water. The line came to a standstill on the mat of weeds, but that extra five feet of tippet landed in perfect coils on the current seam just beyond, some four feet above the nearest trout.

All I could do now was wait as the fly drifted downstream, hoping I had provided enough slack line and leader to allow the ant imitation to reach the trout before drag set in. Under no tension, the fly drifted to within Inches of dragging when the lead trout rose confidently. And a good thing because I could have never made a second such presentation without spooking those trout on the pick-up.

Landing that trout was a different matter. Suffice it to say that I successfully waded downstream through one of the deepest pools on the Ranch (floated through or flailed through might be more accurate). I even found my hat down by Osborn Bridge later that day.

The point of this anecdote is that I considered the appropriate variables and also successfully adjusted my tactics when unanticipated obstacles threatened my efforts. In any event, my initial decisions on approach and positioning were central to hooking that trout. I may have more easily approached the trout from the other bank, but chose not to because of the proximity of other anglers. Rarely, in fact, will you encounter a situation that offers only one approach.

I have read many times that each trout can be approached from only one ideal position, the remaining approaches all being less desireable. In an Orwellian world, where every

angler possessed identical skills, identical physical ability, and identical desires, this might prove true. In reality, however, most trout offer several approach alternatives, any one of which might be perfect for you, but lousy for the next angler simply due to differences in skill, wading ability, casting style or whimsical preferences.

Actually, the key to spring creek situations is to choose an approach that best suits that situation's critical variables. Sometimes the obstacles are few and related only to the appropriate position and cast relative to your skills and desires. Frequently, though, you must consider additional variables, such as other anglers in the area, wind conditions, expected duration of the trout's feeding pattern, and others specific to particular places.

On the bank feeder that I spooked by snagging my fly, I had failed to consider the variable of backcast room. But this variable presented no problem on the giant Henry's Fork rainbow because I had nothing but 100 feet of water behind me.

The physical variables central to that situation included the fact that other anglers were present, forcing me to abandon my plans to cross the river and approach from the other side; the deep, swift water, which dictated how far I could wade; the weedbed and the myriad mini-currents, which accounted for the type of cast and mends I choose to employ, and, to some extent, the expected duration of the feeding pattern. (Bear in mind also that my background as a West-coast steelhead angler, used to wading aggressively in the biggest, swiftest, coldest rivers around, assured me that wading deep in a spring creek posed no problem; another angler, whose wading experience is limited to tiny mountain streams, might have chosen an entirely different approach based simply on not considering such a deep wade as an option.)

Some anglers choose their position based on how they can best fight and land the trout once it is hooked. Certainly this approach is warranted if you place a high priority on landing your catch. I've always felt that actually landing a fish was secondary to the thrill of fooling and rising that trout. Naturally I enjoy landing and admiring a nice trout, but I'm not overly concerned with that end of it. That, of course, is a personal choice, reflecting the personal nature of our sport.

As referred to above, the expected duration of whatever hatch or feeding pattern is in progress is always a significant consideration in how you approach a trout. Some insect emergences are surprisingly brief in duration, requiring that an angler waste no time in choosing and pursuing a trout. Other hatches or insect drifts may last for hours, allowing more time to target and approach various trout.

Spring creek anglers usually go astream with a good

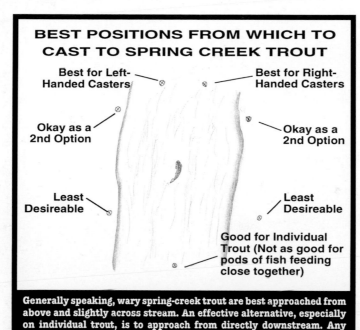

BEST POSITIONS FROM WHICH TO CAST TO SPRING CREEK TROUT

Best for Left-Handed Casters

Best for Right-Handed Casters

Okay as a 2nd Option

Okay as a 2nd Option

Least Desireable

Least Desireable

Good for Individual Trout (Not as good for pods of fish feeding close together)

Generally speaking, wary spring-creek trout are best approached from above and slightly across stream. An effective alternative, especially on individual trout, is to approach from directly downstream. Any position that requires you cast across numerous mixed currents or to throw line within the trout's field of vision should be considered a last resort.

idea of what hatches or insects drifts will occur and when these will occur. But the most experienced anglers soon learn to anticipate the duration of any given feeding pattern. Those lacking the experience to know this information should contact someone who does know—guides, fly shop personnel, or friends who have fished the river.

Finally, in choosing an approach and a position, remember to consider physical variables such as wind, angle of the sun, and the presence, location and attitude of wildlife.

As for the first two, wind and sun, simply choose an approach and a position that will minimize their tendency to be a pain in the neck. The wind, of course, can wreak havoc on our casting performance, but consider also the fact that it can wipe out a good mend just as easily. So select a casting position that will minimize any negative influence on the cast or mends. Certain casts can benefit from the wind. On many occasions I have used upstream winds to aid reach casts and reach mends and various other presentations.

In general, cross-winds tend to be most troublesome; head-winds and tail-winds, least so. A little extra power will drive a tight-looped cast into the wind with reasonable control and laying off a bit will compensated for a tail wind. But crosswinds require you to compensate by adjusting the size and power of the casting loop and by adjusting for lateral fly-line drift that can push your cast too far up or downstream. (Techniques for casting in the wind are covered in chapter 3).

In any event, a familiarity with your own casting skills and limitations will allow you to chose a casting position from which you can best nullify the effects of wind. Just be sure to test the wind and consider its potential effects before wading into any given position.

A bright sun, like wind, also requires your attention when planning an approach and a casting position. The problem with sun is four-fold: First, any shiny objects attached to your person can reflect sunlight in a manner that can spook trout. Second a tiny dry fly is terribly difficult to see if you face directly into surface glare. Third, trout may also have difficulty seeing your fly if they must look toward the sun to do so. Fourth and finally, shadows cast by you or by your rod, line or leader frequently spook wary spring creek trout.

To eliminate the first of these potential problems, just remove as many shiny objects as possible from the outside of your vest and other places. Clip the forceps to the inside of the vest; cover the pin-on reel and clippers with a pocket flap; use a non-glare fly reel if you own one or just be aware of reflections

from a metallic-colored reel; remove shiny pins or other decor from your vest and hat.

Another way to eliminate problems with reflection and also to minimize surface glare is simply to approach trout with the sun at your back. Be aware of your shadow, however, as a long shadow suddenly thrown over a feeding trout will almost always terminate your chance at that fish.

Trout may have trouble with the sun as well, primarily when they must look directly into the glare. Sometimes an oversized fly works wonders on these half-blinded trout; more frequently, though, the trout will simply alter their position or change their feeding pattern to avoid the full brunt of the sun's glare.

Finally, shadows —especially your own—can send a feeding trout scurrying for cover. Like most other elements of approach and positioning, shadow is a foreseeable problem for which you can plan accordingly. Even though you may prefer to keep the sun at your back, don't do so in a careless manner. This is especially critical early and late in the day when shadows are longest. In short, at all costs avoid throwing your shadow over feeding trout.

Like sun and wind, the presence of wildlife on most of our spring creeks is a foregone conclusion. On several occasions I have carefully stalked within range of sipping trout only to have a muskrat or otter swim feverishly across the creek to escape me or to have an unseen heron or waterfowl spook noisily from point-blank range. In many of these cases, the ensuing commotion spooked the trout into inactivity.

Similarly, I've had osprey, pelicans or mergansers fly over feeding trout at close range. Same result: spooked trout.

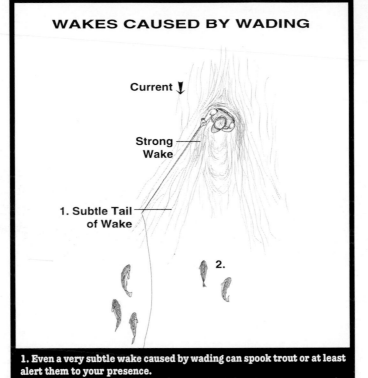

WAKES CAUSED BY WADING

Current

Strong Wake

1. Subtle Tail of Wake

2.

1. Even a very subtle wake caused by wading can spook trout or at least alert them to your presence.
2. Despite being inside the wake, trout holding downstream can be alerted to your presence by the change in current speed or orientation caused by your position in the stream above them. These fish might also be spooked by debris, dislodged by your wading, that drifts downstream.

Trout frightened by wildlife will usually resume feeding after a few minutes, although substantial commotion may put them down for keeps. I once accidentally ran two range bulls across a small spring creek, putting to rest all evidence of feeding activity by every trout within 50 yards. Herefords may not qualify as wildlife (although I've seen a few range bulls that probably should) but the result was the same.

All you can do about these incidents is to try to avoid spooking whatever animals reside on or near the stream. Sometimes by approaching slowly you can stir waterfowl or mammals to make their exit quietly. If not, you may have to rest the trout until they resume feeding. Sometimes luck plays a big role—such as when you don't see the heron in the shoreline grass until its too late or when a pair of pelicans fly lazily down

Aquatic weed and moss beds, especially those that grow to the surface, can provide excellent cover for anglers, allowing for close approach to trout holding on the far side of such growths. This photo shows some of the large weed beds on Idaho's Silver Creek.

the river and right over the trout with no prompting from you.

Undoubtedly the most bizarre incident I've had with regards to wildlife on a spring creek occurred on the Henry's Fork. For several years running I groveled in frustration when a flock of mudhens (coots) would flush noisily from a quiet backwater where several large trout fed. These trout would feed greedily a few feet below the grazing mudhens, benefitting from all the debris stirred up by the constant diving of the birds.

No matter how carefully I approached, the mudhens would either fly away or swim across the river. In either case, the trout would quit feeding. No matter how long I waited, the fish would not resume feeding until the coots returned. I tried everything, ridiculous and otherwise, all to no avail. No mudhens, no feeding trout. The birds created a chum line for the trout and served as an alarm mechanism to boot.

One year the coots disappeared altogether and I haven't seen them in that backwater since. Nor do the trout feed there any more. Too bad, because I had devised one last desperate ploy: I was intent on setting a string of decoys on the water the night before I tried for those trout.

Making The Wade: Get Close!

In any situation imagineable on a spring creek, you will want to get as close as possible to your target fish. This is especially true where dense hatches and narrow feeding lanes are concerned.

In fact, most of the casting tactics and line control techniques discussed in this book are predicated by the assumption that anglers will be positioned as close as possible to the trout. Certain tactics—flip mends, reach casts, slack-line casts—loose much of their inherent applicable value at distances beyond 30 or 40 feet.

Most of us loose some accuracy as casting distance increases, but more importantly, the longer the cast, the more currents the line must cross. Each of these currents, with their varying speeds and orientations, will exact different reactions in the fly line. Simply put, the more currents that your line and leader must absorb, the more likely the fly is to drag.

So get close, but do so with all due stealth. In choosing an appropriate path of approach, take advantage of any structures that can shield your movements from the trout. Voluminous aquatic moss and weedbeds are especially helpful in concealing your approach and, significantly, in buffeting the wake caused by your wading.

Weed and moss beds that grow to the surface, along with lush patches of sub-surface trailing weeds, are in fact, so valuable in concealing your approach that you should plan your wade to utilize these growths whenever possible.

On the lower end of Harriman Park on the Henry's Fork, the weed/moss beds grow so thick by late summer that they form virtual islands at mid-river. These massive weedbeds, while being more-or-less impenetrable to trout, can provide excellent cover for anglers. When trout rise on the perimeter of these extensive "islands," I like to position myself in the middle of the weeds and work one trout at a time, my movements all the while hidden by the lush vegetation.

The weeds are so thick in these mats that moving about is a slow, laborious process. Within five steps I'll be trudging along with 50 pounds of weeds trailing from my legs. Still, the work usually proves worthwhile because I can stalk to within 15 or 20 feet of many trout.

In the absence of such strategically located weedbeds, other structures can help conceal your approach. These might include fallen timber, boulders, shallow gravel bars, grass hummucks, small islands, or various shoreline features.

In many cases, especially on small spring creeks and on remote streams whose trout rarely see anglers, you might do well to stay out of the water. In such cases, any number of shoreline features can conceal your approach, including tall grass, shrubbery, trees, boulders, or any other handy objects.

No matter how you conceal your approach, though, if you wade, do so slowly, quietly and purposefully. Even if the trout don't actually see you, they may spook if a wave or wake from your movements passes over their heads or if you send a debris cloud (mud and debris dislodged by your feet) through them.

Even subtle wakes can spook trout: Sometimes just the very tail end of the V-shaped wake caused by the current pushing against your body can alert trout to your presence. Additionally, trout directly downstream might sense a change in current velocity or orientation caused by water deflecting off your body.

The key is to move slow and watch the trout. If the fish stop rising, then you should stop moving until they again begin to rise regularly. Once you are in position to cast, stop and watch for a few minutes. Are the fish rising in the same place and with the same frequency and intensity they exhibited before you stepped into the water? If not, just hold still until they return to the same rise pattern.

Also, if you have any doubt about being able to approach a trout from above without spooking her, you might consider an upstream wade. As we will discuss in depth in proceeding chapters, the downstream cast is frequently most effective for spring creek trout. Still, sometimes a trout can be caught completely unaware by an upstream approach followed by a cast that delivers the fly and a couple feet of tippet right over the fish's back. (The specifics of this technique are discussed in chapter 2.)

At times, no matter how carefully you wade, trout will move and begin feeding a few feet or a few yards away from their original position. Despite being alerted to and to some extent bothered by your presence, these trout still feed and can still be taken. Readjust your postion if necessary, again moving slowly and quietly.

Above all else, be patient in your wading. Move slowly and quietly, taking advantage of any available cover and don't hesitate to rest the fish if you detect a change in their feeding pattern or rythm.

"Tame" Wild Trout:
The Reality of Today's Spring Creeks

On our most popular spring creeks, trout get used to people: They will continue feeding despite the fact that you are standing within 15 feet and flailing away at them. This is not to say that such trout will in turn readily accept your offering. These fish (Idaho's Silver Creek is a great example) simply must continue feeding. If they quit eating every time an angler

happened by they would soon whither and die of starvation—the spring creeks can be that crowded.

So they continue rising as you approach; continue feeding as you cast from 15 feet away; continue eating as they steadfastly refuse to take your fly. I am convinced these trout become more selective in their feeding when they detect an angler's presence. What can you do? Start by staying farther away: Just because you can sneak within 12 or 15 feet of a pod of Silver Creek rainbows does not mean that you should do so. If they prove totally uncooperative, go find another batch of fish or look for loners. Or just stand still for 10 minutes before making that first cast.

Often, on the most crowded spring creeks, you will take a trout from a school of risers on the first or second good cast and then fail to move another fish. Period. Hooking that initial sacrificial lamb alerted the other trout to your presence. Move on. The surest way to drive a spring-creek guide into the psycho ward is to insist on casting to the same pod of trout all morning just because you hooked one on the first cast. Go find another pod or a single fish; return later and try for another from that initial batch of trout.

Just don't get stuck thinking that the trout or the stream is too tough. These days, with the voluminous fishing activity on our spring creeks, many trout have simply adapted by continuing to feed, in a very selective manner, in the presence of fly casters. Go on to another trout or another school of trout and treat even the tamest of trout as thoroughly wild: If you approach these fish with all the stealth and caution due a wild, timid trout that has never seen a human, you are likely to find them much more cooperative.

"Schooling" Trout

To this point, I've tossed around the concept of trout "schools," or more precisely "pods." These groupings of feeding trout are commonplace on the spring creeks. During a dense insect emergence or drift, big trout gather in groups of eight or ten to 40 or 50 individuals and feed ravenously, frequently moving about the stream in a constant state of flux.

At times these pod trout feed so heavily that their heads and backs constantly bulge through the surface creating a disturbance reminiscent of a huge pack of carp stranded in inches-deep water. When you locate such a pod of trout that remains stationery, you can have some of the best trout fishing on spring creeks: The trout seem to excite and compete with one another, causing them to loose a little of their native caution and allowing you to sneak rather close. (Such sights also have a way of making anglers loose their nerve.)

Play your cards right and you might take half a dozen trout or more from one pod. The key is to forget about flock shooting and work on one individual trout at a time. Think in terms of the perimeters first: Look for some of the largest fish to hold stations on the outside edges of a school of trout. If you spook these trout, you may well spook the entire pod, so, by fishing to them first instead of casting over them, you avoid that problem. All the rules of careful, well-conceived approach apply, but with the added dimension of considering what will happen if you spook one trout. In other words always think in terms of the domino effect: You spook the trout on the outside, he spooks the next two, they spook the rest and so on.

In fact as long as we're on the game analogy, how about comparing your approach to a game of billiards: You decide on a ball that you want to play and then you consider the kind of shot you will make with an eye towards setting up the next

Spring-creek trout often school together to feed, forming "pods" of anywhere from a few to dozens of individual fish. This pod of Silver Creek trout was responding to a hatch of blue-winged olive mayflies.

ball or balls. Screw up the initial shot and your strategy collapses for lack of a second opportunity. Indeed, when fishing to a pod of trout (or when simply fishing a section of stream with many rising individual trout), you may want to consider how your approach will affect other fish in addition to the one you are after.

Although the largest trout sometimes seem to occupy the fringes of these pods, you can never count on such positioning to be the rule. Sometimes a single huge trout will start rising right in the middle of a pod of smaller fish. On the Henry's Fork, Silver Creek and the Metolius, my fishing partner Tim Blount and I have watched trout of five or six pounds begin rising regularly in the middle of large pods of 14- to 20-inch individuals. Tim suggests that, during the course of the season, these huge trout habitually find that the center of the pod is the safest place to feed. Perhaps so.

Luckily, these trout that binge-feed in pods tend to be a little less wary than individual risers, probably as a result of gluttonous excitement and agitation on their part and as result of an otherwise glass-smooth surface temporarily transformed into a choppy riffle by their incessant sipping and gulping. For the same reasons—abundant food and ample opportunity to eat it—these pods of trout rarely stay spooked for very long if they are put off. Frequently they will begin feeding again within minutes, sometimes in the same place, sometimes a few yards up, down, or to one side.

Pods of feeding trout can occur anywhere: mid-stream, against the bank, or anywhere in between. Pin a school of trout against a bank and you've got it made as long as they hold still. Such pods, if they take up a position against the shore, are less likely to move about. On the other hand, mid-river pods are frequently on the move, usually working their way slowly upstream and often being difficult to intercept.

But intercept them, you must. Trying to chase a pod of trout up and down the stream generally results in failure and spooked fish. Instead, watch them for a while. Is the pod working slowly upstream, then across, then drifting downstream again before beginning the whole circuit again? Are they moving upstream, ever so slowly, and then simply backing down again in the same current lanes? Or are they progressing upriver only to disappear, perhaps reappearing downriver a bit later or perhaps simply vanishing?

By determining their general pattern, you can position yourself to intercept the trout. Not to worry if they don't happen your way: Roving pods of rising trout relish in frustrating fly anglers and they are damn good at it, so don't let it get to you. Instead simply play the game as best you can. Take advantage of any stationary pod of trout and do your best to position yourself to intercept those pods that are on the move. Your other option, in the face of roving pods of trout, is simply to ignore them and instead search for individuals or stationery packs of two, three or four fish. These might well prove easier to stalk much in the way that an individual elk is far simpler to approach than is a whole herd.

SPRING CREEK DIARY

August, 1988; Western Montana

Spring creeks weren't really on the agenda this trip, but we took a short cut via an old county road and in the process drove over a culvert through which flowed the prettiest little watercress-filled spring creek I'd ever seen. I slammed on the brakes and backed up for a look.

Reminiscent of a miniature Silver Creek, the stream meandered across a large pasture and was shaded on both banks by chest-high grass and willows. Some thoughtful landowner had fenced the creek to keep stock from destroying the riparian vegetation. This was a landowner we had to find.

On our third try we knocked on the right door. The property owner, himself a fly fisher, not only gave us permission but filled us in on the hatch we could expect that afternoon.

As he promised, *Baetis* mayflies choked the little stream from bank to bank. But it was tough with a capital T. We couldn't get close without sending every trout scurrying for cover. These weren't the tolerant fish of Silver Creek or the Henry's Fork. Our sole take that afternoon was a brace of 12-inch browns.

Again we called on the landowner in hopes of lining up permission for the next day. This he granted over a cup of coffee.

By 10 a.m. the following morning we stood in awe of a Trico spinner fall as dense as any we could remember anywhere. The trikes were too numerous; we fished small black ants and took two more browns.

The Trico's were long finished by noon, when a stiff breeze began whipping the shoreline grass. Hoppers. What a difference a day can make. For the next four hours we killed 'em on hoppers. Sneak through the grass, pitch a live hopper or two into the creek to locate a trout, then follow with the artificial. Brown trout to 16 inches and I didn't bother counting.

Again we called on the landowner, this time to say thank you and good-bye. He greeted us in the driveway as we pulled in, a certain excited glint in his eyes: "Bet you guys killed 'em with the wind blowin' and all!"

What a difference a day can make.

Chapter 2

Casting & Mending Techniques
For the Spring Creek Angler

The smooth, glassy, weed-infested waters characteristic of the spring creeks and the wary trout that inhabit these streams have, over the years, prompted fly anglers to develop innovative casting methods and line control techniques. For years, in fact, a handful of Western spring-creek anglers extoled the virtues of the downstream presentation for skittish flat-water trout. Their voices fell largely on deaf ears as presentation technique continued to focus on the traditional upstream and cross-stream tactics that worked so well on the waters fished by most anglers.

Western spring-creek trout, meanwhile, furthered their already-advanced education in the ways of anglers. The uncrowded spring creeks of the West quite suddenly yielded to the Henry's Fork, Silver Creek, Fall River and Hat Creek of today as fly fishing's popularity exploded during the latter half of the 1970's. Among the countless new inductees to the sport came many who were ready to ply their craft on the most challenging of trout waters, causing spring-creek trout to see exponentially more artificials.

Under these auspices, the downstream cast finally began gaining its deserved reputation as the single most important presentation technique in the arsenal of a Western spring-creek angler. Quite simply, spring-creek anglers realized that the downstream approach offered two overwhelming advantages over any other presentation: The trout always saw the fly first, before the leader and line could drift overhead and the line, leader and fly were never suspended in the air over the trout during the cast.

Spring-creek anglers also devised methods of accomplishing super-accurate drifts (required by narrow feeding lanes) while utilizing a downstream cast. One such method involved sliding the fly into the feeding lane after the line had landed on the water and then feeding slack line. California anglers called it the "Fall River Drift," or "Fall River Twitch," this idea of casting downstream to the fish, then sliding the fly into the exact feeding lane and finally shaking line out the rod tip to extend the drag-free drift well beyond actual casting range. But by whatever name the technique is known, a downstream presentation—especially in the hands of a practiced fly fisher—is deadly. More than that, it is a necessity.

In fact, when combined with various reach casting and mending techniques, the downstream presentation becomes even more formidable an approach for spooky flat-water trout. This is not to say that traditional upstream casts cannot succeed on the Western spring creeks because indeed they can: One effective method that proves its value time and again in certain situations is to cast the tippet directly over the trout's back so the fly lands two feet or less in front of the fish's nose. But this technique requires lots of practice and is not so easily mastered as the downstream presentation. We will, in this section, examine the aforementioned upstream cast. But first let's examine the always-important reach cast and then look at the "slide method" or "Fall River drift" and a variety of other downstream presentation methods.

A word of caution fishing downstream: Many anglers strike too hard when the trout rises, resulting in a broken tippet and lost fish. Don't set the hook! Watch the trout take the fly, then gently raise the rod tip,

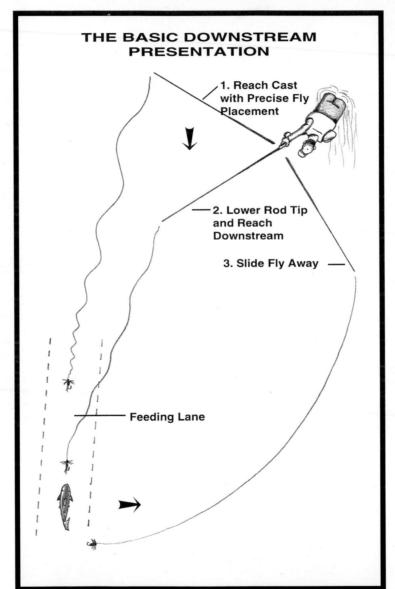

THE BASIC DOWNSTREAM PRESENTATION

1. Reach Cast with Precise Fly Placement

2. Lower Rod Tip and Reach Downstream

3. Slide Fly Away

Feeding Lane

1. Using an upstream reach cast, place the fly directly in the trout's feeding lane. **2.** Immediately lower the rod tip to the water's surface and reach the rod downstream, following the drift of the fly. **3.** If the fish does not take, allow the fly to drift a foot or two beyond the trout's position and then swing the rod toward the opposite side, sliding the fly away before beginning the next cast.

rather slowly, just enough so you feel the weight of the trout. A small, sharp hook needs very little encouragement from the angler to imbed itself securely in the jaw of a trout. Whatever else you do, don't jerk. When presenting a fly downstream, you must allow the trout to turn his head back under water before you tighten the line— otherwise you aren't likely to get a solid hook-up.

The Reach Cast

If you fish spring creeks frequently, reach casts become second nature, or at least they should: This casting technique, in its various forms, is so valuable to spring-creek presentation that to practiced anglers it is as automatic as a double haul is to the steelhead fly fisher.

The reach cast, in whatever way it is employed, helps to extend the drag-free drift of your fly by assuring that, even on a cross-stream presentation, all of the line lands upstream of the fly (and the fish). In accomplishing this, the reach cast necessarily places your line, leader and fly in whatever section of current you deem to be best suited to the type of drift you want.

The basic reach cast is simple to learn. Start by delivering a down-and-across cast, the forestroke aimed at your target. Just as the line straightens out over the water, reach upstream with the rod and with your casting arm. A correctly executed reach cast allows the line, leader and fly to touch down only at the completion of the upstream reach. Then follow the downstream drift of the fly with the rod tip, reaching and leaning downstream as the artificial approaches the target.

Naturally, you can execute both right- and left-side reach casts. Assume you are right handed and are casting down and to the right. As you deliver the cast, extend your arm and the rod across and upstream, leaning the same direction. As the line lands on the water, immediately begin following the drift with the rod tip, which should be lowered to the water's surface. As the drift reaches its end, lean and reach

Executing the basic reach cast: Deliver the forestroke as usual, but as the line straightens over the water, begin reaching the rod upstream (A). Immediately extend the casting arm as far as possible while leaning in the same direction (B), until the line touches down, at which point you should lower the rod tip and follow the drift of the fly (C).

Executing the cross-body reach cast: When your casting arm is on the downstream side and you want to execute an upstream reach cast, you can simply reach the rod and your arm across your body, leaning upstream as well.

downstream, pointing the rod tip at the fly. This is the right reach cast.

The left reach cast works the same way mechanically, but requires that you reach the rod across the left side of your body. Imagine that you are standing in the river, with your right arm and rod on the downstream side, and that you are casting down and across. As the line straightens toward its target, reach your right arm and the rod across your body to the left, leaning upstream and to the left in the process. Again, follow the drift with the rod tip.

If the trout doesn't take, allow the fly to drift three feet or so below the fish and then slide it and the line away before picking up for another cast. If casting to a target down and to the right, slide the fly out of the trout's feeding lane by pointing the rod tip downstream and to the left; if casting down and to the left, reverse the process, the objective being to first, avoid having the fly line and leader butt drift over the trout and second, slide the fly as far away from the trout as possible before

picking up for the next cast.

While steelhead fishing on some of Oregon's large rivers, I began using another reach-cast variation that has proven valuable on the spring creeks as well. Perhaps best labeled the "switch-reach cast," I use the technique to extend even further up and across with a left reach cast. To do this, execute the left reach cast as described above, but as your right (casting) arm reaches its maximum extension across your body, simply pass the rod over to your left hand and continue reaching and leaning. Then you can pass the rod back to your right hand as you follow the downstream drift with the rod tip. This technique, while it does require some practice, allows you to extend the left reach cast a considerable distance. (For left-hand casters, of course, the idea would simply be reversed and would be used to extend a right reach cast).

The reach cast, in whatever form it is employed, is one of the most valuable tactics for spring-creek anglers. We already examined the merits of the downstream approach and

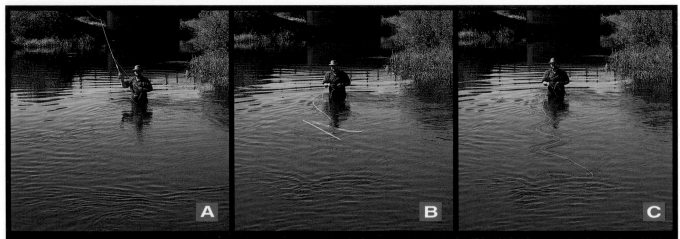

Executing the "serpentine" or "wiggle" cast: begin with a normal back cast (A), but just as the line straightens on the forestroke, wiggle the rod tip side to side with a quick side-to-side motion of the hand and wrist (B), causing the line and leader to land in a series of S-curves (C).

the reach cast can be used very effectively to perform such presentations. In fact, the reach cast allows you to create a downstream presentation even from an across-stream position. Thus the reach cast, in a wide variety of situations, will be your method of choice to accomplish drag-free drifts simply because such casts allow you to control the placement of the fly with considerable accuracy.

The "slide method" or "Fall River drift:"

On wary smooth-water trout, the downstream presentation outperforms more traditional approaches for a very simple reason: The fly arrives in the trout's field of vision before the line and leader. In fact, with a properly executed downstream presentation, you can offer the fly time and time again without ever showing more than two feet of tippet and a fly to the trout.

The "slide method" or "Fall River drift" is a downstream presentation comprised of three components: **1.** casting the fly downstream to the fish, **2.** dragging the fly into the precise feeding lane and **3.** immediately dropping the rod tip and shaking loose line onto the water to extend a drag-free drift.

Initial positioning is paramount to successfully using this technique. Wade in above your target fish. Remember that, because trout face upstream, they stand a better chance of detecting you when approached from above. Not only might they see you, but the fish also might spook at the sight of debris, stirred up by your wading, drifting over them. The general rule is to allow a bit more distance to a trout approached from above than one stalked from the downstream side. In other words, if from below you could sneak to within 20 feet of a trout, you probably should approach no closer than 30 or 35 feet when wading in from above.

Immediate conditions will dictate how close you can approach. Super-clear, slow water holding ridiculously shy trout might require a 60-foot cast. More often, by quietly moving slowly and by taking advantage of natural cover (especially aquatic weedbeds) you can approach to within 30 feet of a trout, sometimes considerably closer. Where voluminous weeds form walls of waving green trailers, you might be able to sneak within 15 feet of feeding trout, assuming, of course, that you keep those weeds between you and the fish.

In any event, an ideal casting position leaves you above and at a rod's length or less across from your target. From such a position, imagine three parallel lines extending downriver. Your position lies along the first line. Less than a rod's length away, the second line intersects the trout's position. The third line is your casting target, which lies beyond but close to the line marking the trout's position. Cast so your fly lands along this imaginary third line and two or three feet above the fish. Raise the rod tip to drag the fly into the trout's feeding lane, represented by the imaginary second line. Immediately lower the rod tip and reach toward the trout, simultaneously shaking slack line from the rod tip. This is the basic downstream presentation, but you're not done yet.

If the fly fails to draw a rise, allow it to drift one to four feet beyond the trout and then reach the rod back across your body, causing the fly and line to quietly slide away from the trout. Carefully dragging the fly away in this manner prevents the trout from seeing the fly line and leader butt overhead.

As soon as the line has drifted well to the side of the trout's position, you can cast again immediately. If you are positioned more than a rod's length across stream from the trout, you can simply pick up the line with a backstroke, change casting direction just slightly and drop the fly back onto that imaginary third line. If a rod's length or slightly less separates your position from the line intersecting the trout's position, you may have to draw the backcast high over your head, turning the cast in a half-circle motion on the forestroke. Under breezy conditions, the rather wide loop of this half-circle cast might prove uncontrollable. Instead, you might try picking up over your opposite shoulder, turning the cast slightly on the backstroke and finishing the realignment on the forestroke. The windiest of conditions (or when you are using a long cast) sometimes require that you make a full false cast prior to the next presentation. When your position is only a few feet away from directly upstream of the trout, you might choose a V-shaped stroke, rather high over your head, to turn the cast for the next presentation.

In any of these scenarios, the idea is to avoid casting over the trout and to drift your fly over the fish as many times as possible in as short a time span as possible. One trout might take your first good drift while another might take on the 50th presentation. If you cannot draw a rise despite numerous good drifts, try resting the trout for a minute or two between casts.

Executing the "switch-reach cast:" To extend the reach farther than is possible with a cross-body reach cast, deliver a normal forestroke (A) and then, as the line straightens toward the target, pass the rod to your opposite (upstream hand in this example) with smooth, fluid motion (B); as you switch hands with the rod, begin reaching and leaning upstream (C) until the line falls on the water with leader in line with target (D).

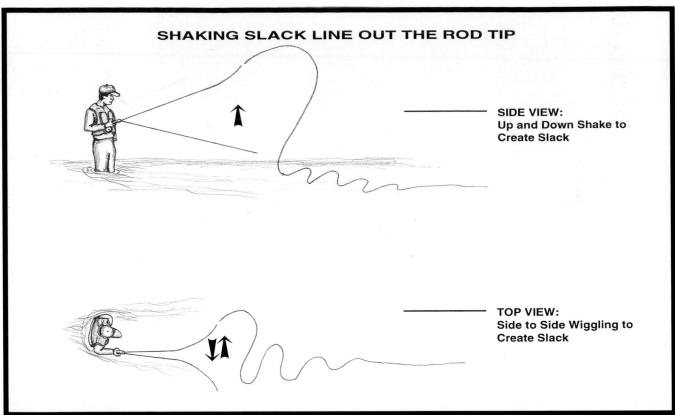

SHAKING SLACK LINE OUT THE ROD TIP

SIDE VIEW:
Up and Down Shake to Create Slack

TOP VIEW:
Side to Side Wiggling to Create Slack

You can extend the drag-free drift of the fly by shaking extra line out the rod tip using either a side-to-side or up-and-down wiggling motion of the rod. 1. Side view of up-and-down motion: this method allows you to keep most of the slack line in the same current seam. 2. Top view of the side-to-side method, which is effective in places where multiple current seams are not a concern.

Remember too that the closer you are to the trout, the lower you should keep the rod during the entire process. On a sunny day, cast sidearm and slide the fly into the feeding lane with a sidearm motion any time you are within 20 feet or so of the fish as they may spook if they catch the glare or motion from your rod.

In its most extreme form, the Fall River Drift is used to extend the drag-free drift of the fly well beyond normal casting distance to reach trout far downstream. On the Fall River, anglers fishing from boats will make a cast relatively in line with the trout's feeding lane, slide the fly into position, and then flip line out the rod tip with up and down motions until the fly reaches the trout—which might be 60, 70 even 90 or 100 feet away.

While the downstream cast is frequently the method of choice, the accompanying "slide method" of positioning the fly in the feeding lane has its liability: By skating the fly into position, you necessarily straighten the leader. No matter how many slack coils grace the fly line, a straight leader can catch in the myriad swirls and currents created by water filtering through and around underwater vegetation, causing the fly to drag ever so slightly—typically an unpardonable offense with spring-creek trout.

Reaching downstream and shaking line out the rod tip usually eliminates drag, but not always. At times the drag caused by the straightened leader may be imperceptible to you, but certainly not to the fish. If you notice drag or suspect that the fly's drift is impeded ever so slightly, you should consider abandoning the "slide method" and instead try to cast directly into the feeding lane with a reach cast or a slack-leader/slack-line presentation of one variety or another. Granted, the slide-

method allows for very precise fly placement, but with just a little practice, most anglers can place a reach cast or slack-line cast with considerable accuracy, eliminating the need for sliding the fly and eliminating that method's inherent liability.

The slide method does, however, offer one distinct advantage when fishing to the pods of feeding trout so common during spring-creek hatches: With a timely "mini-slide" of the fly, you can, at times, present your offering to two or three fish in succession during a single drift. Assume you have singled out a trout laying at the upstream end of a pod of rising trout. You make a cast to this fish using either a slack-leader cast or a slide presentation. Three feet below this trout and slightly outside him, another fish is rising steadily. If you fail to move the target fish, simply allow the fly to drift a foot beyond his position and then slide the fly a few inches over and again lower the rod tip, allowing a dead-drift presentation over the next fish. (see diagram on page 30).

Obviously this technique depends entirely upon how the pod of fish is arranged and on your position relative to that pod of fish. Still, when the opportunity presents itself, you might as well drift a fly by two or three fish on every cast rather than just one.

Downstream Slack-line Casts:

Perhaps the easiest of the slack-line casts to master and certainly among the most useful is the "stop cast," wherein you abruptly check the forward motion of the rod, drawing it toward your body after the line straightens in the air. This causes the line to rebound back towards you and fall on the water with ample slack for a lengthy drift.

The Basic Slide Method executed from an on-shore position: Using a down-and-across cast, the angler places the fly above the target and to the far side of the feeding lane (A). He then holds the rod in place, causing the fly to drag on the surface and swing into the trout's feeding lane (B). Then the angler immediately drops the rod tip and reaches down stream, in this case switching hands to reach the rod as far as possible, allowing the fly to float drag-free over the target (C).

As with any slack-line cast, the stop cast requires practice, especially when accuracy is critical. Still the stop cast allows for more line control than the other slack-line presentations.

To execute the stop cast, aim slightly beyond the trout, but well off to its opposite side, and deliver the forestroke as usual, but don't allow the rod tip to follow the line down to the water. Instead, just as the line straightens, stop the rod abruptly so the line recoils toward you. Immediately draw the rod butt toward your body and toward the water's surface while still leaving the rod tip pointing up at a sharp angle. This last action allows you to place the recoiling line and leader on the water before it can bounce all the way back toward your position. With some practice, you can execute the stop cast and drop your rod hand in a manner that will deliver the fly a few feet above the trout and directly in his feeding lane.

The stop cast often proves to be the best choice on spring creeks, where narrow feeding lanes are the rule, but at times particular situations will dictate that you choose another method for delivering a slack line and leader. The age-old "serpentine cast" (or "wiggle cast") is one such method.

As you deliver a normal forestroke, quickly wiggle the rod tip side to side before the line touches down. Because the fly line follows the path of the rod tip, this wiggling motion results in a series of snake-like curves of line and leader on the water. With any luck, the fly drifts unhindered while the curves of line and leader slowly straighten. The serpentine cast can be combined with a reach cast to further extend the downstream drift. Begin whipping the rod tip side to side immediately prior to and during the reach. This combination is somewhat difficult to master, especially with accuracy, but can prove valuable at times.

A useful presentation in some situations, the serpen-

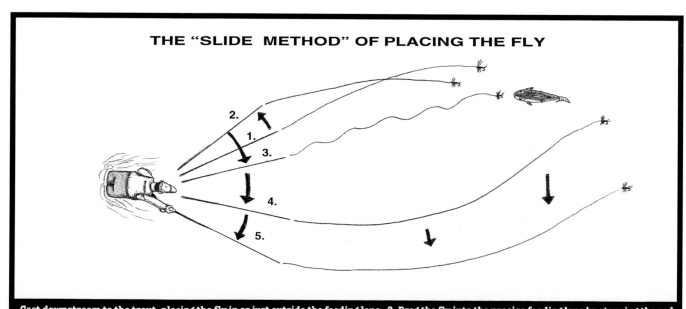

THE "SLIDE METHOD" OF PLACING THE FLY

Cast downstream to the trout, placing the fly in or just outside the feeding lane. 2. Drag the fly into the precise feeding lane by stopping the rod or by moving the rod tip slightly upstream. 3. Immediately lower the rod tip and follow the drift of the fly with the rod tip held at the surface. 4. If the fish does not take, allow the fly to drift a foot or two downstream from the trout and then swing the rod to the opposite side to slide the fly away. 5. When the fly is several feet away from and below the trout, pick up for the next cast, being careful not to false cast over the trout.

THE "MINI SLIDE"

Initial Cast ——

Slide

Feeding Lane

Slide

Feeding Lane

The mini-slide can be used to present a fly to two or three trout during one drift. To use this method effectively, the trout must be aligned in a stairstep arrangement wherein the lower fish is holding downstream and to the side of the first fish. If the first fish fails to rise, allow the fly to drift just beyond that trout's tail and then slide the fly into the feeding lane occupied by the next trout. Immediately lower the rod tip to allow for a drag-free drift over the second fish.

tine cast is unfortunately hindered by its inherent inaccuracy and by the fact that the tiny swirls and mini-currents can easily cause the last couple feet of tippet to drag the fly. The cast itself might be on target, but with the multitude of S-curve in the line and leader, you can never be sure that each S-curve of line is properly aligned to absorb currents. Moreover, with all those serpentine curves in the line, actually placing the fly in a narrow feeding lane becomes a problem not easily solved.

By slightly changing the angle of delivery, however, you can alter the serpentine cast into what might best be labeled a "straight-leader serpentine cast." This technique requires exact timing but otherwise is easy to master. Angle the cast slightly downward: In other words, instead of casting on the horizontal plane, tilt your cast forward so you are casting along a plane that is angled slightly toward the water in front.

Then deliver the cast so the fly and tippet land before the leader and line. Just as the first several feet of tippet and leader catch in the surface film, wiggle the rod tip side to side as before. The result should be a straight leader, precisely placed in the trout's feeding lane, followed by a series of S-curves in the fly line. If you wiggle the rod tip before enough of the leader has landed on the water, the fly and tippet will jump off the surface. Thus the key to timing this cast lies in waiting for the leader to anchor itself in the surface film before you wiggle the rod tip. Obviously, all of this occurs in the matter of a second or so, but with a little practice the straight-leader serpentine cast becomes a useful tool for spring creek anglers.

Similarly, the "parachute" or "steeple cast" proves useful in some spring-creek situations. This cast, while not so accurate as reach casts and stop casts, is easy to execute and lends itself well to places where you must cast across mixed current speeds. Moreover, you can combine the parachute cast with an upstream reach rather easily.

The parachute cast works like this: Tilt the casting plane slightly backward. Then, on the the forestroke, throw a rather wide loop aimed high in the air. As the loop straightens at an angle extending up and away from the water, simply allow the line to pile onto the water in loose curves. This cast is especially useful when you are positioned across and slightly upstream from a trout, with varying current speeds in between.

Line Mending

Line mending is an integral part of spring-creek fishing, allowing fly anglers a measure of control over the manipulations of current characteristics after the fly is on the water. Any of the downstream presentations might (and usually will) benefit from some kind of line mend, depending on the particular situation.

An effective mend might be little more than a simple upstream flip that repositions the belly of the line to allow for a longer drag-free drift. In other situations, namely when a slower current seam runs between you and the faster water where a trout rests, a downstream flip of line might aid in extending the drift of the artificial.

But mending can get complicated, often in direct correspondence to the complexity of the water's surface. In some situations, a series of mends, perhaps three or four in a row, each executed as the line is about to drag or get trapped in a current seam, swirl or "dead spot," will be required to drift a fly over a particular trout. No matter what the situation, though, your ability to anticipate drag before its onset is paramount to effectively mending the line.

Visualize every presentation before you cast. Look for the potential trouble spots and visualize your strategy for dealing

The "stop cast" is one of the easiest methods of creating slack in the line: Begin with a normal cast (A), but as the line straightens on the forestroke, abrubtly stop the forward motion of the rod, leaving the tip rather high in the air (B). The line will rebound slightly, creating some loose curves of line on the water (C). Be sure to lower the rod tip as the fly drifts downstream to maximize the drag-free drift.

with them, both in terms of the cast you employ and the mends you use after the cast. The reach cast, in reality, is kind of an in-the-air mend. Beyond that, you will commonly employ the upstream and downstream flip mends.

In addition, the "roll mend" comes in handy when you need to force fly line into a faster current to prevent the closer slow current from sweeping the fly and line away from the target area. The roll mend can extend your drift enough that the line trapped in the slower water won't pull on the fly until after it has drifted beyond the trout.

The roll mend works as follows: After delivering the cast, shake slack line out the guides and then gently raise the rod tip, simultaneously extending and lowering your casting arm toward the fly. (You must shake enough slack line out of the guides so that only this first few feet of line will be affected when you raise the rod tip.) Immediately after elevating the rod tip, make a "miniature roll cast," causing a small hoop of line to roll into the faster water and then fall in a heap just beyond the current seam.

Another mend, one that I call the "shoot mend" can help in guiding your line around dead spots, swirls and upwellings.

After delivering the cast, keep a loop of several feet of fly line in your free hand and make a firm, sidearm flip across stream. When properly executed, this mend will shoot line out the rod tip, causing this line to land in an arc beyond whatever surface element you are trying to avoid. The shoot mend requires practice, but will prove valuable almost immediately and second nature with enough use.

Cross-Stream Presentations

When a downstream presentation is not possible on a particular fish, one alternative is a cross-stream approach. The various slack-line casts discussed above can also be applied to cross-stream presentations, with the reach cast being especially valuable.

Certainly the greatest obstacle to most cross-stream presentations is the variation in current speeds in any given run or pool. The smooth water of a spring creek may appear to be traveling at a constant and uniform rate, but hidden by the quiet surface are countless current seams, mini-currents and swirls. Cast a straight line directly across a smooth spring creek and you can easily see the affects these surface fluctuations have on

Executing the "parachute cast:" Begin by tilting the casting plane slightly backward and delivering an open loop upward (A). Stop the rod tip fairly high, allowing the casting loop to collapse and the line to fall straight downward (B). As the line falls, you may want to lower the rod butt to gain more control over how the line falls (C). That part of the fly line closest to the leader should land with small curves and the fly will usually touch down last; be sure to lower the rod tip as you follow the drift of the fly (D).

The "straight-leader serpentine cast," illustrated here, can be used to place S-curves in the fly line while maintaining a fairly straight leader: Tilt the casting plane slightly forward so the fly lands on water ahead of the line and leader (A). Just as the leader and first few feet of fly line land on the water impart a quick side-to-side wiggling motion on the rod tip, causing the belly of the line to land in a series of S-curves (B).

a fly line.

The reach cast is so valuable on cross-stream presentations because, in many situations, it allows you to deliver what is in essence a downstream drift. Therefore, the reach cast should always be your first choice when delivering a fly cross stream. But the other slack-line casts may also help counter the effects of various currents.

When a fast current runs between you and the trout's position, you must devise a presentation that will compensate for the faster water in the middle. A reach cast thrown so that the belly of the fly line lands in the fast water and well above the fly (which lands in the slow water beyond) combined with one or more upstream mends generally serves as the best way to deal with these situations. In addition, you can use your rod to suspend the first few feet of line above troublesome currents, especially when you are reasonably close to the fish. Incidentally, the ability to suspend line above such currents and other obstacles makes a strong argument for using 9- to 10-foot rods on some spring creeks.

Just as often, the scenario works in the opposite manner when a slower current seam or weed mat lies between you and the faster water where a trout holds. Get more line in the fast water than on the slow water and you can handle these obstacles. Although difficult to master, a pile cast will usually do the trick. The pile cast simply results in a heap of line landing in the faster currents across stream and above the trout. To make this cast, either overpower the forestroke while tilting the casting plane forward or, better still, execute a parachute cast combined with a reach cast, allowing the majority of fly line to pile up in the intended current seam. In some instances, you can mend downstream to help the line trapped in the slower currents keep pace with that drifting more rapidly in the faster water.

Also, a positive curve cast, usually combined with an upstream reach, can help place the fly downstream of the leader and line. This curve cast, called positive because the loop is allowed to curve around

Executing the upstream roll mend: Immediately upon delivering the cast, raise the rod tip enough that you can effectively deliver the roll, but not enough that you pull the fly off target (A-B). With the rod slightly upstream from the line, deliver a quick downward forestroke as if you were roll casting, making sure that this rod action occurs on the upstream side of the line (C-D). The result will be a single large S-curve of line, the curves extending upstream (E-F).

the left of a right-handed caster or right for a left-handed caster, is performed by a sidearm stroke wherein you abruptly stop an overpowered forecast, causing the end of the line and leader to whip around in an arc. The positive curve is effective only when you're casting arm is on the upstream side; from the downstream side, the positive curve cast will result in the fly and leader curving upstream, which leads, of course, to drifting the line ahead of the fly. With practice and considerable casting-stroke power, you can throw a curve-cast with an over-the-opposite-shoulder delivery or by turning your back to the target and releasing the cast on the backstroke—in both cases the idea is to curve the line and leader downstream.

Because the positive curve cast requires an overpowered casting stroke, the amount of curve is partially determined by how suddenly you can stop the forestroke. In fact, if you can develop the habit of abruptly stopping the rod motion and also pulling back slightly on the rod but, you can create a more prominent curve in the line. The sudden stop and subtle reversal works something like a bull-whip when properly executed: Just as a slight backward check snaps a whip, it will also deliver more snap to the curve cast.

In addition, a slight "line haul," performed by tugging at the line with your free hand as the loop straightens, will add momentum to the forestroke and thus aid in forming the curve at the end of the line. This haul works much like the "foreword" or "forestroke haul" in a double-hauled cast: As you drive the forestroke forward and the loop begins to straighten, add a quick, sharp tug on the line with your free hand. Combine this haul with the bull-whip effect described above and you can maximize the curve effect of this cast.

The curve cast, when combined with an upstream reach, is a versatile technique in skilled hands, but it does require practice and, unfortunately, is rendered useless with even a slight breeze (mainly because of the long, light leaders used on spring creeks). Given a still day and/or a leader less than 12 feet

DEALING WITH MULTIPLE CURRENTS

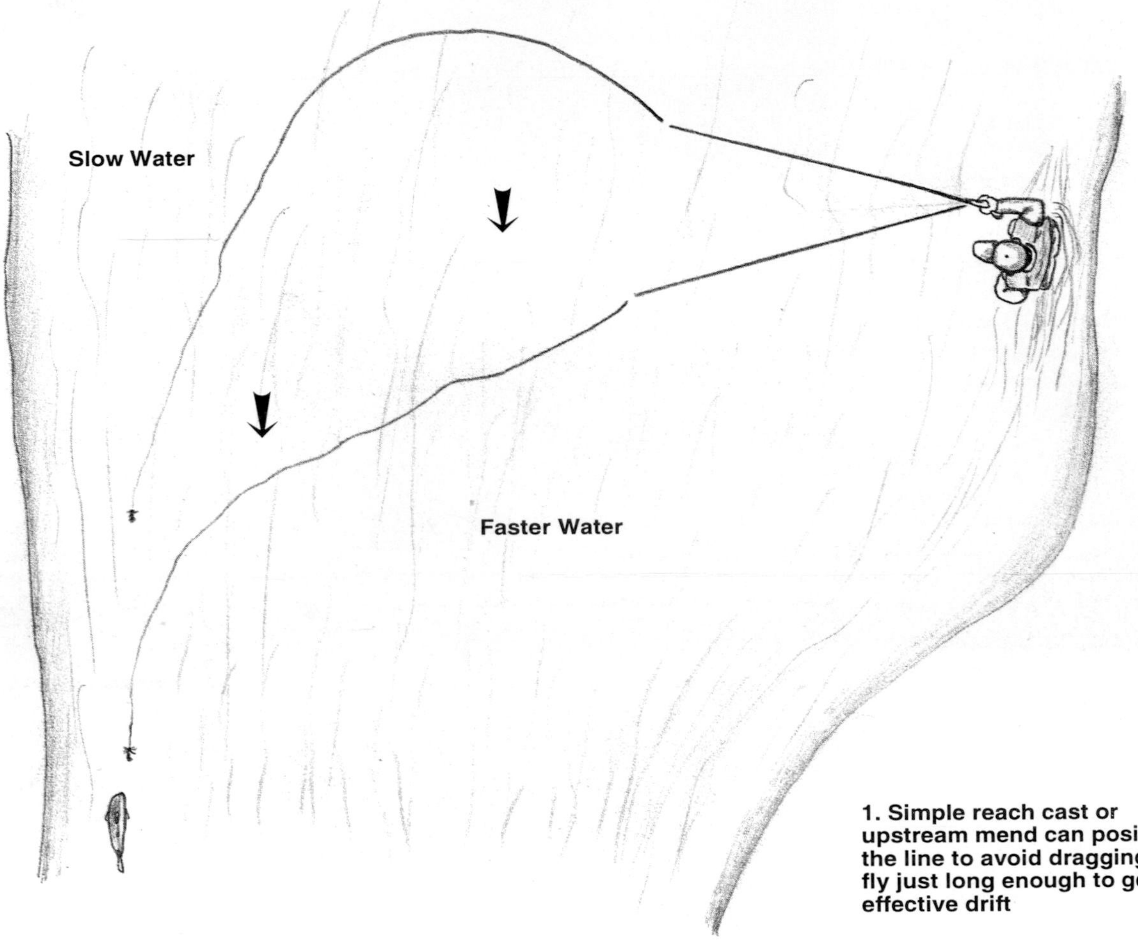

Slow Water

Faster Water

1. Simple reach cast or upstream mend can position the line to avoid dragging the fly just long enough to get an effective drift

2. If feasible, you can use the rod to suspend the line away from troublesome currents.

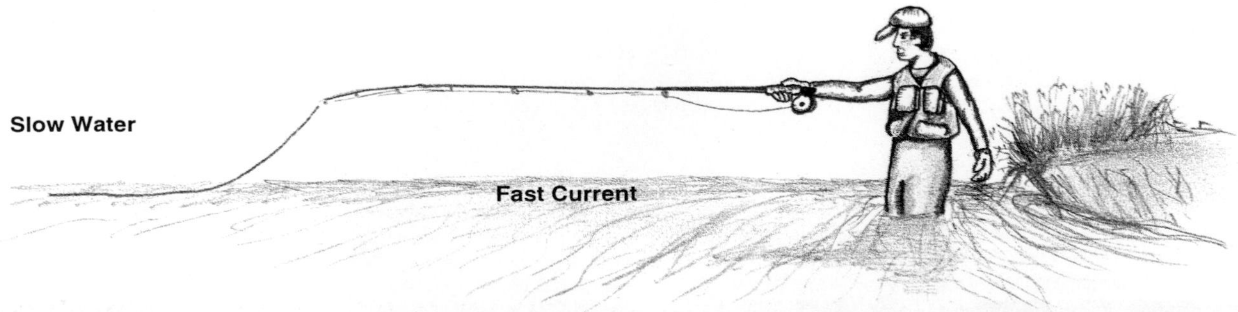

Slow Water

Fast Current

ROLL MENDS

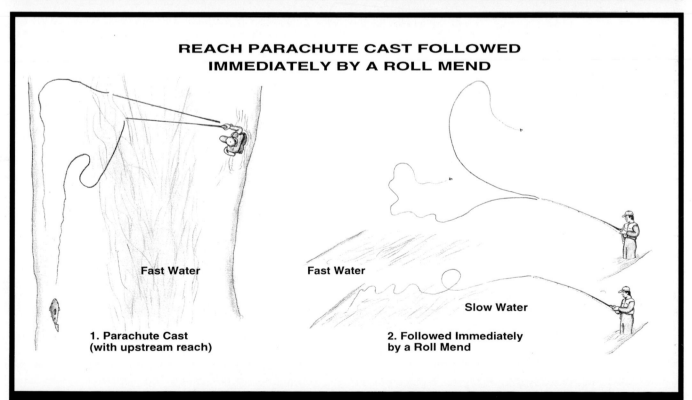

Slow Water **Faster Water** **Upstream Roll Mend**

Fast Water **Slow Water**

Downtream Roll Mend

Upstream Roll Mend **Faster Water** **Slow Water**

Roll mends, which are like mini roll casts, can be used to prevent multiple currents from dragging the fly: The roll mend can be made to the downstream or upstream side and can be extended well out the line or can be placed on the water just a few feet away, all depending on the characteristics of the currents you encounter in a given situation.

REACH PARACHUTE CAST FOLLOWED IMMEDIATELY BY A ROLL MEND

Fast Water

1. Parachute Cast (with upstream reach)

Fast Water

Slow Water

2. Followed Immediately by a Roll Mend

By combining a variety of mending and casting techniques, you can present a drag-free drift in virtually any situation: 1. Upstream reach cast followed immediately by a roll mend to conquer a fast current running alongside a slow current. 2. A parachute-reach cast (parachute cast combined with an upstream reach.) followed by a roll mend to deal with a trout holding in faster water just beyond a slow current. These are just two examples of numerous technique combinations that can help in dealing with multiple currents.

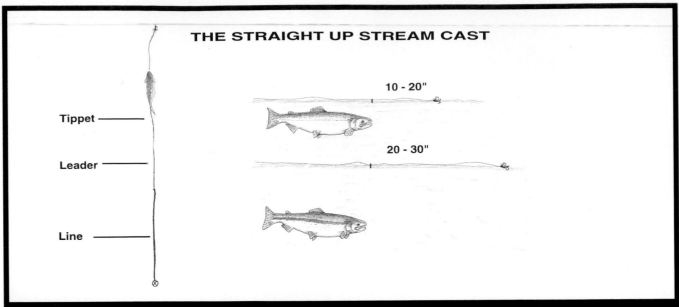

THE STRAIGHT UP STREAM CAST

Tippet ———

Leader ———

Line ———

10 - 20"

20 - 30"

In some situations, a direct upstream cast, wherein you place the tippet directly over the trout's back, will prove to be the best approach. If the fish is holding at the surface, cast the fly 10 to 20 inches beyond its nose; if the trout is holding deeper in the water, place the fly 20 to 30 inches above its nose.

long, however, the reach-curve cast is a valuable and effective delivery for cross-stream presentations. The arced leader places the fly ahead of the leader and the upstream reach allows for maximum absorption of tricky current seams and swirls before the fly drags.

For the record, a negative curve cast—one that curves to the right for a right-handed caster—is accomplished by underpowering a wide-open, side-arm loop. Start by casting a wide, lazy sidearm loop, perhaps tilted slightly downward on the forestroke. Before the loop staightens, drop the line to the water, thus leaving the fly and leader still arced around in the unfinished stroke. Because the negative curve cast requires a wide-open loop, it is virtually impossible to control in the wind and is never reliably accurate, especially when you are dealing with long leaders and feeding lanes only a few inches wide. Practice the negative curve if you must, but forget about it for most of your spring-creek angling.

In any case, cross-current presentations leave you more at the mercy of current seams and other surface characteristics than does a downstream cast. But at times, the cross-stream cast may be all that is possible; other times it may even offer an advantage. Naturally, if you can get close to the trout, you can eliminate many of the problems inherent to casting across myriad current seams and if you combine proximity with a long, coiled leader, so much the better. Remember, your success hinges on delivering a fly-first presentation devoid of drag, so any advantages you can gain before actually casting will make the game that much easier.

Upstream Presentations

Having already extoled the virtues of the downstream presentation I should hasten to add that your choice of presentation is frequently limited by the particular characteristics of a given situation. Sometimes you have no choice but to cast upstream to a trout and other times you may want to cast upstream.

At the age of 15 I fished over some nice-sized browns in a small Rocky Mountain spring creek. They cooperated nicely when given a No. 16 beetle on a downstream cast. But the two biggest trout I found all day were, naturally, holed up in the refuge of the least accessible pool on the stream. Willows and other shrubs grew thick enough on both sides of this long, 20-foot wide pool to form a virtual tunnel that excluded any hope of approaching from either bank. I couldn't wade down on the fish either. Having tried that approach when I first spotted those fish at mid-morning, I only succeeded in spooking them by way of a cloud of silt, stirred by my wading, that drifted toward and over them. I could find no way of avoiding that cloud of debris, so I opted, later that afternoon, for an upstream approach.

In the minds of many anglers, the upstream approach will require a curve cast of some kind. And those who have tried to master the curve cast know well that such tactics work considerably better in the backyard than on a spring creek during a windy day. Given the normal Western winds (a windless day is a rarity on the Rocky Mountain streams) the curve cast is an exercise in uncertainty because you can never be certain how accurate each such cast will be nor how much it will actually curve.

I tried a curve cast on those big browns. The cast went well. It was pretty. It curved nicely around to the left and the fly drifted downstream, completely unimpeded by drag, to where the trout had been rising. They had quit feeding just as soon as that curve cast hit the water. They just didn't like the leader and line touching down to their flank side, no matter that it landed ever so delicately.

A few years later I learned a better way: Cast directly over the trout's back. Position yourself directly downstream from the rising trout, sneak to within reasonable range (say 15-30 feet), and deliver the cast so that the tippet runs directly above the trout's back—right between his eyes being ideal—and the fly lands 10 to 30 inches ahead of his nose. In essence, you are taking advantage of the fact that a trout doesn't see particularly well directly above her back and that she probably will not detect your fine tippet extending a foot or more in front.

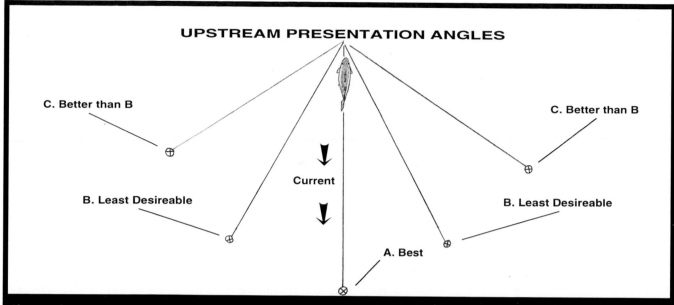

UPSTREAM PRESENTATION ANGLES

C. Better than B

C. Better than B

Current

B. Least Desireable

B. Least Desireable

A. Best

If you opt for an upstream presentation, choose a position from which you can cast directly over the trout's back. If this is not possible, then position yourself as far to the side of the trout as possible so you can employ a reach cast or other technique to assure a fly-first presentation.

Obviously this method requires extreme delicacy, not to mention considerable practice. In addition to making an accurate cast, with the tippet running directly above the trout and the fly landing just ahead of its nose, you will want a few S-curves in the leader and line behind the trout. How's that for a tall order? Given efficiency in its delivery, the method works, even on the selective trout of the Western spring creeks. This upstream presentation is especially useful on individual trout feeding close to the bank or in narrow slots between mats of aquatic moss and weeds. Unfortunately, if you are forced to cast from a position even a few feet to the side of directly downstream from your target, you will have to employ a reach cast or a side-arm cast to place the tippet properly. In either case, most of us lose a little accuracy.

Also, because the upstream cast requires a very precise amount of line, you may want to measure the distance by purposely throwing a cast that lands short and below the fish. Then strip off enough line to extend the cast to a point where the last foot or two of tippet will land ahead of the trout.

On those ocassional situations where you have little choice but to opt for an upstream approach and yet the direct upstream cast as described above is impossible, at least give yourself the advantage of staying as much to the side of the trout as possible. In such a place, where you simply cannot position yourself to make the upstream presentation directly over the trout's back, then the farther your lateral position from directly downstream from the trout, the better your chances for delivering an effective cast. If you are a right-handed caster, opt for the right side of the trout as you look upstream. If you are left-handed, try for the left side. This left versus right positioning is intended to put you into position to throw a reach cast or, failing that, a positive curve cast, which will hook to the inside.

In addition, the direct upstream cast offers a distinct advantage when dealing with a stiff upstream wind. Such winds, blowing directly upstream, tend to make downstream presentations rather difficult. An upstream cast, however, is fairly simply to deliver with a tailwind, so under such conditions you might consider approaching from below and casting directly over the trout's back.

As previously discussed, some trout on the popular spring creeks are conditioned to continue rising and feeding even as you cast over them. They know you are there—they tolerate you—but they also know better than to eat anything except the most convincing artificial presented in the most convincing manner, a qualification that doesn't really fit the up-and-across approach. Tim Blount and I once found a big rainbow on the Henry's Fork that would continue feeding even if you stood in the water four feet away. If you inched any closer, the fish would swim away (rather lazily), but from four feet or more away you could do jumping jacks in the water without interrupting that trout's dinner. Talk about a tough customer.

Incidentally, I eventually rose one of the big browns that I spooked with my upstream cast. Take this for what it's worth, but the next day, trying the upstream tact again, I accidentally threw a cast into the willows above the fish only to have the leader and fly slip onto the water and immediately draw a rise. Not knowing what else to do, I pulled on the line, which was still draped over the willow limbs, and actually fought the fish, willows and all, for a few seconds before the tippet gave up the ghost.

Bank Casting

English anglers, traditionally at least, consider wading in a trout stream to be somewhat barbaric. At times we would do well to follow their example. Effective wading on a spring creek means knowing how to best approach a trout and sometimes just staying the hell out of the water gives you a tremendous advantage. This is especially true of bank-hugging trout and of small creeks.

Some of my favorite spring-creek trout are those that hold tight against a steep bank, nonchalantly sipping terrestrials, caddis and other morsels while, in the middle of the river, their counterparts feed on whatever hatch is currently in progress. Bank huggers are smart and thus they tend to be big fish that

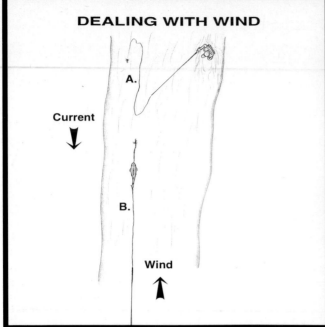

DEALING WITH WIND

Current

A.

B.

Wind

A. Strong upstream winds cause the leader and fly to blow up-stream, ruining the fly-first drift. B. One solution is to use the direct upstream cast, keeping the wind at your back.

DEALING WITH WIND

2. Upstream Mend & Slide

3. Drag-Free Drift

1. Initial Cast: Wind Forces Much of Leader/Tippet to Land in a Single Large S-Curve

Current

Wind

If conditions dictate that you cast downstream even in the face of an upstream breeze, you can use the wind to your advantage in placing the leader on the water in a single S-curve. To do this, deliver a slightly overpowered sidearm cast aimed toward the water's surface. 1. Properly executed, this cast will cause the fly to catch in the surface film and thus remain slightly downstream from tippet, which will blow upstream. 2. Then employ a quick flip mend to reposition the belly of the line and the leader butt followed by a slide to position the fly in the trout's feeding lane. 3. Lastly, lower the rod tip and follow the drift of the fly to assure a drag-free drift, shaking extra line onto the water if necessary.

have been around the block a time or two. A careless approach by a fly fisher results in a subtle wake marking the path of a large trout as she glides into deeper water.

These bank-huggers get spooked via walking and wading more often than they get cast over as anglers, intent on pursuing the rising trout farther out in the stream, simply miss fish that quietly feed in the shadow of shoreline grass. But anglers who pay attention, scanning the banks for subtle rises or nervous water, may well have a chance to cast to the largest trout in a given spring creek.

Sometimes a cross-stream wade, where you approach from the opposite bank and position yourself above and a rod length or so out from the trout, gives you the best casting angle for a bank-feeder. In these cases, the presentation techniques previously discussed will prove effective. Some situations, however, might require you to approach from the same bank under which the trout is feeding. In doing so, you can, at times get remarkably close to the fish. Imagine crawling up to a grassy bank and carefully peering through the weeds only to see a trout so close that you can count its spots.

The best place for casting to such a trout varies with each individual situation, but often a position just a few feet behind the fish can work wonders. From such a position, deliver a sidearm cast, keeping the rod and line over the shore and not over the water. (Glare from the rod or reel, not to mention the line in the air over their heads can easily spook these bank-hugging trout). For a right-handed caster looking upstream with river on his or her left, this cast is easy. But cross the river and that same right-handed angler must cast over the opposite shoulder to keep the line and rod away from the water.

Deliver a reach cast that allows the fly and tippet to land on the water two to four feet above the trout while the line lands on the grass above. Then don't twitch. Keep your rod and your head as low as possible. Assuming you have accurately judged the amount of tippet needed on the water to allow for a drag-free drift, you stand a good chance.

A similar delivery, with the line being draped over the grass and the fly and tippet on the water, can be made from upstream or immediately beside the trout. With the line draped over the grass, however, all these angles are essentially equal in terms of how you eliminate drag: You must accurately judge the amount of tippet needed on the water to assure an effective drift. Thus none of these angles really betters the others in terms of the actual cast, but positioning yourself downstream of the fish at least allows you a better chance of not being seen by your quarry.

Some bank feeders lend themselves better to an approach from well upstream where you reach your rod out over the river to cast. Sneak to within 30 feet or so of the trout (the exact distance, of course, will vary with each opportunity) and reach the first third or half of your rod out over the river, executing a sidearm cast. Employ a reach cast or the slide method (or one of the slack-line casts) to ensure an accurate, fly-first drift. If the trout refuses, extend your entire rod length out over the river to slide the fly and leader out of the trout's feeding lane. Then pick up for the next delivery. If you have any doubts as to whether you can pick up the fly without any disturbance on the water, slowly strip in line, rod held well out away from the bank, until the fly is far enough upstream of the fish to facilitate a quiet, easy backstroke.

Finally, some bank-hugging trout are suckers for a dabbled fly. Belly-crawl up to the bank, just close enough so that you can barely see the fish when you carefully part the grass in front of your face. Having located the target, back off a bit, reach the end of the rod, with just the leader and fly hanging from the tip, over the grass—ever so slowly—and drop the fly on the water a foot above the trout (or use a bow cast). Allow the artificial to float dead drift for two or three feet and then quietly pluck the fly from the surface and try again.

Not everyone would agree that these bank-huggers are best approached from the bank. I'm not even sure I believe that. More than anything else, I enjoy approaching these trout from the bank if only for the reason that I can usually watch the fish react to the fly. The disadvantage to this approach is obvious if you make even one wrong move—too hard a foot-fall, raise your head too high to look, wave the rod within the trout's window, etc.

If you choose to cast to a bank-hugger from astream, use the downstream angle or the direct upstream cast. About the only approaches you can rule out are those that, either on the bank or just off the bank near shore, require you to stalk downriver. If you decide to cast from the bank well above the trout as mentioned above, your approach to that casting position should be from inland and should be concealed by vegetation and a low profile—hands and knees being the rule.

Dealing with Wind

Wind is a fact of life on the Western spring creeks, especially on the larger streams like the Henry's Fork, where virtually every day of the season a wind will begin between late morning and mid-afternoon and last until late afternoon. Some days the winds are stronger than others, but their presence, to one degree or another, is a foregone conclusion.

Fly anglers simply must learn to cope with the wind if they intend to fish during the afternoon. But therein lies one advantage of a windy day: Many anglers get frustrated with casting in the wind and simply give up until evening, leaving the streams less crowded during the time of day when terrestrial fishing is best and when some mayflies emerge.

To make the most of a windy day, simply add a bit more zip to your casts, creating tighter casting loops that will penetrate the wind more effectively or choose a position that will keep the wind at your back, where, in some cases, it can help your cast. In addition, you may want to employ a sidearm delivery when possible because the wind is always stronger a few yards above the water than near the surface.

The wind's direction will determine the type of delivery you should use. If a strong wind blows into your face, the forestroke must be tilted slightly toward the water and driven hard with a tight casting loop; if the wind blows from behind, the backstroke must be overpowered while the forestroke will often benefit from the breeze.

An upstream wind, blowing into your face, is reasonably easy to overcome if you combine the slide method with a short down-and-across cast (say 20 feet or so) that is forced into a single large S-curve with the fly on the down-current end of a straight tippet. Accomplishing this set-up requires a low, short, overpowered sidearm cast that is tilted toward the water with the intent of driving the fly rather hard toward the surface. After the fly lands, throw a short mend upstream and then slide the fly into the feeding lane (see diagram page 38). Without an upstream wind, this over-powered cast would result in a big splash and a drowned fly. But a breeze cushions the fly's landing and blows much of the leader upstream from the fly. This cast requires only a little practice and can prove valuable in the face of a headwind (the only condition under which it will perform as intended).

As discussed previously, an upstream wind that is too troublesome for a downstream cast can be tamed rather easily by wading in behind the trout and delivering the direct upstream cast.

Unless you have the option of choosing either the left or right hand side from which to approach a given trout, strong cross-winds blowing from your casting-arm side often pose more difficulty than all but the stronger head and tailwinds. A right-handed caster, when fishing in a gentle cross-breeze blowing from his or her right side, can usually compensate with an overpowered sidearm cast. But during stronger winds, a "circle cast," opposite shoulder cast or a backward cast may be the only ways to combat the wind without getting a fly in the face.

The circle cast is a valuable technique when the wind is just too strong. A standard backstroke might seem harmless, but throughout the stroke, your line is being blown toward your body only to blow into your head and potentially pierce an ear on the ensuing forestroke. To avoid this problem in a strong cross wind, simply follow the standard backstroke with a forestroke originating from the other side of your body. For a right-handed angler, the cast works like this: As the backstroke straightens behind you, allow your casting arm to drift upward and above your head, simultaneously tilting the rod to the left so it extends beyond the left side of your body. Begin the forestroke from this position, driving a hard, tight loop from the opposite side. (Left handers, of course, can simply reverse the process).

Cross-winds strong enough to completely disallow any kind of cast from the normal side of the body require that both the forestroke and backstroke be switched to the other side. In such a situation, you have three choices: 1. learn to cast with both arms. 2. Use an opposite-shoulder cast by reaching your rod across the other side of your body and casting from there. 3. Turn around and cast backward, delivering the fly on the backstroke.

Don't rule out the first of these options (casting with the opposite arm): With a little practice, you might be surprised how easily you can deliver a short, accurate cast with your "off" arm. The ability to do so will most certainly make you a more versatile and effective angler. Moreover, teaching yourself to cast with your "off" arm can help you discover and correct minor flaws in your dominant-arm cast.

As for the other two options, The opposite-shoulder cast is never quite as powerful as a regular backcast, but with practice you should be able to effectively and accurately work with 30 or 40 feet of line. Not much more than that is needed in most spring-creek situations. The backward cast, on the other hand, is capable of every bit as much power (and thus distance) as the standard backcast, although most anglers require lots of practice to learn accuracy with this method.

The opposite-shoulder cast is an integral part of your arsenal on the spring creeks and, despite the practice required, I recommend that all casters practice and learn the backward delivery. For me, it has proven valuable in countless angling situations, from spring creeks to surf fishing. The backward cast is mechanically identical to the standard overhead cast, but you are delivering the fly on the backstroke. With practice, you can easily and accurately throw double-hauls, curve casts, reach casts and all of the slack-line casts.

When possible, of course, you will want to keep the wind at your off-hand shoulder, blowing across your body toward the casting arm. From that side, the wind is much easier to deal with since you needn't worry about loosing a piece of scalp. Therefore, if you can approach a certain trout from either side, you can eliminate the hastle of crosswinds by simply choosing the side that will allow for the easiest cast. Thus the wind becomes an important variable not only in choosing a casting method, but also in determining your initial positioning.

Consider also that windy days usually create the best terrestrial-fishing opportunities, especially where grasshoppers are concerned. In other words, don't let the wind frustrate you into giving up a good afternoon's fishing on the spring creeks. Learn to deal with it on a strategical and tactical level and you can enjoy mid-afternoon fishing even on the biggest and windiest spring creeks.

Tackle Considerations

The leader and tippet constitute the critical part of your fly tackle for spring creek fishing. For the most part, you will want long leaders and long tippets because spring-creek trout tend to be terribly line shy—a long leader and tippet will prevent the fish from ever seeing the fly line. Moreover, a long leader and tippet aid substantially in executing a drag-free drift.

During still days, 12- to 18-foot leaders (including tippet) are often preferable. I usually buy knotless tapered leaders of 9- and 12-foot length and then add more tippet to them. A typical set-up of this kind might begin with a 12-foot, 5X leader, to which I will add another four to six feet of 6X tippet material (the six-foot-long tippets are advantageous when fishing areas replete with surface weed growths and mixed currents). I prefer the tapered leader to be of a rather stiff material and the additional tippet to be of a soft monofilament. The stiff leader butt seems to help turn over the long tippet.

Windy days, may force you to go with a shorter leader. Luckily, however, the same breeze that demands a shortened leader also tends to ripple the water enough to make trout more approachable and less likely to spook if the line or leader butt passes too close.

Choose your tippet to compliment the size and style of fly you intend to employ. If you are fishing tiny hooks (No. 22-24, for example) 7X tippet might be required to make the fly look natural on the water. Hooks ranging from No. 16-20, on the other hand, perform just fine with 6X tippet. A few years ago I experimented with tippet size in an effort to determine just how tippet-shy trout might act. Even when using 5X tippet on No. 20 patterns, the trout seemed confident in the take. Thus your choice of tippet is probably better made in relation to the fly than out of concern for leader-shy trout. Most of the time, with small flies, I will opt for 6X tippet and only employ 7X tippet on the tiniest of patterns.

Incidentally, I prefer to use a perfection loop to attach many flies to the tippet, especially when I use sub-surface patterns and large dry flies. A loop knot allows the fly to play freely at the end of the tippet, resulting in a more animated, life-like appearance.

As for rods, I'd like to suggest a long rod, say 9- to 9-1/2 feet, for the big spring creeks where line control is so important and a shorter rod (7-1/2-8-1/2 feet) for the small spring creeks. Although I own both kinds of rods, I am quite guilty of being a virtual one-rod man in my trout fishing, whether it be spring creeks, big freestone rivers, tiny brooks or high mountain lakes. That one rod is a nine-foot six-weight model with which I have grown so comfortable that it feels like just another bodily appendage.

If you own a trout rod like that, one that does most of your fishing and one that feels utterly comfortable and familiar, by all means stick with it for your spring creek fishing. If you don't have any particular loyalty to one rod, however, then consider something in the four- to six-weight category, perhaps eight to nine feet long. I've seen a few three-weight rods that might make good spring-creek tools, but I have yet to see a two-weight or even worse, a one-weight that I would use to torture a spring-creek trout (or any trout) of more than a foot in length: No matter what reel or tippet you use, I don't think one and two-weight rods have a place on the Western spring creeks. The big, wild trout of the Western spring creeks deserve to be hooked, beached, handled, and released with all due efficiency.

One disadvantage of a long rod is that those who are

Casting to a bank-hugging trout from above, the angler maintains a low profile while delivering the fly to the target (A). in this case with a positive curve cast (if necessary, the angler can slide the fly into the exact feeding lane) (B). Immediately upon completing the cast, the angler lowers the rod and, with tip, follows the drift of the fly (C-D).

not used to fishing a 10-foot rod all day will likely experience some casting fatigue. Thus, if most of your days astream are spent casting small trout rods, by all means stick with a rod of nine feet or less. On the other hand, if you spend a lot of time casting steelhead, salmon or saltwater rods, a 10-foot five-weight will cast effortlessly all day long.

Dave McNeese, a fine rod-builder and one of the best technical casters I've ever met, points out another important consideration in choosing between slow-action rods or fast-action rods: Fairly short (8- to 8-1/2-foot), fast-action rods might be a better choice on the Western spring creeks for the simple reason that rod motion stops more quickly at the completion of each cast, resulting in increased line control and decreased potential for drag. Moreover, fast-action rods tend to be easier to cast in the wind. One could certainly make an arguement for slow-action rods. They probably protect light tippets better.

Fast or slow, though, the rod you choose for spring-creek fishing should be one that feels utterly comfortable in your hands. I own a lovely little 8-1/2-foot five weight that would make a nice spring-creek rod except for the fact that I never use it; My nine-foot, six-weight rod, does virtually all of my trout fishing (not to mention all my bream fishing, smallmouth fishing, and some saltwater fishing) and is wonderful in the wind. Being so comfortable with that one rod, I just can't see any advantage in changing rods when I visit the spring creeks.

Other tackle is pretty straight forward. Use a reel with a good, smooth drag. Click drags are fine, so long as they are reasonably smooth and high-quality disk drags do a nice job of protecting fine tippets as well. Load the reel with, for most

3/4" Wood Dowels

Aquarium Net

Window Screen Material

A seine of some kind can be a tremendous help in determining what insects are present in the drift at any given time.

instances, a double-taper floating fly line. I carry a weight-forward line on an extra spool for those places where an extra-long cast might be required. I load my vest with everything I'll need for a day on the stream, I also carry a tiny, 6-compartment fly box full of flies This small box, along with nippers, tippet, fly floatant and forceps, goes in the pocket on the outside of my neoprene waders. Wading beyond the top of my chest waders seems to be rather habitual for me, so I leave the vest ashore when I find fish and carry only those few necessary items into the river.

Also, some kind of small seine or net for sampling the drift can save your bacon at times. I usually carry a large size aquarium net with an opening about eight inches by six inches. Even better is a piece of window-screen material stapled between two wood dowels. Cut a three-foot by one-foot piece of screen and attach a foot-long, 3/4-inch dowel to each end. This seine will roll up and fit nicely into the pocket on the back of your vest. For sampling deep, however, you will need a larger version, made with three-foot or four-foot dowels and a comparable sized piece of screen material. I prefer the small version because most of the time I am interested in sampling the upper foot of water. In any case, some kind of insect net or seine can prove invaluable on the spring creeks.

Lastly, a pair of polarized glasses and a brimmed hat (the brim preferably having a dark-colored underside) will aid substantially in spotting fish and in following the drift of your fly. A net with a soft cotton mesh bag can help land trout quickly and efficiently, although the net can be something of a bother to pack around with you.

SPRING CREEK DIARY

late August, 1986; Railroad Ranch

God damn little bugs. *Pseudocleons*—tiny Western olives, true 24's and millions of them, choking the surface in a huge flotilla that looked like a football field cloaked in faded green Astroturf.

This was silly. I had just made several dozen casts to two big rainbows who were confidently gorging themselves on the puny mayflies. Still not entirely convinced of the futility in this, I picked out a pod of eight or ten nice trout, whose snouts were visibly breaking the surface every time they devoured a chunk of that Astroturf—and believe me, with every opening of the mouth, those trout certainly inhaled half a gross of mayflies. I counted: 44 casts with nothing to show for it.

Too many naturals—without a doubt the most awesome emergence of tiny Western olives I will ever witness on the Henry's Fork or anywhere else.

Now I was convinced of the futility. I pulled up a shoreline rock. Timmy reappeared from around the island and joined me. We just watched as dozens of big trout chomped away at that green carpet of mayflies.

Chapter 3

Choosing the Right Fly

Tim Blount and I found a pod of 15 or 20 big rainbows devouring flying ants that had blown en masse onto the smooth water's of the Henry's Fork downstream from the old ranch bridge. We could see clearly that the hapless ants, their wings held aloft and glistening in the sun, were being picked off eagerly by the trout. We knew what the fish were eating, so we just had to choose the right fly to match those ants.

On that particular day, our little fur ants proved more or less useless. Tim was first to switch to one of the new McMurray ants, which had recently been touted in one of the fly fishing magazines. The results were impressive: Tim's little balsa-body ant drew a confident rise on the first cast. Within 15 minutes, Timmy had enticed three trout to the ant, landing two. I'd like to offer a comparative analysis as to the relative effectiveness of the fur ant I was using and the McMurray ant Tim was fishing, but before Tim had landed the first of those trout, I too had switched to a black McMurray ant.

Timmy had chosen the right fly. We now consider the McMurray ant, in its various forms, to be the franchise player amongst our ant patterns. We still carry fur ants. At times they will outfish the McMurray ants.

Same trip, two days later: The ants were back on the water, along with a rather sparse drift of Callibaetis mayflies ("speckled duns"). No problem. We located a few persistent risers (not nearly so persistent as they had been two days earlier), and tossed those same McMurray ants at them for an hour or so without touching a fish. Part of the problem lay in the fact that, unlike the first day of our trip, the pods of trout were roving about, constantly shifting positions and making themselves very difficult targets in the process.

Finally we regrouped ashore and decided to get things figured out anew. That the trout were taking Callibaetis emergers and duns should have been obvious, but the exceptional ant-fishing we had experienced over the past two days had obviously skewed our judgement. Just to make sure, we hauled out the sampling nets and seined a few current lanes. Sure enough, ants and Callibaetis comprised the bulk of the drift, but the Callibaetis had not been present until that day. Apparently the trout welcomed the new menu item.

We still had tremendous difficulty intercepting the constantly roving trout, but those we could get a drift over took the Callibaetis pattern without hesitation. We had again found the right fly, but only as a result of floundering uselessly for more than an hour.

Five years later. Silver Creek under cloudy morning skies. Tricos danced above the water in huge swarms. Trout took up feeding stations. I waded in above a pod of some 10 or 12 fish, a No. 20 Trico hackle spinner attached to a long tippet. I made three presentations before deciding I had better set up my camera tripod on the bank so I could get a few self-portrait shots. That trip back to shore probably saved the morning for me: Sitting on the bank assembling camera gear, with my legs dangling in the creek, I noticed a clutch of little Baetis mayflies clinging to my waders.

The Tricos, in huge dancing swarms above the water,

had captured my attention immediately—after all, I had come here to fish over the little Tricos. But the rising trout had yet to see one of those Tricos actually fall to the water. Instead, the rainbows were eating the little Baetis mayflies. I seined the drift at mid-river just to be certain. Sure enough, little blue-winged olives—emergers, nymphs, duns and cripples—clogged the mesh. I dug out a tiny floating Baetis nymph and enjoyed a memorable hour of good fishing before the trout started keying on the Tricos. By way of luck, I had discovered the right fly.

The right fly. That can mean a lot of different things. The right fly, first and foremost, is one that will take fish. On a swift-water freestone river, the right fly for a caddis hatch might be a fully hackled elkhair caddis; on a spring creek, that same elkhair might well prove useless. Instead, a downwing spent caddis pattern might be the right fly.

In choosing the right fly, you must consider the trout's environment: Flat-water trout have the opportunity to inspect, very closely, anything that drifts by. I have watched spring-creek trout drift downstream under a fly (real ones and imitations) for five or six feet before either taking the bug or rejecting it and looking for something more appealing.

This opportunity for trout to get a really good look at your fly requires that it be as suggestive as possible of the actual insect. Do not, however, confuse the term "suggestive" with the phrase "imitative." An ultra-realistic mayfly pattern, such as those artistic gems tied by Russ Spain of Portland, Oregon wherein every minute body part is exactly duplicated to scale, are truly and precisely imitative. They are not, however, very suggestive simply because, to the trout, they don't look like the real insect on the water. Russ Spain would be the first to agree that, despite their dazzling intricacy and artistic value, ultra-realism in flies does not equate to a better fishing fly.

What, then, does make an effective, suggestive fishing fly for spring creeks? The no-hackle duns are good examples: simple in design, precisely representative of the size and silhouette of the natural, and constructed in a way that enables them to float much in the way of the natural insect. The same can be said of virtually every effective spring-creek pattern, from the highly effective Juracek/Mathews sparkle emergers to the partridge caddis. Certainly there are a few patterns of somewhat complex design (e.g. the para-drake), but even these retain the two most signifcant characteristics of an effective spring-creek fly—they are the right size and shape and, just as importantly, they ride the water in a realistic manner.

Indeed, to fool spring creek trout day in and day out, your patterns must pass each of those two tests: They must mimic the size and shape of the natural (not to mention color) and they must act natural. Passing only one of these tests and failing the other generally means doom for a fly fished on the spring creeks.

That, of course, is the big difference between flies we fish on the riffle waters so common throughout the West and those we fish on the flat waters over ultra-selective trout: The two styles of patterns are not especially inter-changeable in many cases. Fast-water flies need be tied in a manner that keeps them

afloat, but the very act of adding the materials required to accomplish that task render such flies rather ineffective on the spring creeks. (likewise, the lightly-dressed, frequently unhackled flies we use on the spring creeks would simply sink under the rigors of riffles and rapids).

Beyond specific dressing, however, the right fly means one in which you, as the angler, has confidence. Even the best pattern is virtually useless unless you fish it with utter confidence: You must believe in the fly you choose to be at your best as an angler.

Craig Mathews and John Juracek, in their informative book *Fishing Yellowstone Hatches,* make a crucial point in saying, "an important lesson. . . is that fishing the correct fly removes a critical variable, freeing you to concentrate on your approach and presentation, and eliminating worry about whether you should be changing flies."

That day on Silver Creek, after I discovered that *Baetis* occupied the drift almost exclusively, I had no doubt that a floating nymph of the right size and color would take trout. I still had to make the ideal presentation because, as is typical during a heavy spring-creek hatch, the trout fed in very narrow feeding lanes and with very regular rise intervals. But even after 20 drifts I maintained utter confidence in the fly I had chosen, knowing full well that the floating nymph is the best choice for a flat-water *Baetis* hatch and that I might very well have to cast 20, 30 or 40 times before fly and trout collided at a riseform simultaneously.

Thus, choosing the right fly requires a knowledge of the particular insect you are imitating and an understanding of how trout feed on that insect. Some mayflies (like *Baetis*) are almost always more effectively imitated with an emerger pattern (like a floating nymph) than a dun pattern. In other cases, the dun pattern might prove as or more useful than any kind of emerger. In a few cases, spinner patterns are the appropriate choice.

Even specific pattern can make a difference, as was the case between the fur ants and the McMurray ants that Tim and I employed that week on the Henry's Fork. Thousands of effective patterns have come about over the years: How is the

newcomer to spring-creek fly fishing to choose the best from the countless effective flies available? Ask questions at the local fly shop. Ask them what is hatching and what flies have been most productive. Talk to other anglers on the stream. Read information on the subject, especially about specific hatches. Then go fishing. I started fishing the Henry's Fork at the age of eight when my dad would let me tag along on his appraisal-business trips to the Island Park area. Despite all those years, I still have a hell of a lot to learn about that river and I have always learned more per day spent fishing than per day spent reading about it, if for no other reason that, on the water, I can apply what I have read. So read what is available, but don't forget the application part: You can read everything there is to read, talk to everyone there is to talk to, but without some time spent astream applying what you have learned, most of the knowledge gained through secondary sources is of limited value.

Anyone who has spent considerable time fishing over certain hatches or on certain waters eventually settles on a few favorite patterns. In the next section, in which we discuss spring creek trout foods and flies to match, I offer a variety of patterns that will work on the flat water and, for what it is worth, I have highlighted my preferred patterns with an asterisk. Perhaps that can serve as a starting point for you when you pursue a new hatch, but going afield in search of that hatch will prove most educational of all, especially if you are prepared with patterns that you will fish with confidence.

When you get right down to the act of picking a fly from your box of spring-creek patterns, you have already eliminated those that are not meant for flat water and highly selective trout. Now it is only a matter of choosing the correct fly to match the insect on which the trout are currently feeding.

Sometimes this is the most difficult task of all, especially when myriad insects are adrift on the water and trout are rising everywhere. If you are not sure what the trout are eating, sample the drift with your handy seine or aquarium net—this simple 5-minute task will take a lot of the guess-work (and the inherent frustration that frequently accompanies guessing) out of choosing a fly.

Much has been said over the years about reading riseforms and in doing so, determining what the trout are eating. In fact, an understanding of riseforms can be useful, but much more so in determining what stage of an insect is being preyed upon than in discovering exactly what insect is being eaten by the fish. If, for instance, you can clearly see a trout's snout above the water during the rise, you can be fairly certain the fish is eating something on top or in the film. Conversely, if you see fins and tails breaking the surface, but not heads or noses, the trout are feeding just below the surface.

Traditional fly angling literature tells us that splashy rises indicate that trout are eating caddis, stoneflies or hoppers; sipping and gulping rises indicate predation on mayflies, midges and small terrestrials. Despite its value on riffles water and freestone streams, such advice should be regarded as suspect on the flat waters of the spring creeks where trout tend to sip and gulp just about everything. In fact, on the best spring creeks, splashy rises tend to mark the efforts of small trout or whitefish.

In any event, do study the riseforms: watch for heads or noses or bubbles to indicate surface or surface-film feeding; watch for fins and tails to tell you the trout are eating emergers just below the surface. Watch for the porpoising rises that might indicate trout eating caddis pupa at the surface; pay close attention to sipping rises, where the only sign is a few subtle rings on the surface, as these can indicate the presence of a very large trout quietly sucking morsels out of the film. Just don't make the mistake of assuming a splashy rise is a big trout chasing adult caddis or that a subtle gulp couldn't reveal a trout eating hoppers.

When in doubt (which is fairly often for most of us on the spring creeks), get out the seine and sample the drift.

Remember also that different trout may be feeding on different foods. Indeed, understanding that fact and then properly responding to compound and complex hatches wherein a variety of trout foods are available and are being preyed upon in various measure by individual trout, goes a long way toward redoubling your success on the spring creeks.

An example: A pod of trout in front of you might be contently sipping *Baetis* mayflies (blue-winged olives) while another pod across-stream has given up on the *Baetis* in favor of a drift of flying ants. Meanwhile, a single large trout at mid-river is taking only the few *Callibaetis* mayflies that are present. If that were not enough, you begin to notice different feeding strategies within the single pod of trout to which you are casting: Most are taking only *Baetis*; some seem to be taking both *Baetis* and *Callibaetis*; still others are eating anything and everything that looks edible.

So what fly do you choose for that pod of monster rainbows? Perhaps a *Baetis* floating nymph because every trout in the pod seems to be taking the little blue-winged olives, which are currently the dominant part of the drift. But the light is bad and the *Baetis* are a No. 20 and you have all kinds of trouble seeing those little flies even 30 feet away. Perhaps a *Callibaetis* pattern, being a little larger and thus easier to see, might make a better choice. But thus far you have seen only a few of these larger mayflies eaten by trout and then seemingly only by an individual trout rising at the far edge of the pod. Maybe an ant pattern—you've noticed a few on the water, you are well aware of the taste trout seem to have for terrestrials.

Such are the thoughts that will occupy your mind come fly-choice time. And by way of tidying things up, let's say you go with the ant pattern and rise two fish in the first 10 casts. You have done well, but over the next 20 minutes, the ant pattern fails

to move another trout. Perhaps then, bad light and all, you switch to the *Baetis* floating nymph. After 20 drifts you finally time one just right and the tiny fly, which you can actually see on the water for the first time in the last six casts, arrives at a trout's nose just as that fish rises. Welcome to spring-creek fishing.

When Selectivity Breaks Down

Given everything we have deduced about selective fish and spring-creek fishing, why, during the midst of a heavy hatch of tiny mayflies, does a trout still ocassionally gobble down a No. 12 Royal Wulff that is dragging badly on the water?

In short, we don't know. We—meaning the angling community—don't really understand the trout's world nearly so well as we might believe. Indeed, despite the voluminous information we have compiled over the years, trout still befuddle us. They eat a big, bushy dry fly or a wooly bugger during a blanket hatch of little mayflies or caddisflies or they devour a fly that is dragging horribly on the surface when our angling insights suggest these things should not occur.

By our very nature we assign logic to the behavior of trout. But this is our logic, not their's and no matter how in-depth and technical our studies of fish, some trout somewhere will always do something to blow away our carefully crafted theories. Such is the intrigue of the trout.

I've heard all the theories on why selectivity breaks down when logic (our logic) suggests that it should not: Maybe the trout have been feeding so heavily on a certain insect that something totally different appeals to them; perhaps they've seen so many imitations of the predominant insects that something new and different fools them completely; maybe a streamer stirs an instinctive reaction to attack or maybe the "wrong" fly just looks good to them at the time.

Perhaps all these notions hold true at one time or another. Perhaps none has any validity. Either way, when trout defy our sense of logic, we can only guess as to why. But we should not be surprised that trout march to their own tune and we should avoid the trap of over-analyzing them. A trout, after all, is simply a trout and it's ability to constantly surprise and fool us is what allures us most.

This point suggests that instead of trying to figure out why a spring-creek trout ate your No. 12 Royal Wulff when you couldn't touch a fish on the "right" fly, just file that day away in your memory and file a few of those Wulff's away in your fly boxes. Then, the next time your perfect flies and perfect presentations fail to entice a trout, dig out one of those Royal Wulff's (or trudes, or wooly buggers, or humpy's, or muddlers, or whatever did the trick last time) and see what happens. After all, you can't do any worse and at times you might be pleasantly surprised.

Spring-creek anglers tend to forget those days of their infancy in this sport—days when bucktail caddis, Royal Wulff's and muddler minnows always seemed to catch a few fish. I wonder myself whether I was a better angler at the age of 10 or 12, loose on the Henry's Fork and unencumbered by knowledge of hatches and feeding patterns and all the other stuff we fly fishers cram into our brains. Those were simple times and trout didn't seem so smart then.

So I don't forget the lessons learned a long time ago; I carry a box full of the old standbys and when things don't follow the scripts I've learned to expect on the spring creeks, I'm not afraid to revert back to the tactics of old. The worst that can occur is that I won't rise any fish, which is exactly the reason I switched from the "right" fly to the "wrong" fly in the first place.

Green Drake *(Drunella grandis).*

Pale Morning Dun

Slate-winged Olive, or "Flav" *(Drunella flavilinea).*

Speckled-wing Dun *(Callibaetis).*

SPRING CREEK DIARY

Sept. 1993, Railroad Ranch

Paradise found. They were big this year—that much was obvious by the snouts, backs and tails breaking the surface ever so deliberately. Intermittent thunder showers and crummy weather in general had driven most folks off the river, not that late September is a crowded time anyway on the Henry's Fork.

Mahogany duns. God, I love those mayflies—they so rarely let me down as the trout seem to relish them above everything else that time of year. Lots of them that day—a full-blown regatta of lovely reddish-brown mayflies—but as per usual, not really a dense enough hatch to make things difficult. They drove the trout nuts and I had the whole incredible thing to myself and it was easy.

I hope to live long enough to enjoy a day like that one again.

Spring Creek Mayflies

From the stately green drakes and *Hexagenias* to the tiny Western olives and Tricos, mayflies traditionally define the spring-creek experience. The mayflies hatch in a reasonably predictable procession of species throughout the season, starting with blue-winged olives (*Baetis*), pale morning duns and green drakes; ending with the Tricos, mahogany duns and finally the *Baetis* once again.

The mayflies are reliable, perhaps more so than any other spring-creek trout foods. Year in and year out they follow the same general emergence schedule, varying only slightly with annual weather and climate variations. And they emerge in the same orderly fashion each season, allowing anglers to plan entire spring-creek trips around a particular mayfly.

Despite their abundance and predictability, the mayflies of our spring creeks can produce some tough fishing simply due to the selectivity with which trout will feed on many of the hatches. Tradition dictates that dry-fly anglers use upright, hackled patterns to represent these mayflies when, on the flat waters of the spring creeks, surface-film emerger or nymph patterns frequently outfish standard dries. The transition from classic hackled flies to emerger and surface-nymph artificials is probably the single most important adaptation in pattern that a spring-creek angler can make with respect to mayflies.

Make no mistake—when, in the course of fishing a spring-creek mayfly emergence, you employ emergers, cripples, stillborns or floating nymph patterns, you are indeed fishing dry or, at the very least, damp. During reasonably dense emergences of any kind, spring-creek trout (at least the large ones) will hover just below the surface, waiting for emerging insects to reach the surface film. Referring to caddisflies, Gary LaFontaine coined the phrase "hesitation" in reference to the time at which an emerger reaches the surface film. He meant that the emerging insect, after swimming or being bouyed to the surface, necessarily hesitated during the period of time required for the adult insect to remove itself from the surface film. The same principle is applicable to the mayflies. They too must hesitate at the surface—sometimes for a considerable amount of time (e.g. several seconds)—in order to escape their nymphal shucks.

Without a doubt spring-creek trout have learned to take advantage of the highly vulnerable emerger stage of the mayfly. By hanging just below the surface, trout can simply pick off nymphs as they reach the surface and duns as they struggle to escape their exoskeleton. The smooth, slow currents typical of spring creeks allow the trout to pursue this feeding strategy: They can hold near the surface in such water without expending much energy. Conversely, fast-water trout must either feed on nymphs as they leave the bottom or must hold deep and make sudden dashes to the surface to eat emergers or dries.

During research for his book *Mayflies the Angler and the Trout,* Fred Arbona sampled the stomach contents of more than 1,000 trout after the fish had fed during various mayfly hatches. Arbona writes:

"Nymphs and emerging duns, according to the stomach contents examined, do turn out to be the most frequently found and apparently the most vulnerable stages of emerging mayflies. . .Fortunately for the dry fly purist, artificial imitations of both of these stages are designed to be fished just under or on the surface film during the hatch, and thus will still provide the lover of the dry fly the thrill of seeing the ring of a trout rising to his imitation."

Arbona also suggests that ". . . it may behoove anglers to develop the habit of matching the hatch at the start of any hatch, and then concentrating fully on proper presentation."

Indeed, proper presentation is essential to the success of any spring-creek fishing situation. But the right fly is critical as well. In fact, proper fly and correct presentation are inextricably bound in successful spring-creek angling, mayflies being no exception. This is precisely what Arbona says. Learn to choose the right fly for the hatch in progress early on and then concentrate on presenting that fly in the logical manner. By doing so, you can be confident in your fly, thus eliminating the variable of pattern choice and allowing yourself the chance to succeed or fail on the merits of the variable of presentation.

Spring creeks host a tremendous variety of mayfly species. Thus, learning which patterns produce best on particular mayfly emergences is critical. But you needn't tie and carry imitations for every species of mayfly. Instead, focus on two things: 1. Tie flies to imitate the major mayfly groups (families and genera) rather than species and 2. Learn which mayflies will be emerging on the spring creek you intend to fish at that particular time.

An example of the first of these considerations might be the *Baetis* mayflies (blue-winged olives, tiny Western olives). More than a dozen species occur in the West, yet all are so similar that tying imitations for each of the species would be absurd. Instead, a selection of imitations in two or three shades and three or four sizes will handle any and all *Baetis* activity you encounter. This chapter lists the most important mayflies found on our spring creeks. Only on occasion does the identification of these insects go beyond the level of genus. *Hexagenia limbata*, for example, is the only giant yellow mayfly—the only *Hexagenia*—found on any of the Western spring creeks. Thus, the species name, *limbata*, might deserve mention only for the sake of interest but certainly not for clarity's sake.

The *Drunella* mayflies, on the other hand, might offer an example of species identification being necessary. *Drunella grandis* and *Drunella flavilinea* are important mayflies on our spring creeks. Both are green drakes, the former being the big green drake that emerges in May and June, drawing anglers from the far reaches of the globe to places like the Henry's Fork. *Drunella flavilinea*, despite offering excellent hatches, does not command such attention from anglers. *D. flavilinea* has long been called the "small Western green drake" or the "slate-winged olive." If you see this insect astream, its physical characteristics and time of emergence will identify it for you. At that point you may not care whether it is a *Drunella flavilinea* or a small Western green drake. But suppose you are calling around for some information about hatches on a particular spring creek and the name "flav" is tossed around? *D. flavilinea* is often called "flav" by some anglers. If you didn't know what a

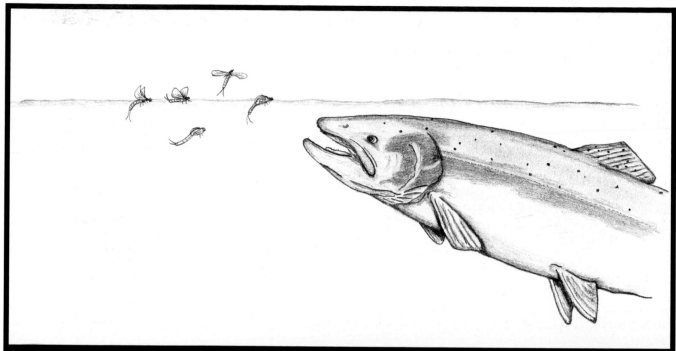

By hanging just below the surface, trout can take advantage of the most vulnerable stage of an emergence as nymphs, stillborns, and newly hatched duns are concentrated at the top and in the film.

D. flavilinea was, then you probably wouldn't know what a "flav" is either—despite the fact that you might well be able to identify the mayfly as a "small Western green drake" or "slate-winged olive" on sight.

In other words, the Latin identifications of certain mayflies can be helpful when communicating with other anglers especially when planning trips to particular waters. Another classic example might be my first encounter with the Williamson River. I called a friend to get some information about the gray drakes. He said they didn't have gray drakes but that the black drake spinner fall had been excellent the past week. Having never heard of a black drake at that time, I said as much and asked the follow-up question: "Is the black drake a *Siphlonurus* mayfly?" The answer was yes and my suspicion proved correct. Black drake was simply a local name for the gray drake spinner.

Having said all that, let's back up a bit and remember that trout could care less about Latin or any other labels we humans attach to their food. The trout see's things differently: Adequate quantities of one mayfly will cause the fish to feed exclusively on that insect because such a strategy is the wisest use of the trout's energy. Trout, obviously, don't know this. They just react instinctively in a selective manner to an abundance of food. Arbona gathered evidence with his stomach sampling to support another common-sense theory: The denser the emergence, the higher the incidence of selective feeding. In other words, if you fish over a blanket hatch of *Baetis* mayflies that are mixed with a sparse handful of some larger mayfly it will be a rare trout that will not respond by feeding selectively on the *Baetis* to the exclusion of the larger insect.

Certainly there are some exceptions to patterns of selective feeding. Some trout will take ants or beetles better than Trico patterns or tiny Western olive patterns during the course of these mayfly hatches. But such cases frequently involve trout that live in a section of stream where they see a lot of terrestrials. When the Trico activity gets them looking up,

these trout are still apt to eat an ant or beetle simply because they have developed a strong reflex to do so. Another trout—one that lives in the middle of the river—might not have seen enough terrestrials to develop a taste, or rather a habit, for them. It is worth noting, as well, that trout tend to be less selective during the early and late stages of a hatch than during its peak.

As my friend Brent Snow of Eugene, Oregon, notes, sometimes a tiny non-imitative fly can work wonders during a heavy hatch. Brent suggests that in some sense maybe the trout get bored looking at the same tiny mayflies for days on end. Thus, he sometimes tries a No. 20 royal Wulff or renegade with excellent results. I've experienced similar success once in a while with a tiny Griffith's Gnat fished during the height of a heavy mayfly hatch. Perhaps the trout see these flies as terrestrials or maybe just as something to break up the monotony, but whatever the case, once in a while a small, non-imitative pattern can work wonders. (Interestingly, Brent's two favorite flies for this purpose, the royal Wulff and the renegade, and my favorite, the Griffith's gnat, all share a body made from peacock herl, a material which I have always found to produce highly effective patterns.)

In any event, the most important aspects of spring-creek mayflies is their ability to cause trout to feed selectively and to do so while holding just below the surface. These two things dictate our pattern choice. Obviously you could tie flies to mimic every important stage of every important type of spring-creek mayfly. But you would be wasting time at the tying table unless you planned to spend the entire season fishing a particular river. For most of us, spring-creek angling is a process of choosing a destination and then going there for a few days during the season. Therefore, it makes considerably more sense to find out what mayflies will be hatching at the time you will be fishing and then tying just those patterns. In this manner you are prepared to anticipate the hatches.

With that, let's examine the important spring-creek mayflies, beginning with the "Big Three:" pale morning duns, blue-winged olives and the Trico's or white-winged blacks. These three types are found on every spring creek and, more importantly, comprise the most significant hatches on most of the spring creeks. From there, we will move on to cover the other significant spring-creek mayflies. Fly patterns marked by an asterisk denote patterns that I rely on constantly. Patterns listed without the asterisk are simply those that I use infrequently or not at all, but which have been developed by experienced spring-creek anglers and exhibit the essential qualities of successful spring-creek patterns.

Many of the best mayfly patterns can be tied in whatever sizes and colors are required to mimic particular hatches. The sparkle dun, for example, is effective on most of the spring-creek mayfly hatches. You can tie this fly on a No. 20 hook with an olive body and olive-brown Z-lon for a trailing shuck to imitate a *Baetis* (blue-winged olive) or on a No. 14 hook with a tan body and gray shuck to imitate the *Callibaetis* (speckled wing dun). The pattern is the same. Only the size and color changes. The same can be said of all the patterns listed below: Each can be used to imitate any number of mayflies with slight changes in size and color (appropriate sizes and colors for each pattern are listed under the different mayflies described hereafter).

Sparckle-Dun *(Juracek/Mathews)*
hook: dry fly
tail: Z-lon or similar material (represents the trailing nymphal shuck of the emerging mayfly)
body: fine dubbing
wing: fine natural deer hair, tied compara-dun style

Compara-Dun
hook: dry fly
tail: micro-fibets or hackle fibers
body: fine dubbing
wing: fine natural deer hair

No-Hackle Dun
hook: dry fly
tails: micro-fibets or hackle fibers
body: fine dubbing
wings: duck quill segments

CDC No Hackle
hook: dry fly
tails: micro-fibets
body: fine dubbing
wings: CDC feathers

Emergent Cripple *(Shewey)*
hook: dry fly
tail: fine sparkle yarn as a trailing shuck
body: fine dubbing
wings: Z-lon or CDC tied short, spent in delta position
hackle: two turns in front of wings, undersized by one hook size

Quigley Cripple *(Bob Quigley)*
hook: dry fly
tail: ostrich herl
body: fine ostrich herl
thorax: rabbit dubbing

wing: fine natural deer hair, butt ends showing at front
hackle: dyed grizzly

Floating Nymph
hook: dry fly
tails: hackle fibers, short
body: fine dubbing
legs: hackle fibers, short
wing: ball of grey synthetic dubbing

Bunse Natural Dun *(Richard Bunse)*
tails: beaver guard hairs
wing: natural fine deer hair
body: closed cell packing foam, colored with permanent marker

Sparkle Spinner *(Juracek/Mathews)*
hook: dry fly
tails: hackle fibers
body: fine dubbing
wings: white or pale gray Z-lon

Hackle Spinner
hook: dry fly
tails: micro-fibets or hackle fibers
body: fine dubbing and/or stripped peacock herl
wing: hackle, clipped bottom and V-clipped top

Hen-wing Spinner
hook: dry fly
tails: micro-fibets or hackle fibers
body: fine dubbing or stripped peacock herl
thorax: fine dubbing
wings: hen hackle tips or CDC feathers, spent

Krystal Spinner *(Shewey)*
hook: dry fly
tails: micro-fibets or hackle fibers
body: fine dubbing and/or stripped herl
wings: a few strands of Krystal Flash
hackle: a few wraps of dry fly hackle, clipped top and bottom

Pale Morning Duns
The pale morning duns (especially *Ephemerella inermis* and *E. infrequens*) comprise perhaps the most important of spring-creek mayflies. Their emergences span the season from late May through August; at every stage of their life—nymphs, emerger, dun, spinner— the PMD's are heavily preyed upon by trout; finally, they are widespread throughout the West, offering good hatches on virtually all spring creeks and many other rivers to boot.

The season's initial emergences of pale morning duns can be frustratingly brief, perhaps half an hour. Later, the PMD hatches might span several hours. In fact, once the emergence begins, it quickly gathers momentum and becomes very dependable. The PMD's generally hatch between late morning and early afternoon and always tend to hatch during the most comfortable time of the day. Thus, on hot days, hatches may be earlier in the morning or at times during the evening. On warm days, in fact, PMD's sometimes emerge for a short time only to reappear later in the afternoon. Cold days might delay the hatch until noon or 1 p.m. and see it last through late afternoon.

MAYFLY PATTERNS

NO-HACKLE DUN   SPARKLE DUN   COMPARA-DUN

QUIGLEY CRIPPLE   FLOATING NYMPH   EMERGENT CRIPPLE

CDC NO-HACKLE DUN   BUNSE PARACHUTE DUN   BUNSE NATURAL DUN

MAYFLY SPINNER PATTERNS

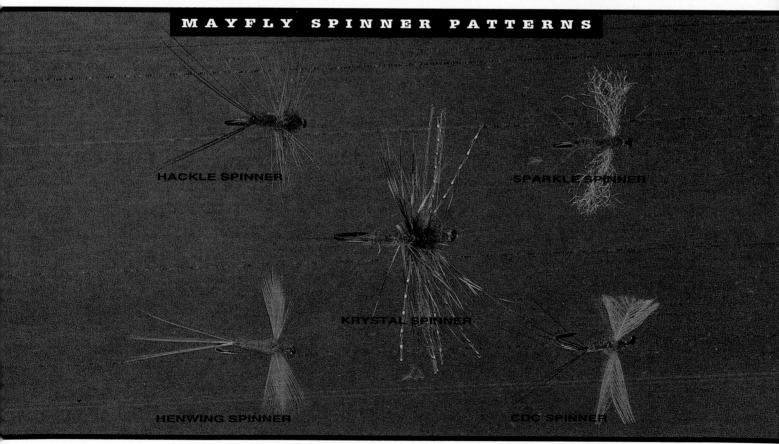

HACKLE SPINNER   SPARKLE SPINNER

KRYSTAL SPINNER

HENWING SPINNER   CDC SPINNER

The PMD hatches are predictable, following the same general pattern and time schedule each day unless the weather changes drastically. As with other mayflies, inclement weather can only improve the hatch of pale morning duns, sometimes prompting immense "blanket hatches."

During a good year on the Henry's Fork, *Ephemerella* activity can consume every day, virtually all day, for a month or two. Other bugs are always present as well, but some fish lock into the PMD's—emergers, duns, spinners—for most of their surface feeding throughout the day. These Henry's Fork PMD hatches are as profuse as they get, but all the spring creeks host major emergences of these mayflies, often lasting for a good portion of the season.

The earlier hatches, usually *E. inermis*, are larger than the later insects, with a No. 14 or 16 (sometimes 18) pattern mimicking them. Later, during the end of June and during July and August, the PMD's are smaller, usually requiring a No 18 imitation (on occasion, a No. 20). On some streams, these later hatches are frequently comprised of *E. infrequens*, but Mike Lawson, owner of Henry's Fork Angler's Inc., notes some interesting information regarding PMD's on the Henry's Fork:

I have corresponded with George Edmunds for the past few years and he has set me straight on several mayfly species. According to his findings, E. infrequens *is not a recorded species on the Henry's Fork. Of course he realizes that this species has been written about by numerous fly fishing writers, but according to his research, only inermis is found in the Henry's Fork. Several years ago he asked me to send him as many male spinners as I could which I identified as* infrequens.

He wrote back identifying each as E. inermis. *He explained that in waters which contain both species, they are separated by a difference in the elevation of their habitat. He has explained the vast differences in size and coloration of individual specimens of inermis. They get smaller as the season goes on, from about a size 14 in early June to as small as a 20 in mid August. There is also great differences in coloration partly due to difference in habitat and also the difference in gender.*

Indeed, pale morning duns vary widely in color, with shades of light olive, pale or even bright yellow or tannish olive being common. They also occur in shades of orange and olive-brown. In their book *Western Hatches,* Rick Hafele and Dave Hughes note that "*Ephemerella* duns change color quickly after emerging."

Hafele and Hughes observed this tendency in *Ephemerella doddsi,* a green drake species of the Pacific coast streams, whose dark brown bodies they attempted to match with their flies. They write that "our patterns met with little success until we caught a freshly emerged dun: It was a pale yellowish-olive, with just a tinge of brown. Within an hour or two, brown became the dominant color."

"To imitate *Ephemerella* duns accurately," conclude Hafele and Hughes, "one must observe a dun within minutes of emergence."

Though the body color of PMD's varies considerably, their wings are always a very pale gray, sometimes tinged on the leading edge with yellow or light olive. Unlike a large *Baetis* specimen, with which a PMD might be confused, the *Ephemerella's* hind wings are rather well developed and easily noticeable.

PMD spinners, as one would expect from reading Hafele and Hughes, have a darker coloration, females being medium olive to olive-brown, males displaying a rusty-brown shade. Both have clear wings and trout seem to care little whether they eat the olive female or the rust-colored male spinners.

Similarly, exact duplication of the dun's color is only rarely required. Carry imitations in two or three shades, perhaps pale olive, yellowish, and medium olive.

The emergence of PMD's and the spinner fall are both capable of causing voluminous surface activity. During the peak of the season, both hatch and spinner fall can be remarkably dense.

Trout often feed readily on the duns because the newly emerged PMD's tend to ride the water for a while, making easy targets of themselves. Nonetheless, emerger patterns and stillborn patterns often elicit more rises than flies mimicking the duns. Emerger patterns can be fished just below the surface or flush in the surface film. Stillborns or cripple patterns, especially productive during heavy emergences, are easier to see on the water and are therefore the choice of many spring creek veterans.

The spinner falls occur morning or evening and in many places both morning and evening. These spinner falls can be dense to the point of absurdity. Tim Blount and I worked a week's worth of PMD activity on the Henry's Fork one year with excellent fishing during the mid-day emergence. But the evening spinner falls were ridiculous: Huge flotillas of spinners drifted over countless rising trout and during a week's time I think we managed three or four fish during those evening spinner falls.

We were competing with too many naturals. In fact, competing isn't an accurate description of the drubbing we took that week. Every square foot of water must have contained hundreds of dead PMD's. The sheer quantity of spinners was awesome. The hatch itself was good, but not dense enough to lead us to expect such unbelievable numbers of spinners.

In fact, any time a tremendous hatch of PMD's occurs during cloudy weather, you can expect the first day of sunshine to produce an outstanding morning spinner fall. This is especially true of the late-season pale morning dun hatches of August.

Huge numbers of these mayflies, in both the dun form and spinner form, are not unusual. The fish will feed heavily during both the emergence and spinner drift, although during lengthy hatches of several hours, the best fishing may be early with rise activity decreasing during the hatch's latter stages. Observant anglers, however, can find some of the largest trout in any given spring creek quietly sipping PMD's towards the end of the hatch when smaller fish have apparently satisfied their appetites.

*PMD Sparkle Dun: No. 14-18, light brown Z-lon shuck, pale olive-yellow body, light deer hair wing
*PMD Emergent Cripple: No. 14-18, tan shuck, pale olive or yellow-olive body, pale gray wings, cream hackle
*PMD Floating Nymph: No. 14-18, light dun tail & legs, light olive-yellow body, olive rib, gray wingcase
CDC Floating Nymph: No. 14-18, yellowish-olive body and thorax, pale gray wing
Quigley PMD Cripple: No. 14-18, light olive tail, light green body & thorax, light green grizzly hackle
PMD No-Hackle: No. 14-18, pale olive or ginger tails, pale olive or pale yellow body, light gray wings

**CDC FLOATING NYMPH/
EMERGER**

**PMD SOFT HACKLE
EMERGER**

**LAWSON DROWNED
PMD**

**PMD SLOW-WATER
EMERGER**

PMD NYMPH

LAWSON PMD NYMPH

Compara-Dun: No. 14-18, olive or dun tails, pale olive-yellow body, light gray wing

Bunse Natural Dun: No. 14-18, pale olive-yellow body or colored on-stream to match naturals

*PMD Hackle Spinner: No. 14-18, dun tails, olive tan to rust body, tan rib, dun hackle wings

PMD Sparkle Spinner: No. 14-18, dun tails, light brown to pale olive body, white wings

Pale Morning Dun Nymph

hook: wet fly for deep-fished patterns, dry fly for those fished just below the surface; No. 14-18
tail: wood duck fibers
body: pale yellow or pale olive-yellow dubbing
rib: olive thread
wingcase: light gray mallard quill segment
legs: wood duck

Pale Morning Dun Nymph *(Mike Lawson)*

hook: 2XL nymph, No. 14-16
thread: pale olive
tails: lemon woodduck fibers
abdomen: light olive-tan hare's mask fur
rib: fine gold wire
thorax: pale olive-brown ostrich herl
wingcase: dark grey mallard quill segment

PMD Slow-water Emerger *(Rene Harrop/McKenzie Flies)*

hook: dry fly, No. 14-18
tails: lemon woodduck fibers
body: pale olive dubbing
rib: fine gold wire
wings: mallard quill sections, tied to the sides and fairly short
legs: a few light partridge fibers
thorax: same as body

Drowned PMD *(Mike Lawson)*

hook: dry fly, No. 14-18
tail: pale olive-yellow Z-lon or similar
body: pale olive-yellow dubbing
wings: mallard quill segments tied spent

PMD Soft-Hackle Emerger *(Mike Lawson)*

hook: dry fly, No. 14-18
tails: lemon woodduck fibers
body: pale olive-yellow hare's ear dubbing
rib: light olive mono-cord
hackle: medium gray hen hackle (wet fly style)

PMD CDC Floating Nymph Emerger

(Rene Harrop/tied by McKenzie Flies)
hook: dry fly, No. 14-18
tail: woodduck fibers
body: pale olive-yellow dubbing
rib: olive tying thread
wing/legs: light dun CDC flanked by partridge hackle fibers
thorax: pale olive-yellow dubbing

Blue-winged Olives and Tiny Western Olives

The *Baetis* mayflies, often called "blue-winged olives," "tiny Western olives," or simply "olives," comprise one of the most abundant mayflies in our streams. Trout love them. At times fish even seem to prefer these mayflies over other insects hatching simultaneously.

Entomologists recognize numerous *Baetis* species. The differences among these species are insignificant to anglers. Just match the size, mimic the color reasonably well and fish the stage of emergence on which the trout are feeding (nymphs, emergers or duns).

Baetis tend towards the small range as mayflies go. Hatches of larger *Baetis* (No. 14-16) occur from time to time, but flies tied on No. 18, 20 and 22 hooks will match most emergences. The tiny Western olives (formerly classified in a now-defunct genus called *Pseudocleon*) may run as small as a No. 26, although No. 24's and 22's are more common.

Baetis mayflies emerge throughout the year. They constitute something of a Godsend at times during February or March, October or November, when a surprisingly heavy hatch might tempt trout to the surface, giving nymph-wielding off-season anglers a welcome chance to fish on top. In fact, these little mayflies can emerge any time of year. Many spring creeks host their best *Baetis* hatches during May and June and again during September and October.

The duns are recognizable by their dun-colored wings, the hind pair of which are so small as to appear non-existent. True to their name, these mayflies usually sport a body of an olive cast, sometimes tending toward brown or gray, but usually with an olive cast nonetheless. The tiny Western olives are often pale light green, sometimes tending towards cream, other times, towards chartreuse. In addition, tiny Western olives have light gray wings (sometimes almost white).

Blue-winged olives and tiny Western olives can hatch in tremendous densities. Emergence can occur virtually any time of day, with late morning through mid-evening hatches being common. On cold days, mid-afternoon hatches, coinciding with the warmest part of the day, are the norm. Likewise, hot weather prompts early and late emergences.

Cool, drizzly days are traditional *Baetis* days and indeed such conditions are ideal because they cause the duns to ride the surface for a considerable distance before flying away. Under such circumstances, trout may feed heavily on the duns. But pleasant days offer *Baetis* hatches as well and even during sunny weather trout will at times feed heavily on the duns.

Still, emerger patterns, especially the Swisher-Richards floating nymph, often outfish dun patterns. Luckily you needn't worry about tying flies to match each of the different *Baetis* species. Instead, for blue-winged olives, tie duns and floating nymphs (or other emerger patterns) in No.16 through 22. Tie two or three different colors (e.g. medium olive, pale olive-brown and gray-brown) all with dun-colored wings. For the tiny Western olive, tie the same patterns, but on No. 20-24 hooks and with light wings and a light bright green body. With such a selection of flies, you can handle *Baetis* activity anywhere.

During a *Baetis* hatch, some large trout may feed exclusively on nymphs, often in very shallow water. These fish may take a floating nymph pattern, but their feeding strategy of capturing the nymphs just below the surface often renders dry flies useless, including the floating nymphs. These nymph feeders are very active. They usually stir up a commotion with side-to-side feeding that often exposes their back or tail and in general roils the surface into classic "nervous water."

You may encounter these nymphing trout during any spring-creek *Baetis* hatch. Luckily, however, good blue-winged olive emergences will cause most trout to concentrate on insects in the surface film. The trout will sip away at emergers and stillborns, taking an occasional dun as well. I've seen *Baetis*

Thousands of stillborn Baetis mayflies collect along a weed bed on the Henry's Fork.

**BAETIS EMERGER
(BLUE-WINGED OLIVES)**

BAETIS NYMPH

**CDC BAETIS EMERGER
(TINY WESTERN OLIVE)**

hatches where floating nymphs worked wonders while dun imitations went unnoticed, but rarely have I found a trout who would take duns to the total exclusion of floating nymphs. In other words, if you single out a trout feeding on *Baetis* duns, by all means offer him a like imitation. But if you have any doubt about a trout's preference, go with the floating nymph or cripple imitation, or offer the dun a few times and then switch to the floating nymph.

Baetis mayflies, incidentally, are the culprits in many masking hatch situations: A perfectly good drake hatch is coming off. You single out a nice, steadily rising trout and make the perfect presentation a dozen times with no response. You take a closer look only to discover little olives, outnumbering the drakes forty to one and parading endlessly over the fish. Like usual, close observation and a sampling net can really come in handy. Heavy *Baetis* hatches turn another peculiar trick as well. Sometimes the largest trout won't respond too well to the tiny No. 20 or 22 olive imitation, despite a voluminous hatch. But the frenzied hatch activity gets these big trout looking skyward anyway and a well-placed ant or beetle imitation might very well take them.

Such situations occur with regularity during the hatch of tiny western olives on the Henry's Fork. Tim Blount and I were fishing opposite sides of one of the islands on the lower end of Harriman Park when the river let fly with a tremendous hatch of tiny western olives. Every trout and whitefish in the river came up and just getting the fly past small trout to get to the big fish was a problem. We soon determined that the best fish didn't want the floating nymphs or dun patterns anyway.

Tim switched to a No. 14 red flying ant and cast to what looked like a decent rainbow. It was far beyond decent. With the ant pattern entrenched in its lower jaw, a huge rainbow tore downriver, porpoised twice, completely spooled Tim's reel and broke off, all in a matter of seconds. We figured that this trout was between six and eight pounds—no wonder the tiny olives didn't interest him. But the surface activity got his attention and the ant proved irresistible.

These tiny Western olives, the ones formerly known as *Pseudocleon*, can emerge in unbelievable numbers during late August and September. Unlike the larger *Baetis* species, trout don't seem too eager to feed on nymphs but will instead take emergers and some duns. Regardless, I've developed the habit of choosing first an ant or beetle during a heavy hatch of tiny olives and switching to imitative patterns only if the terrestrials fail. The larger *Baetis*, those imitated by No. 18 and 20 flies, are easier to mimic than the tiny Western olives. Nonetheless, during mid summer and fall, I keep the ant and beetle patterns handy. If a particular trout steadfastly refuses my *Baetis* patterns after what seems like an adequate number of drifts, I'll switch to the terrestrial.

Incidentally, when the late summer/fall emergences of *Baetis* get into full swing, they generally follow a unique and predictable schedule on most of the spring creeks with strong populations of these mayflies: First, during early afternoon, the larger blue-winged olives (commonly *B. parvus* and/or *B. tricaudatus*) begin to emerge (typically No. 18-20). Then on the heels of this hatch begins the emergence of the tiny western olives (*B. punctiventrus*), typically about 4 p.m. In short order, the tiny Western olives (No. 22-24) take over and may hatch for two hours or so. Though particular species vary, this pattern is common to most of the Western spring creeks.

In any case, look for the best *Baetis* hatches during inclement weather. Or, if you are in the vicinity of a spring creek, look for inclement weather and when it appears, go find a *Baetis* hatch. During stormy days of September I've been astream as early as 8 a.m. only to be greeted by a *Baetis* hatch in full progression, so watch for that wonderful "*Baetis* weather" anytime you are within reach of a spring creek.

*Sparkle Dun: No. 18-24, olive brown shuck, grayish- or brownish-olive body, grayish wing (switch from deer hair to CDC feather for smallest sizes to simplify the tying process)

*Sparkle Dun, Tiny Western Olive: No. 20-24, pale olive or pale chartreuse body, pale gray or white CDC wing

*Baetis Floating Nymph: No. 18-22, cream or watery dun tails and legs, light olive-brown or olive-tan body (or to match naturals), gray wingcase (substitute CDC for "CDC floating nymph")

Baetis No-Hackle: No. 18-22, light dun tails, light olive-tan body (or to match naturals), gray wings

*Emergent Cripple: No. 18-22, brown shuck, olive-brown body, gray wings, dun hackle

*Emergent Cripple, Tiny Western Olive: No. 22, olive shuck, light green body, white wings, no hackle

*Tiny Western Olive Floating Nymph: No. 20-24, cream tails, light olive body, pale gray or white wingcase (substitute CDC for CDC floating nymph)

Baetis Hackle Spinner: No. 18-22, dun tail, dark olive-brown or olive-gray body, dun hackle wings

Quigley Cripple: No. 16-20, light olive tail, light olive body, medium olive thorax, olive grizzly legs

Bunse Natural Dun: No. 16-20, olive-tan or olive-brown body

Baetis Emerger *(Juracek/Mathews)*
hook: dry fly, No. 18-24
tail: woodduck fibers
body: grayish- or brownish-olive dubbing
hackle: two turns of a mallard shoulder or snipe feather
Note: for tiny western olive, use pale olive or chartreuse dubbing for body

Baetis Nymph *(Arbona)*
hook: wet fly or nymph, No. 16-20
tail: ginger wood duck fibers
body: light olive brown dubbing
wingcase: dark mallard quill fibers
legs: ginger wood duck fibers

Harrop CDC Baetis Emerger *(Rene' Harrop)*
hook: dry fly, No. 18-20
tail: teal flank fibers
rib: fine gold wire
body: olive rabbit dubbing
legs: brown partridge hackle fibers
wing: dark dun CDC feathers, short
thorax: olive rabbit dubbing

Tricos ("white-winged blacks")

On the spring creeks of Idaho, one mayfly of August captivates the attention of spring-creek anglers above all others. This tiny mayfly is the "Trico," or *Tricorythodes*, sometimes called the "white-winged black" or simply "Trike." In the Rockies, Tricos begin their emergence between late July and early August, a time when most of the spring creeks are less crowded. Trico emergences in California, Oregon and Washington can begin as early as late May or June, with their significance increasing as summer progresses.

Tricos are small. Their imitations must be tied on hooks ranging from No. 18 through 22 (I use No. 20's most of the time). Male Tricos, which average a bit smaller than females, sport a black body. Female Tricos have olive bodies. Both sexes have a single pair of whitish-colored wings and three tails. In the spinner stage, the wings turn clear.

The male Tricos emerge during late evening on most streams, although apparently not in dense enough numbers to command widespread attention from the trout. (On a couple of occasions I have found a few of these Tricos hatching alongside more abundant *Baetis* mayflies on cool overcast evenings during September.) The males remain in the dun stage throughout the night. The next morning, female Trico duns emerge and quickly molt into spinners. The males do likewise, forming large swarms that hover over shallow water. The female Trico spinners then join the swarms of males and mating ensues.

This emergence and mating pattern offers trout extensive opportunity to feed on the Tricos because duns and spinners are on the water almost simultaneously. Some trout will feed exclusively on the nymphs and emergers; others key in on duns or spinners and many trout feed on all of the above.

During the early stages of the morning emergence, before the spinner fall really begins, determining which stage—duns, emergers or nymphs—is being eaten by individual trout requires careful observation and often a little trial and error. Or you can wait until the hatch is heavy enough that the majority of nymph-feeding trout switch to duns and spinners.

I used to try very hard to take trout on tiny nymphs and emergers during the earliest stages of the morning Trico emergence on the Henry's Fork. My efforts yielded far more frustration than trout. Since that time I've become convinced that an angler can do a lot more harm than good by trying to anticipate the Trico hatch by being in the water early with nymphs and emergers.

From those days on the Henry's Fork, I learned to stay out of the water until the trout were rising steadily, even greedily. Despite clouds of male Trico spinners swarming near shore, I learned to plant my butt on a rock above the pool and wait. Only when the trout had settled into feeding rhythms and the female Tricos were hatching, molting and falling spent, along with the males, would I enter the water.

My success during the Trico drift increased dramatically and I'm certain it is because I quit spooking trout by wading

around prior to the hatch. Consequently, when I've fished Tricos on other streams, I have followed the same ploy: Forget nymphs and stay out of the water until the Trico drift is in full swing.

In fact, when the duns have molted into spinners and hordes of the tiny mayflies (duns and spinners alike quite often) invade the water's surface, presentation usually becomes more significant than imitating one stage or the other.

As with any heavy concentration of insects, trout feeding on Tricos may hold just under the surface, rising at regular and usually frequent intervals. During these heavy Trico drifts you may well do better to stick with one fly, whether dun or spinner, and make as many presentations as necessary. Should a particular trout prove utterly uncooperative, your time is usually better spent finding another fish than making countless pattern changes.

I have generally had best results with a hackle-spinner pattern, which I tie on a No. 20 hook. During heavy Trico drifts, I will at times try a double fly—two flies tied on one hook. This arrangement allows you to get away with a slightly larger hook (a No. 16), which will hold fish better. Other than that, I have not found the double patterns to be any more or any less effective than standard patterns: When trout feed heavily on Tricos, they simply open their mouths every few seconds and inhale whatever is there, including your fly if your timing is perfect.

The late Ken Miyata was a proponent of what he called "anting the hatch." This technique, which I've seen employed by Henry's Fork veterans for years, simply involves casting an ant or beetle imitation to trout feeding on Tricos (or other tiny mayflies). Trout see ants and beetles regularly throughout the year and they get used to feeding on them. By casting an ant or beetle pattern to Trico-sipping trout you may be able to trigger a rise because the terrestrial fly is different from and thus distinguished from all the Tricos and yet is still familiar to the fish.

Next time you're having trouble rising a trout to a Trico pattern, try switching to a small ant or beetle. You still must time the rise and present the fly accurately, but sometimes the trick really works.

Trico Sparkle Dun: No. 20-24, brown shuck, olive or black body, light wing (CDC on small sizes)
Trico Sparkle Spinner: No. 18-24, white tails, black body, white wings
*Trico Hackle Spinner *(Shewey)*
hook: dry fly, No. 20-22
thread: white 8/0
tails: 3 white or cream hackle fibers, tied long
abdomen: tying thread
thorax: black mole fur

hackle: white or very light dun, wound through thorax (4-5 wraps), clipped flat below and V-clipped above

*Wing-fly Spinner (Datus C. Proper)
hook: dry fly, No. 20-24
thread: black
tails: dun hackle fibers, split, tied long
wing: stiff white hackle fibers covering 2/3 hook shank, trimmed on bottom
body: black dubbing wound through hackle

*Trico Antron-Dun (Shewey)
hook: dry fly, No. 18-22
tails: white hackle fibers, divided
body: black or olive dubbing
wing: white antron, tied compara-dun style (two turns of dun hackle optional)

Harrop Trico CDC Tailwater Dun
(Rene Harrop/McKenzie Flies)
hook: dry fly, No. 18-22
tails: white hackle fibers, divided
body: olive dubbing
thorax: black or dark brown dubbing
wing: white CDC feather

Green Drakes

They come from all over. I've met anglers from Maine and from Florida; from Texas and Alaska; from Japan and from England; from dozens of other places. I've met them on the spring creeks—especially on the Henry's Fork—all timing their trips for a common goal: to cast over the green drake hatch.

These grand mayflies might aptly be labeled the kings of the spring creek insects simply because of the attention they garner from fly anglers. Probably no other spring creek hatch is more popular and surely none draws so many anglers from far away places.

The green drakes are actually comprised of several species, including *Drunella grandis* (formerly *Ephemerella grandis*), the famous drake of the Henry's Fork. On most spring creeks these large mayflies emerge between early May and mid June, largely depending on elevation. A few streams also host late hatches, usually during September.

The hatches don't last long, usually a week or two. Yet fishing can be superb, with the largest fish feeding ravenously on the big mayflies. This is dry fly time. I've tried nymphs prior to the actual emergence, always with marginal success at best. Nymphs fished just below the film during the actual hatch can be very productive, while dun and emerger patterns always work when the trout get turned on to green drakes.

During the heaviest of green drake hatches, emerger patterns usually produce better than anything else, even when trout seem content to take duns. When the emergence is sparse (often the first and last few days of the hatch), dun patterns are very effective.

On most rivers, the green drakes emerge in limited numbers each morning for a few days before finally and suddenly busting loose on a subsequent morning. The peak of the hatch can mean thousands of duns covering the river's surface with the emergence lasting anywhere from two hours to most of the day. Finally, after a few days, maybe a week or a little more of heavy daily emergences, the green drakes will taper off. On rivers with good hatches, trout can often be tempted to eat a green drake pattern several days after the hatch has ended.

The green drakes are easily recognizable. Their body color, upon emergence, can vary from a bright green with olive-brown markings to a lovely olive with yellow trim. The wings are dark gray. As with the pale morning duns, the green drake's body color changes rather soon after emergence. In *Selective Trout*, Swisher and Richards note that a "freshly hatched female has a bright green body with slight brown markings on the back. However, the same dun one hour later is much darker, mostly dark reddish brown with light olive rings. The fish see the bright green, not the later darker fly."

In addition to their attractive color, the green drakes are distinguishable by their large size. A No. 10 fly will imitate them most of the time.

A typical time frame for the green drake emergence would be from late morning through early afternoon. Cool, overcast days sometimes cause the hatch to begin later, perhaps at 2 or 3 p.m. The very best days might offer a hatch lasting from 10 a.m. until 3 or 4 in the afternoon.

As with any good spring creek mayfly hatch, the green drake emergence requires that you concentrate on one fish and not worry about all the others. Pick your trout; approach carefully, positioning yourself upstream and slightly across; then concentrate on that one fish.

You needn't worry about spinners with green drakes and I've quit tying nymph imitations: When the hatch is on, trout feed on top or on insects in the surface film. Extended-body dun patterns fish well, but often the emerger patterns are a better choice.

*Bunse Natural Dun: No. 10-12, olive-green body
*Emergent Cripple: No. 10-12, brown shuck, olive-green body, light green rib, gray wings, grizzly dyed olive hackle
Quigley Cripple: No. 10-12, olive tail, olive-green body and thorax, tan-gray wing, light green grizzly hackle
Compara-dun: No. 10-12, light dun or cream tails, olive-green body, dark wing
*Sparkle Dun: No. 10-12, light brown shuck, olive-green body, dark wing

Trico spinner.

TRICO PATTERNS

TRICO HACKLE SPINNER

TRICO WING-FLY SPINNER

TRICO ANTRON DUN

TRICO CDC TAILWATER DUN

GREEN DRAKE PATTERNS

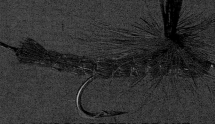

HARROP DOWNWING GREEN DRAKE

LAWSON GREEN DRAKE PARADRAKE

ARBONA GREEN DRAKE NYMPH

LAWSON GREEN DRAKE NYMPH

HARROP CDC CAPTIVE DUN

*Green Drake Emerging Dun (Arbona)
hook: dry fly, 2x-long, No. 10-12
thread: brown
tails: grizzly hackle dyed light olive
body: dark olive dubbing
rib: yellow floss or moncord thread
wings: 2 hackles—4 turns of dark dun for wings followed by two turns of grizzly dyed chartreuse for legs
(not pictured)

*Lawson Green Drake Paradrake
(Mike Lawson/Umpqua Feather Merchants)
hook: dry fly, No. 10-14
thread: yellow or chartreuse
tails: dark moose hairs
body: elk hair dyed dark olive
wings: dark gray deer hair
hackle: (parachute style) grizzly saddle, dyed chartreuse

Lawson Green Drake Nymph
(Mike Lawson/Umpqua Feather Merchants)
hook: wet fly or nymph, No. 10-12
tail: partridge or woodduck fibers
rib: fine gold wire
body: blended 50% hare's ear fur, 25% gold-dyed hare's ear fur and 25% olive-dyed hare's ear fur
thorax: same as body
legs: brown partridge fibers
wingcase: dark turkey tail section

Green Drake Nymph (Arbona)
hook: wet fly for deep patterns; dry fly for patterns fished just under surface; No. 8-10
thread: olive
tail: dark olive-brown partridge fibers
abdomen: olive brown dubbing, tied fuzzy, with olive ostrich herl for gills
rib: fine gold wire
thorax: olive-brown dubbing, tied fuzzy
wingpads: dark gray goose quill segment
legs: dark brownish amber partridge fibers

Harrop Downwing Green Drake
(Rene Harrop/Umpqua F.M.)
hook: dry fly, No. 8-12
tail: dyed olive grizzly hackle fibers, divided
rib: bright green floss
body: olive dubbing
hackle: dyed olive grizzly, clipped on bottom
wing: black moose body hair with clipped butts forming head

Harrop Green Drake CDC Captive Dun
(Rene Harrop/McKenzie Flies)
hook: dry fly, No. 10
tail: brown partridge fibers and a few CDC fibers (dark gray)
abdomen: brown marabou wrapped up shank
thorax: light olive dubbing
legs: dark dun CDC protruding from both sides of thorax
wing: dark dun CDC tied in as wingpad

Small Western Green Drakes
("slate-winged olives," "Flavs" or *"Flavilineas"*)
As the green drake hatch draws to a close, a very

similar and closely related mayfly, the small Western green drake, begins its emergence on some of our spring creeks. Scientifically named *Drunella flavilinea*, this mayfly is sometimes called "Flav" or *"Flavilinea,"* though perhaps another of its common names, "slate-winged olive," is more stately. Trout, of course, could care less about names, so long as they can eat these mayflies.

Indeed, trout usually react eagerly to the evening emergences of slate-winged olives, with large fish feeding confidently at the surface. The emergence can stimulate good rises for days on end, making it one of the most significant summer hatches on certain rivers.

Drunella flavilinea looks like a small version of *Drunella grandis*, the green drake. Where green drakes run towards a No. 10 hook in size, the slate-winged olives are imitated with No. 14 and 16 patterns. In color, however, the two species are very similar. As their name suggests, slate-winged olive duns feature slate-gray wings and attractive greenish-olive bodies (although, like other members of the genus, the body color becomes darker as time passes after the insect's emergence).

On some waters the hatch is an important one and can last for nearly two months. Mid- to late June through early to mid August is a common time frame. Unlike green drakes, *D. flavilinea* emerges late, usually between late afternoon and sunset. Inclement weather often changes the hatch schedule: as early as 2 or 3 p.m. under some conditions and commonly around 5 or 6 p.m.

Being surface emergers, the duns are often heavily preyed upon by trout. Still, an emerger pattern, fished on top, often outfishes more traditional dun patterns. Also, if you can accurately gauge the timing of the hatch, a nymph pattern can prove effective the hour or so preceding emergence.

I have yet to encounter what I would call an overwhelming spinner fall of flavs. At times I've found the reddish-brown spinners during the evening and even during late morning a time or two. But in most of these instances, the trout seemed interested in some other insect present in greater abundance. Still, I have no doubt that the spinners are of major importance on some streams. In *Selective Trout*, Swisher and Richards say, "a brown-bodied hen spinner is killing in the morning after a hatch the previous evening."

Similarly, Juracek and Mathews (*Fishing Yellowstone Hatches*) note that "Flav spinners fall in the evenings and, when concentrated alone, can stimulate good rises of fish."

They go on to say that these spinners are "often overshadowed by the simultaneous emergences of caddisflies. . ." Perhaps this best describes my experience with *flavilinea* spinners: Although I've taken fish on them on the Henry's Fork, often some other insect gets in the way of what could otherwise be a good fishable spinner fall. Nonetheless, the wise spring creek angler is prepared for just about anything, so I always carry a row of slate-winged olive spinner imitations. (Note: virtually any dressing tied to imitate green drakes can be sized down to work on the slate-winged olives).

*Sparkle Dun: No. 14-16, brown shuck, medium olive body
*Floating Nymph: dun tails and legs, medium olive body, gray wingcase
***Flavilinea* Emerging Dun:** Same dressing as per Green Drake, but on No. 14-16 hooks
No-Hackle: No. 14-16, dun tails, medium olive body, dark slate wings

*Emergent Cripple: No 14-16, brown shuck, medium olive body, gray wings, pale watery dun hackle

Sparkle Spinner: No. 14-16, dun tails, medium olive or rust body, white wings

Hen Hackle Spinner: No. 14-16, dun tails, med rust-brown body, pale watery dun hackle or CDC for wings

Compara-dun: No. 14-16, dun tails, medium olive body, gray wing

Quigley Cripple: same dressing as Green Drake, but on No. 14-16 hooks

Flavilinea Nymph (Arbona): (dressing as per Arbona's green drake nymph, but tied on No. 12-14 hooks)

Callibaetis
("Speckled-wing spinners;" "speckled-wing duns")

Often called speckled duns, speckled spinners or speckled-wing duns, the *Callibaetis* mayflies emerge between mid summer and mid autumn on the spring creeks and can offer some exciting and productive fishing. The *Callibaetis* is primarily known as a stillwater mayfly so it should come as no surprise that the emergence occurs on the slowest reaches of the spring creeks. At times the hatch can be heavy; more often it is rather sparse, causing interested trout to patrol wider feeding lanes or to prowl about somewhat.

The *Callibaetis* emergence generally begins during late morning or early afternoon, often coinciding with the start of the mid-day winds common on Western waters. You've just watched the mid-morning Trico hatch wane and you have switched to an ant pattern hoping to find a smorgasboarding trout. About that time you notice the first big mayfly dun parading downriver. Then you see another and then a few more, scattered over the surface and large in appearance compared to the tiny Tricos you fished over earlier.

This is how *Callibaetis* hatches begin. They tend to sneak up on you, starting slowly and innocently but sometimes exploding into truly respectable emergences. Trout seem to like the *Callibaetis*. Only a handful of the insects need emerge to bring a few trout up to feed.

The mottled wings of the *Callibaetis* duns are characteristic. Body color ranges from pale olive-tan to grayish-brown to pale cream. *Callibaetis* spinners can be darker, sometimes approaching deep gray, other times appearing more of an ashy gray-brown. No matter how dark the spinner's body is on the back, the underside is always lighter, sometimes drastically so (and thus imitations should be tied to imitate this lighter underside). The wings of the spinners are clear, but the characteristic mottling remains. A No. 16 fly will serve well during most *Callibaetis* hatches, although a No. 14 may be required for some emergences and is the size best suited to mimic the nymphs.

On the larger spring creeks, *Callibaetis* hatches frequently cause trout to feed in roving pods of a half dozen or more individuals. These small schools of trout can be very difficult to track down. Just as you get into position to cast, the fish will move far enough away that you must begin stalking again. You are never really sure if you have spooked them or if they have simply decided to seek greener pastures for whatever obscure reason.

On the Henry's Fork, where *Callibaetis* emergences quite often equate to wandering schools of trout, I've learned to just sit tight and wait for the trout to come to me. This strategy helps me avoid spooking both the pods of trout and any individual fish that might begin feeding nearby as the hatch intensifies.

Spring-creek trout often feed readily on speckled wing duns, especially during cool days. In addition, the spinners may be present at about the same time and trout will eat them too. On a few occasions I've encountered *Callibaetis* spinner falls during mid-morning and at dusk.

When the *Callibaetis* hatch is in full swing, many trout will begin eating more and more emergers while still picking off a few duns. This feeding strategy is tailor-made for a two-fly approach, incorporating a compara-dun dry accompanied by a surface-film or subsurface emerger pattern.

The nymphs of these mayflies are excellent swimmers, capable of rapid ascent to the surface during emergence. On spring creeks, however, the nymphs inhabit weedbeds that often grow to within a few inches of the surface. When a *Callibaetis* nymph leaves the safety of this weedbed, the insect may only need a swim of several inches to reach the surface. In such situations, duns, surface emergers and stillborns are especially effective because trout have little chance to pursue nymphs as they leave the bottom. Thus, the downstream or downwind side of a large weedbed is usually an ideal place to find and fish *Callibaetis* emergers and duns.

However, on waters where nymphs must drift and swim through open water, they become very vulnerable to trout. Thus a nymph pattern, fished below weedbeds in several feet of water, can be productive prior to the emergence or during its early stages. On lakes, the usual habitat of the *Callibaetis*, the nymphs become quite active as much as two hours prior to emergence, sometimes triggering substantial feeding activity by trout. I suspect a similar scenario unfolds on the spring creeks, though I've never gone in search of empirical evidence to prove as much.

If you are to fish the *Callibaetis* nymph with any confidence and any success, the actual emergence and nymph activity must be heavy enough to interest trout. Moreover, you must be able to anticipate the hatch—its time, duration and intensity—to know when to fish the nymphs. Anticipating the hatch can be a big guessing game with *Callibaetis* because their emergence often fluctuates in duration and intensity from day to day and can begin anytime between mid morning on hot days and late afternoon on cool days.

Still, if you are familiar with a particular stream and a particular hatch, or if you can get reliable local information and predict when *Callibaetis* activity will occur, the nymphs can prove deadly. Fish the nymphs, one or two at a time, on a long leader. A tiny split shot might be required to get the flies down in deeper water. Concentrate on channels between weedbeds and the downstream edge of such weedbeds. Fish the flies dead drift, but don't worry about incidental drag because a little movement in the flies won't offend the trout. I've had trout take the nymphs as they ascended toward the surface at the end of the drift, so I try to lift them slowly at the end of each presentation.

Also, ants and beetles can tempt trout during all but the heaviest *Callibaetis* emergences. Larger than most other late summer mayflies, the *Callibaetis*, even in limited numbers, get trout looking up. But sometimes, when the actual mayfly hatch is relatively sparse, the trout will take any number of other patterns.

In fact, the *Callibaetis* is rather straightforward as mayfly hatches go. The habitual wandering pods of trout and even individual trout on some streams generally pose the largest problem for anglers. Be wary, however, of *Callibaetis* emergences that mask other hatches. Sometimes trout will feed on more abundant but smaller mayflies or caddisflies that are less visible

CALLIBAETIS
THORAX DUN

CDC CALLIBAETIS
FLOATING NYMPH/
EMERGER

CALLIBAETIS
TAILWATER DUN

CALLIBAETIS
NYMPH

WESTERN
CALLIBAETIS
NYMPH

to the angler. The presence of a few big *Callibaetis* tempts us to believe this is what the rising trout are eating, when in fact a smaller bug has drawn their attention. Often the only way to be certain is to employ your sampling net.

*Sparkle Dun: No. 14-16, pale gray shuck, tan body
*Emergent Cripple: No. 14-16, tan shuck, pale tan-olive body, tan wings, watery dun hackle
Sparkle Spinner: No. 14-16, dun tail, light tan body, gray or white wings
*Compara-dun: No. 14-16, brown tails, tan-gray dubbing, tan wing
Quigley Cripple: No. 14-16, gray or tan tails, body and thorax; grizzly hackle
Krystal Spinner: No. 14-16, brown tails, tan-gray body, pearl Krystal Flash, light dun/grizzly hackle
No-Hackle Dun: No. 14-16, cream tails, tanish-olive body (or to match natural), gray wings
Bunse Natural Dun: No. 14-16, tan body

Callibaetis Nymph *(Juracek/Mathews)*
hook: dry fly, No. 14-16
thread: tan
tails: gray partridge fibers
body: tan dubbing
wingcase: gray polycelon
thorax: tan dubbing, picked out

Western *Callibaetis* Nymph *(Shewey)*
hook: wet fly, No. 12-16
thread: brown
tails: gadwall flank fibers
body: tannish-olive dubbing
rib: fine gold wire
wingcase: medium brown partridge or grouse pulled over thorax
thorax: natural gray-brown ostrich
legs: partridge fibers

CDC *Callibaetis* Floating Nymph/emerger
(R. Harrop/Umpqua F.M.)
hook: dry fly, No. 12-16
tail: woodduck or gadwall flank fibers
body: tan rabbit dubbing
rib: fine copper wire
legs: brown partridge fibers
wing: white or pale gray CDC feathers, short
thorax: tan rabbit dubbing

Callibaetis Thorax Dun *(Mike Lawson/Umpqua F.M.)*
hook: dry fly, No. 14-16
tails: dun hackle fibers, split
body: grayish-tan dubbing
wings: gray partridge feathers, upright
hackle: a few turns of grizzly

SHEWEY'S MAHOGANY
EMERGER

MAHOGONY DUN FUR
NYMPH

BLUE QUILL SPINNER

***Callibaetis* CDC Tailwater Dun**
(Rene' Harrop/McKenzie Flies)
hook: dry fly, No. 14-16
tails: dun hackle fibers, divided
body: pale tan-olive dubbing
wings: gray CDC feathers tied (butt ends are left
protruding along the sides of the tip ends)
thorax: same as body

Mahogany Duns (*Paraleptophlebia*)

Paraleptophlebia species are amongst the most wide-spread and abundant of Western mayflies. They inhabit virtually every kind of stream, from fast mountain creeks to the largest rivers. On the spring creeks, however, although several species may be present and emerging throughout the season, the important mahogany dun hatches occur in the late summer and fall. At this time, the mahogany duns may well comprise, along with the much smaller Tricos and *Baetis*, the most significant hatch activity on the spring creeks.

The Henry's Fork hosts perhaps the best mahogany dun hatch of any Western spring creek. On the Harriman section (as well as other sections) the emergence begins late in August and lasts until at least the end of September. In typical mahogany dun style, this emergence is never dense, but the trout eagerly devour the mayflies. The duns emerge in the mid morning and early afternoon, often hatching sporadically for two or three hours (even longer on inclement-weather days).

As their name suggests, the *Paraleptophlebia* duns (specifically *P. debilis* and *P. bicornuta*) exhibit a mahogany-colored body and slate-gray wings. They can almost always be imitated with a No. 16 pattern, with floating nymphs, emergent cripples, and dun patterns being most effective. The adult mahogany duns tend to ride the water for a considerable distance before taking flight and are thus preyed upon readily by many trout. Still, the floating nymph or emerger often proves more effective. Many trout will take both nymphs and duns while others feed selectively on nymphs in the surface film. Only rarely, however, will you find a trout feeding selectively on duns to the exclusion of floating nymphs.

Paraleptophlebia spinners can be important on some freestone streams, but I have yet to see a significant rise to these spinners on the spring creeks. Still, a couple of mahogany dun spinner imitations won't occupy much space in the corner of a fly box and they just might save a day sometime.

Fred Arbona, in *Mayflies, the Angler, and the Trout* reports that *Paraleptophlebia* nymphs make "practice runs" of sorts during the hour prior to emergence by swimming toward the surface and then descending again. This motion might easily be imitated in relatively open water, but the weed-infested areas of spring creeks where these mayflies often emerge are inherently hard on nymphing techniques. Besides, it seems as though the mahogany duns, at least on some waters, emerge from the tops of the weeds that grow to or almost to the surface.

The floating nymph pattern makes an effective all-around pattern for late-season fishing on the Henry's Fork and probably on other streams as well. Trout seem to be on the lookout for them just about anytime between mid morning and mid afternoon, so if you find a rising trout that seems to be feeding on whatever happens by, the mahogany dun nymph, fished in the film, might well draw a strike.

In recent years, the mahogany dun hatch has become one of my favorites, primarily because it occurs during the late season when few people are on the water. I've enjoyed some September days when the first mahogany duns appeared at 8:30 a.m. and the hatch continued until late afternoon, always sporadically, but always accompanied by feeding trout.

*Sparkle Dun: No. 16, brown shuck, brown body, dark wing
*Floating Nymph: No. 16, brown legs and tail, brown body, medium gray wingcase
*Emergent Cripple: No. 16, mahogany body, tan shuck, gray wings, watery dun or brown hackle
Compara-dun: No. 16, brown tails, reddish-brown body, medium-dark wing
No-Hackle Dun: No. 16, brown tails, reddish-brown body, dark slate wings
Bunse Natural Dun: No. 16, brown body

Mahogany Dun Fur Nymph *(Juracek/Mathews)*
hook: dry fly, No. 16
thread: brown 8/0
tail: brown partridge fibers
body: brown dubbing
wingcase: gray polycelon
thorax: brown dubbing, picked out slightly

*Mahogany Emerger *(Shewey)*
hook: dry fly, No. 16
tail: brown antron dubbing (fine)
body: brown dubbing, sparse
wing: gray Z-lon or sparkle yarn, fanned like a compara-dun and clipped shorter than traditional dry fly

Blue Quill Spinner *(Ernest Schwiebert)*
hook: dry fly, No. 16
thread: white
tails: two long dun hackle fibers
body: bleached peacock quill with tan tip at rear
wings: white hackle tips, tied spent
hackle: medium brown, clipped top and bottom
Note: Z-lon can be substituted for the wings

Brown Drakes

Brown Drakes *(Ephemera simulans)* can produce some terrific twilight fishing on some Western rivers. Large mayflies (as big as the green drakes), the brown drakes often bring the best trout to the surface.

Depending on water temperature and elevation, the brown drakes emerge as early as May or as late as September. On Silver Creek and the Henry's Fork, which offer some of the best brown drake activity in the West, the hatch occurs between mid June and early July. The actual hatch, even on these rivers, can at times be sporadic. Thus the spinner falls frequently offer better fishing.

The brown drake emergence can and often does begin at the same time of year as the green drake hatch. Both insects are about the same size and a fly angler can easily be caught unaware on those cold, overcast days when green drakes hatch late and brown drakes hatch early. At any distance, the two mayflies look identical on the water, but the

ARBONA BROWN DRAKE

LAIBLE'S BROWN DRAKE EMERGER

MCNEESE GRAY DRAKE
(SIPHLONURUS) SPINNER

SHEWEY'S GRAY DRAKE
KRYSTAL SPINNER

JURACEK/MATHEWS
GRAY DRAKE SPINNER

trout can easily tell the difference. On those occasions when the trout turn selective to brown drakes, the green drake patterns often prove unproductive.

More often, perhaps, anglers on the Henry's Fork mistake the large brown drakes for green drakes, which hatched earlier the same day. They confidently tie on the green drake pattern, sometimes fooling fish with it; other times not. I know because I've made that mistake. These days, if I see big mayflies on the water in the late afternoon or evening, I think brown drake first and then go catch one to make certain.

The brown drakes are distinguishable by their heavily patterned wings. In both the dun and spinner stages, the wings retain this attractive mottling. The spinner's wings are otherwise clear, whereas the duns have gray wings. The body, as one might expect, ranges from a rich chocolate brown with tannish trim to a very light brown with dark brown markings.

Predictability is never the brown drake's strong point. Sometimes the emergence is heavy and offers fabulous fishing. Other times it is sporadic, but even during sparse emergences the large size of the insects is usually enough to interest a few trout. The spinner activity is equally unpredictable, but when good, the spinner fall is exceptionally good. When spinners and duns are both available, the spinners tend to be most effective.

I've had only marginal success trying the nymphs during the early stages of the emergence, but this may be a function of the kind of waters on which I've tried sub-surface tactics. John Juracek and Craig Mathews, in their book *Fishing Yellowstone Hatches*, report similar unimpressive results with brown drake nymphs.

Hafele and Hughes, however, write in *Western Hatches* that "the nymph is available to fish longer than the dun or spinner. The importance of nymph patterns is greater than that of dun patterns in most situations. This is especially true when the quarry is large trout, which tend to confine their feeding to the ascending nymphs while smaller fish feed on the surface."

Likely Hafele and Hughes have encountered brown drakes on a wide enough variety of streams to observe this hatch in substantial detail. My experience with brown drakes is limited to a few spring creeks in Idaho and Wyoming (and, oddly enough, a couple of 9,000-foot alpine lakes in Wyoming). Still, I've had my best success on this hatch with a floating emergent cripple pattern. More than anything else, however, I look forward to the occasional encounter with a brown drake spinner fall, right at dark, to horde a half hour's worth of magical dry fly fishing.

Although evening is the typical period of spinner activity, Nelson Ishiyama, owner of Henry's Fork Lodge near Last Chance, Idaho, reports one occasion on which a tremendous spinner fall occurred early in the morning near Osborn Bridge.

Incidentally, the brown drake nymphs, like the giant *Hexagenia* mayfly nymphs, dig burrows in the stream bottom. Unlike *Hexagenia*, however, the brown drakes burrow in sand or very fine gravel. Thus their distribution is largely dependant on the right kind of bottom material.

Sparkle Spinner: No. 8-10, medium brown body, light tan wings
*Krystal Spinner: medium brown body, pearl K.F. wings, brown/grizzly mixed hackle

CDC Spinner: medium brown body, tan wings
***Brown Drake Emergent Cripple:** brown shuck, light brown body, brown wings, watery dun and grizzly hackle mixed

***Brown Drake Spinner** (Arbona et al)
hook: dry fly, No. 8-10
tails: dark microfibets or moose hairs (3)
body: rusty tan, ribbed with brown monocord
wings: light tan hen or partridge tied spent; or light ginger hackle mixed with grizzly hackle, clipped flush on bottom, V-clipped above (not pictured)

Brown Drake Nymph (Arbona)
hook: nymph hook, No. 8
tails: light brown ostrich
abdomen: light yellowish-tan dubbing and gray ostrich herl ribbed with fine gold wire
thorax: light yellowish fuzzy dubbing blend
wingcase: brown turkey
legs: grouse or partridge hackle fibers dyed olive-brown
Note: Arbona's wiggle nymph calls for the same dressing, but the abdomen is tied on a ring-eye hook whose bend has been cut off leaving a shank of 12mm. This abdomen is attached with wire or monofilament to a No. 14-16 wet fly hook on which is tied the thorax.

***Brown Drake Paradrake** (Mike Lawson)
hook: dry fly, No. 12
tails: 3 moose hairs
body: elk hair dyed yellowish-tan
rib: brown tying thread
wings: medium brown deer hair
hackle: grizzly dyed olive-brown, tied parachute style (not pictured)

Brown Drake Parachute (Juracek/Mathews)
hook: dry fly, No. 10-12
thread: 3/0 brown monocord
tails: moose body hairs
body: light brown dubbing
rib: 3/0 brown monocord
wing: natural deer hair
hackle: grizzly dyed amber, parachute style (not pictured)

Laible's Brown Drake Emerger (Umpqua F.M.)
hook: 2XL dry fly or nymph, No. 8-10
tails: pheasant tail fibers
body: tannish brown dubbing
thorax: same as body
wing: gray-brown CDC feather forming loop over thorax

Gray Drakes ("black drake")

If you want to see an awesome sight, visit Oregon's Williamson River during the "black drake" hatch in June or July. The hatch itself may be uninspiring, but the spinner fall can be nothing short of unbelievable with countless thousands of mayflies clogging the water's surface.

More commonly known in their dun stage as gray drakes, this king of the Williamson River hatches is the *Siphlonurus* mayfly. The gray drakes are large, being best imitated with a No. 10 hook (sometimes No. 12). Their color varies considerably (because there are four different species), ranging from dark gray to pale yellowish with darker markings.

Interestingly, the gray drake duns are mostly insignificant to trout. The nymphs migrate to shallow shoreline margins and backwaters to emerge, so the duns are not usually available to the fish. Sometimes a strong wind will dump some of the duns on the water where trout will take them, but usually the dun stage is unimportant to anglers and fish alike.

The nymphs, being relatively active feeders, do fall prey to trout. Patterns designed to mimic these nymphs can be effective searching patterns on rivers with good *Siphlonurus* populations.

The gray drake spinner, however, can cause gluttonous feeding binges by trout, with even the largest fish rising freely at the surface. On rivers like the Williamson, however, the spinner fall can be so dense as to make fishing an exercise in futility. More sparse spinner falls, or the early stages of dense ones, can provide relatively easy fishing given a good imitation and presentation. During the super-heavy *Siphlonurus* spinner drifts, concentrate on timing the rise so your fly arrives at the trout's mouth the exact moment of the rise. Undoubtedly you can see the inherent difficulty in this strategy, especially when the spinners are so thick that they are piled on top of one another.

The spinner falls generally occur during mid morning and evening, but inclement weather can prompt afternoon activity instead or as well. Also, *Siphlonurus* spinner falls can effectively mask emergences of smaller mayflies or other insects, so, by applying your sampling net, be sure that the trout are taking the gray drake spinners.

June and July are the gray drake months on the Williamson, but other rivers, especially in the Rockies, can offer hatches as late as mid September.

***Gray Drake Spinner** (Shewey)
hook: dry fly, No. 8 or 2XL No. 10
tails: medium dun hackle fibers or microfibets
body: dark gray-brown dubbing, ribbed with dark brown thread
wings: 6-8 strands of dun or pearl Krystalflash tied spent and then six turns of mixed dun and grizzly hackles, clipped flush below and V-clipped above

Gray Drake Nymph (Arbona)
hook: nymph, No. 8-10
thread: gray
tails: three gray ostrich herls
abdomen: tanish gray dubbing with gray ostrich herl fibers for gills and ribbed with brown monocord
thorax: tannish gray dubbing or gray ostrich herl
wingcase: mallard flank dyed dark gray
legs: drake gray partridge hackle

Black Drake Spinner (Polly Rosborough)
hook: dry fly, No. 8-10
thread: black
tails: purplish-dun hackle fibers
body: purplish-brown synthetic yarn
hackle: purplish dun (not pictured)

POLLY'S BLACK DRAKE NYMPH

ARBONA GRAY DRAKE NYMPH

*Black Drake Nymph (Rosborough)
hook: 3XL nymph hook, No. 10
thread: gray
tail: speckled guinea fibers, short
body: beaver belly fur retaining guard hairs
legs: speckled guinea fibers, tied in on each side
wingcase: small clump of natural black ostrich herl

*Gray Drake Spinner (Juracek/Mathews)
hook: dry fly, No. 8-14
thread: gray
tails: dun hackle fibers
body: tan dubbing (or to match natural in your area)
rib: brown polyester thread
wing: "dun hackle wound and clipped on top. A strip of
gray polycelon is then pulled over the top and tied
off at the head. This aids in floatation on large
spinner patterns. A wing of light dun Zelon tied spent
may also be used." (from *Fishing Yellowstone
Hatches*)

*McNeese Gray Drake Spinner (Dave McNeese)
hook: #8 or 10 standard dry fly
tail: dun hackle fibers, fanned
body: 3-4 stripped peacock herls wound to form a
tapering body
wings: light dun hackle tips, V-shape or spent
hackle: dun and grizzly mixed, clipped flush top and
bottom

Hexagenia limbata
("giant yellow may")

Only a few of our spring creeks offer hatches of these amazing mayflies, perhaps California's Fall River being the best known. The *Hexagenia* is huge—the largest of our mayflies. No. 6 paradrakes represent the awesome inch-and-a-half-long, yellowish-colored naturals.

The *Hexagenia* is a burrowing mayfly like the brown drake. The nymphs require mud of just the right consistency (soft enough to burrow in but firm enough not to collapse on the tunnels). The hatch begins at dusk or just after dark and can occur anytime from May to October depending on location. Hafele and Huges say that water temperature is probably the major factor controlling emergence. When the emergence ensues, large trout discard caution and feed voraciously on the swimming nymphs and on the duns. Mating flights occur in the evenings as well, usually as the emergence winds down (usually meaning after dark).

In *Western Hatches*, Hafele and Hughes describe Polly Rosborough's system of fishing the Hexagenia as follows:

Polly Rosborough has worked out a system for fishing the Hexagenia limbata hatch with his Big Yellow May nymph, dun, and spinner patterns. He begins fishing in the pre-hatch period with a nymph and a three-pound test tippet. As soon as the hatch starts and the duns appear, he switches to a pre-tied leader with a dun attached. The change is sped by the use of connecting loops; in no time he is back to fishing. The effectiveness of the dun lasts about half an hour, Polly tells us, then he switches again, taking off the entire leader and quickly looping on a five-pound leader and a spinner imitation. With this he fishes out the last legal light.

Perhaps the most perplexing problem with *Hexagenia* is their late-evening emergence. In many places, night-fishing for trout is not legal (including Rosborough's home state of Oregon). At times the *Hexagenia* hatch occurs entirely after dark. I was once driving along the Columbia River near Hermiston, Oregon, when I pulled into a gas station at midnight on a July evening. *Hexagenia's*, attracted to the station's fluorescent lights, were everywhere and were still arriving in droves.

The Fall River Hex hatch, which occurs on the lower river, generally begins at dusk with the spinner fall arriving after dark. This is an extremely prolific Hex hatch—so much so that Bill Sunderland and Dale Lackey, in their book *California Blue Ribbon Trout Streams*, say that the chances of a trout choosing your fly from amongst all the naturals is pure luck. They go on to say, "Fishing the Hex hatch is more of a social event, a happening, than good fishing. Fall River regulars admit that few fish are actually caught during this period, but the rising fish make it an incredible time to be on the river."

Hexagenia Paradrake
hook: dry fly, No. 8
tail: two dark moose hairs
body: elk hair dyed yellowish-tan
rib: yellow 3/0 thread
wings: dark deer hair
hackle: light ginger or grizzly dyed yellowish-tan, parachute

Hexagenia Spinner
hook: dry fly, No. 4-6
tails: two black moose hairs
body: yellowish tan dubbing
rib: brown thread
wings: light tan Z-lon mixed with clipped light dun hackle
wingcase: yellow foam to aid in floatation (not pictured)

Hexagenia Emergent Cripple *(Shewey)*
hook: No. 6, 2XL
tail: pale tan Z-lon or sparkle dubbing
body: yellowish-tan dubbing
rib: peacock herl, stripped
wings: light tan Z-lon or similar, tied delta-style, spent and slightly short
hackle: three turns of watery dun or light ginger

*Big Yellow May Nymph *(Rosborough)*
hook: 3XL nymph hook, No. 6-8

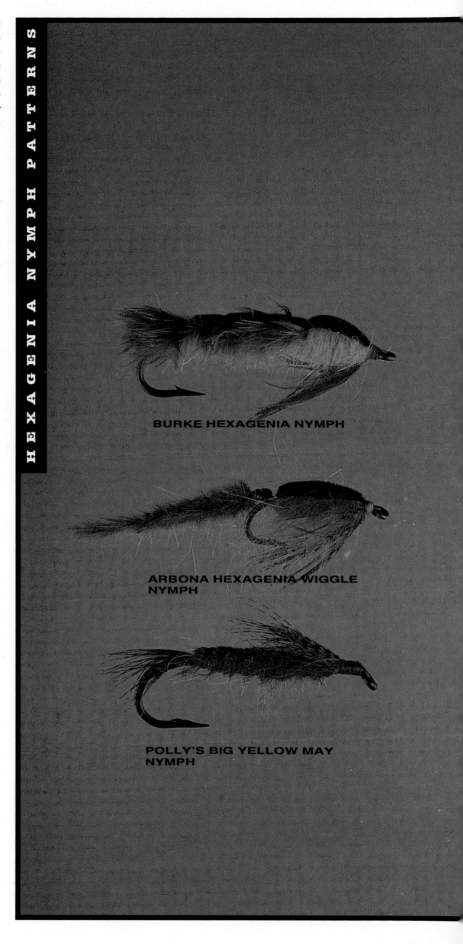

BURKE HEXAGENIA NYMPH

ARBONA HEXAGENIA WIGGLE NYMPH

POLLY'S BIG YELLOW MAY NYMPH

HEXAGENIA PATTERNS

HEXAGENIA EMERGENT
CRIPPLE

HEXAGENIA PARADRAKE

MARCH BROWN EMERGER PATTERNS

MARCH BROWN FLYMPH

MARCH BROWN
SOFT-HACKLE EMERGER

thread: yellow
tail: lemon woodduck fibers
shellback: teal flank, dyed lemon woodduck
rib: yellow synthetic yarn
legs: teal dyed lemon woodduck, fibers tied in as a throat
wingcase: a small bunch of teal fibers, dyed lemon woodduck tied in over body and extending to mid-shank

*Hexagenia Wiggle Nymph (Arbona)
hook: ring eye hook cut to 15mm; thorax: wet fly, No. 10-12, attached with mono or wireloop
thread: tan or yellow monocord
tails: 3 tan ostrich herls, about 1/2 hook length
abdomen: olive-brown dubbing and dark slate ostrich for gills, ribbed with fine gold wire
thorax: olive-brown dubbing
wingcase: dark mottled turkey tail section
legs: light brown partridge fibers

Burke *Hexagenia* Nymph (Umpqua F.M.)
hook: nymph, 3XL
tail: gray ostrich herl
body: tan-yellow dubbing
thorax: same as body
gills: gray ostrich herl
shellback: dark turkey quill section tied length of body and then pulled over thorax
rib: fine gold wire through body
legs: brown partridge or hen hackle

March Brown (*Rithrogenia*)

Other Mayflies

Any number of other mayfly species might be encountered on certain spring creeks, especially on those streams whose character changes from stretch to stretch, going from slow, smooth, weed-choked classic spring-creek water to gentle riffle to gliding run to sand- or gravel-bottom backwaters and eddies. Many of the smaller spring creeks offer a variety of water types and even the largest spring creeks, like the Henry's Fork on Harriman Park include segments of faster water with different insects.

The classic spring-creek mayflies—green drakes and pale morning duns; Tricos and *Baetis*; gray drakes and mahogany duns—comprise the hatches of major significance on Western spring creeks and thus draw the attention of anglers who fish these waters. But on certain stretches of some streams, spring creek anglers might well encounter a hatch of March Browns (*Rithrogenia*) early in the year or perhaps *Centroptilium* or some other mayfly later on. In any case, it pays to be ready for just about anything. Since March Browns are widespread in the West and since *Centroptilium* mayflies are of importance to anglers on the private Paradise Valley spring creeks in Montana, imitations for these are listed here.

In addition, spring-creek anglers should study works listed in Appendix B for information on other mayfly hatches that occur on specific waters.

*March Brown Soft Hackle Emerger (Shewey)
hook: wet fly or dry fly, No. 12-16

thread: tan 6/0
tails: brown partridge fibers
body: pale tan-olive dubbing
hackle: two turns of brown partridge hackle
wing: sparse bunch of tan antron yarn or dubbing, wet fly style

March Brown Flymph (Hafele/Hughes)
hook: dry fly or wet fly, No. 14-16
thread: crimson silk (Pearsall's)
tails: 2-3 pheasant tail fibers
body: dark hare's ear fur, spun on silk
hackle: furnace or brown hen hackle

Rithrogenia Emerger (Juracek/Mathews)
hook: dry fly, No. 14-16
thread: olive 8/0
tails: gray partridge fibers
body: pale olive dubbing
hackle: mottled gray partridge, 2-3 turns, trimmed on bottom (not pictured)

*Rithrogenia Sparkle Dun: No. 14-16, brown shuck, pale olive or tan body
*March Brown Compara-dun: No. 12-16, ginger or gray tails, tan body, tan wing
*Emergent Cripple: No. 12-16, tan shuck, tan body, tan wings, watery dun or olive-dun hackle
*Rithrogenia Sparkle Spinner: No. 14-16, brown tails, olive-brown body, white wings
Bunse Natural Dun, March Brown: No. 12-16, tan body, medium-dark wing

Centroptilium Sparkle Dun
(Juracek/Mathews/Umpqua F.M.)
hook: dry fly, No. 18
tail: cream Z-lon or sparkle dubbing
body: cream dubbing
wing: bleached elk or deer

Brant's Sulpher Emerger
(Brant Oswald/John Greene)
hook: dry fly, No. 18-20
tail: pheasant tail fibers
body: pheasant tail fibers
rib: fine copper wire
thorax: pale yellow dubbing
wing: white foam, short
hackle: cream, parachute-style (sparse)

Swimming Sulpher Emerger
(Brant Oswald)
hook: ring-eye dry fly, No. 18
tail: pale yellowish-orange marabou fibers
body: pale yellowish-orange marabou fibers, wrapped up shank

Sulpher Thorax Dun (Brant Oswald)
hook: dry fly, No. 18-20
tails: cream hackle fibers, divided
body: pale yellow dubbing
wing: white hen hackle fibers or CDC fibers, tied upright
hackle: pale watery dun, clipped below

SWIMMING SULPHER EMERGER

SULPHER EMERGER (BRANT OSWALD)

SULPHER EMERGER (JOHN GREENE)

SULPHER SPARKLE DUN

SULPHER THORAX DUN

Identification Charts for Spring Creek Mayflies

SPECIES	SIZE	NO. of TAILS	COLOR	EMERGENCE TIMES
Green Drakes (Drunella grandis et al)	large No. 8-12	3	olive-green to yellowish-olive to olive-brown slate-gray wings	late May-Sept. mid morning to early afternoon dun is important/spinner fall typically insignificant.
Pale Morning Dun (Ephemerella inermis and E. infrequens)	med to small No. 14-18	3	dun: body varies: olives, olive-brown, yellowish, etc. wings gray. spinners: males have rust-colored bodies; females, olive bodies; wings clear	early June through August emergence: mid morning to late afternoon, depending on weather. spinner fall: early to mid morning and/or evening
Baetis "blue-winged olive," "olive," "western olive," "tiny western olive," etc.	small No. 18-24	2	bright green to olive to olive-brown to gray with gray wings (very light gray in the case of B. punctiventris, formerly known as Pseudocloeon edmundsi) spinners: olive to olive-brown to brown or gray with clear wings. Note: highly reduced hind wings of all Baetis, a characteristic shared only with the readily distinguishable Trico	virtually any time of year, especially March-May and Sept-November; any time of day, depending on weather--best hatches occur during cloudy, wet weather in most cases spinner falls morning and evening
March Brown (Rithrogenia sp.)	medium No. 12-16	2	dun: body ranges from pale cream to pale olive; wings are grayish and highly marked with dark brown mottling. spinner: light to medium brownish bodies with clear, heavily veined wings	March-Sept., depending on particular species and on region (early season hatches of R. morrisoni probably most significant to spring-creek anglers.) Hatch occurs mid-morning to mid-afternoon; spinner falls morning and evening, but only significant on occasion.
Brown Drake (Ephemera simulans)	large No. 8-12	3	dun: brownish body with dark markings on each abdominal segment; wings gray-brown with brown mottling spinner about the same color as dun, but wings are clear with dark mottling	Usually June-July; hatches and spinner falls usually occur during mid- to late evening, sometimes at or after dark.
Gray Drake "black drake" (Siphlonurus sp)	large No. 8-12	2	dun: ranges from dark gray to creamy-olive with dark brown markings at the rear of each abdominal segment; wings are pale grey. spinner is similar but with clear wings	coastal: mid April-mid June Rockies: July-Sept. spinner fall most important, occurring mid- to late morning or during the evening

SPECIES	SIZE	NO. of TAILS	COLOR	EMERGENCE TIMES
Callibaetis "speckled spinner" "speckled dun"	medium No. 14-16	2	dun: varies--tan, pale olive; cream, tannish-gray. wings mottled gray and brown spinner: similar in color to dun with wings that are clear with dark mottling	June-September; most common mid July-Sept. emerges mid morning to mid-afternoon; spinner fall is usually late morning to mid-afternoon, occasionally early evening
Trico's (Tricorythodes) "white-winged black"	small, No. 18-24	3	duns: females have olive bodies, males have black bodies; both have white (very pale gray) wings; spinners have very long tails and clear wings. Note that Trico's have no hind wings.	early July through mid-Sept. mid-July-early Sept most common; emergence and spinner fall at mid-morning. (males actually emerge the previous night, but join the newly emerged females during mid-morning at which time mating and consequently spinner fall occurs.)
Mahogany Dun (Paraleptophlebia)	medium No. 16	3	duns have mahogany-colored body and gray wings; spinners have clear wings.	August-Sept; hatch occurs mid-morning through mid or late afternoon. Spinners active mornings, but not of importance.
Hexagenia limbata Giant Yellow Mayfly	very large No. 6-8	2	duns are cream to bright yellow with dark markings; wings light brownish; body is 3/4 to 1-1/2 inches long, tails excluded. spinner: male ranges from yellowish-tan to reddish-brown; female yellowish-tan; wings clear or tinged brown.	Hatch can occur from June through October, depending on location. Famous "Hex" hatch on California's Fall River generally runs from about June 15 to July 15, sometimes into early August. Hatches late evening, just before and after dark.
Drunella flavilinea "Small Western Green Drake," "Flav," "Slate-winged Olive"	medium No. 14-16	3	looks like a smaller version of the green drake (D. grandis): greenish body with slate gray wings. spinner has reddish-brown body and clear wings	Hatches June through Sept., depending on location. Evening emergence, sometimes mid- to late afternoon on cool, overcast days. Spinner falls can occur morning or evening.
Centroptilum "Sulpher,"	small No. 20-22	2	light tan with a slight orange cast ranging to yellowish; wings light dun	Hatches July-August, earlier where it occurs on West coast. An afternoon hatch, typically mid to late afternoon

SPRING CREEK DIARY

March, 1990; Eastern Oregon

*C*allibaetis in March—this was a new one on me, but then again it had been a strange year anyway, so why not. Despite unusually warm early spring weather and despite the speckled duns and a smattering of *Baetis*, Timmy and I had yet to rise a trout. We just couldn't find a consistent feeder.

A rise here and rise there, but all isolated and random. We struggled through the brush to get to a long pool. A big rooster pheasant exploded from the shoreline willows—Raider, my springer spaniel, would have gone ballistic over that. Timmy experienced those willows up close and personal: He gouged out a nice chunk of leg on a beaver-chewed stub. Hell of a scar to this day.

The pool proved totally uncooperative. We were all but done. In the car, on the way downriver, we crossed a bridge, just upstream from which flowed a nice little channel feeding a small pool. I was sure I'd seen a riseform. Timmy backed up. Sure enough, a consistent riser.

Tim was kind enough to give me the shot. *Callibaetis* paraded down the shallow, four-foot-wide channel, which was guarded on both sides by lush green aquatic weeds. I chose a No. 14 compara-dun and missed short and to the left with the first cast. Kneeling on the fine gravel, almost directly downstream from the trout, I cast again, this time right up over his back. No hesitation. The trout gulped the fly and shortly thereafter we admired a lovely 14-inch brown. It was the day's only fish and one much appreciated.

SECTION II

Spring Creek Terrestrials

As much as I enjoy a heavy spring-creek mayfly emergence, I will readily admit to getting as much enjoyment pursuing trout that are actively feeding on ants, beetles, hoppers or other terrestrials.

My reasoning is simple: Terrestrial feeders tend to be easier to dupe than hatch feeders. You needn't often worry whether the trout is feeding on the surface or just under the surface as is frequently the case during hatches. Moreover, terrestrial feeders are sometimes less selective to precise size and color.

Certainly, terrestrial-feeding trout have their ultra-selective moments. At times these trout become amazingly selective to one size or color of ant, beetle or hopper. Sometimes they even show a marked preference for drowned terrestrials rather than those floating on top.

On numerous occasions I've seen trout ignore large flying hoppers in apparent preference for small, immature ones not yet able to take to the wing efficiently. One year I fished Slough Creek in Yellowstone National Park during the peak of the hopper season. Every time I approached the bank, a cloud of hoppers erupted from the shoreline grass. A stiff breeze catapulted many of them into the water.

Normally those Slough Creek cutthroat wouldn't be too picky in eating hoppers. That particular afternoon, however, they ignored the one-inch-long-plus flying hoppers in preference for the small greenish-tan specimens, which either couldn't fly at all or could just barely fly.

Despite voluminous numbers of hoppers in all sizes, it was pretty easy to figure out what was going on. Large trout repeatedly refused my No. 6 hopper but would continue rising all round the fly. I caught a big flying hopper, pitched it in the river, and watched it meander downstream untouched. Then I repeated the process with two small, immature hoppers and watched both disappear within seconds to gulping rises. I switched to a No. 12 hopper and enjoyed a successful afternoon.

Only later, during the hike back to the car, did I really start wondering why the trout ignored the big hoppers. The best I could come up with was this: Because of their superior flying ability, those big hoppers probably landed on the water only infrequently, whereas any decent breeze would launch small, flightless hoppers to their inescapable demise in the creek. In other words, the trout probably hadn't seen as many of the big hoppers, but were well-versed on the smaller hoppers and therefore recognized them instantly as an easy meal.

If you really want picky trout, however, try the flying ants on the Henry's Fork—not the small brown ants, but the big black ones with the upright wings. The last time I encountered a heavy dose of those ants, every monster trout on the Railroad Ranch was feeding on top.

But every one of them ignored my black fur ants that usually fish quite well during sparse ant drifts. This was no sparse drift, however, and I eventually switched to a No. 10 McMurray ant and took two fish amongst countless refusals.

That evening I tried something new: I cut small pieces of cellophane wrapping and tied it as an upright wing on those big McMurray ants. The glossy, clear wings on the naturals had seemed awfully noticeable to me, so perhaps the trout looked for that characteristic as well.

The next afternoon's ant flight was far more sparse, but I had much better fishing. The wing apparently made a difference. I also experimented with size. The trout would largely ignore a No. 14 imitation and completely ignore anything smaller. They devoured my No. 10's, even though these flies were slightly larger than the actual ants.

Despite their size, though, my McMurray's were dressed sparse: two turns of hackle, clipped on the bottom, and just enough cellophane to give the impression of a wing. In fact, sparse dressings, whether for terrestrials or for mayflies, caddis or other insects, almost always outfish heavily dressed patterns on the flat waters of our spring creeks. Indeed, a heavily-dressed hopper works wonders on a swift freestone river, but on the glassy surface of a spring creek, such a fly often drifts unscathed and frequently puts fish down.

Terrestrial Timing

Traditionally, late summer is considered terrestrial time on our spring creeks and to an extent this is true. Hopper densities peak during July, August and September. But other terrestrials, most notably ants and beetles, are available throughout the summer.

Spring Creeks host some amazing hatches during late spring and early summer, the green drake and pale morning dun being excellent examples. Anglers often focus their attention on these impressive early-season hatches. Yet despite the myriad mayfly and caddis hatches of May and June, ants, beetles and other terrestrials are eagerly taken by many trout, especially those feeding during non-hatch hours and by smorgasboarding trout (trout that are actively feeding on whatever happens to drift by).

The point is this: Carry a few ant and beetle imitations; maybe a few inchworm and cricket patterns even during May and June when your focus is the famous mayfly emergences. You never know when the terrestrials might save a day of fishing for you.

Despite their presence throughout the season, ants, beetles and other terrestrials increase in stature as the primary mayfly hatches wain. In the presence of tiny Trico and *Baetis* mayflies, terrestrials suddenly seem a lot less obscure—both to fish and the fly angler. About the same time (mid-summer), the hoppers begin to appear in appreciable numbers and flying ants become more and more common.

In all honesty, these are the days of my fondest spring creek memories: Monster spring creek trout eagerly devouring ants, beetles and hoppers, sometimes feeding so voraciously on the terrestrials that they suspend all caution and allow close approach and imperfect presentation—I've always felt that smart trout are over-rated. Sometimes I like dumb trout, especially big dumb trout.

That's not to say that terrestrials necessarily make spring creek fishing easier, but they do give fly anglers a break from the difficulties inherently involved in fishing those late-

Likely places to find terrestrial-feeding trout on a spring creek: 1. below over-hanging trees and shrubs, 2. below grassy banks, 3. near fallen timber.

season hatches of tiny mayflies. You still must make a thoughtful, well-conceived presentation with the right fly, but at least you needn't strain to see a No. 22 floating nymph pattern 40 feet away drifting amongst thousands of naturals.

Terrestrial Tactics

Terrestrial fishing is frequently a matter of recognizing places where land-born insects might end up in the water and where trout can easily feed on them. Cut banks with overhanging grass, shoreline shrubbery and trees, timber fallen in the river and other such structures present excellent opportunities for terrestrial fishing.

Occasionally terrestrials become so abundant that trout rise for them as regularly as if feeding on a good mayfly hatch. Swarms of flying ants, for example, descend on many of our spring creeks during mid- and late-summer, frequently driven streamward by the wind.

Under such circumstances, trout can be highly selective, requiring precise imitation on the angler's part. Ant swarms (along with the uncommon termite or beetle swarm) can be difficult to recognize. These insects float in the surface film and are nearly impossible to see at any distance.

The exception to this is the large flying ants previously mentioned. These insects commonly drift along the water's surface with wings held aloft, looking much like mayflies from even a short distance away. In several instances I have been fooled into tying on a *Callibaetis* mayfly imitation after watching big trout gulp these upright-winged ants. Unfortunately, mayfly imitations don't mimic ants very well and selective trout will largely ignore such patterns during heavy ant flights.

Swarming ant flights rarely last long so recognizing the

phenomena quickly will allow you to take full advantage. On many occasions, however, I've enjoyed heavy ant drifts that lasted all afternoon and seemed to bring every trout to the surface.

Ant and beetle imitations, especially when fished during a heavy terrestrial drift, should closely resemble the natural in size, shape and even color. Small black ants (No. 16-18), red flying ants in No. 14-16, fire ants (black and red) in No. 12-14 and beetles in No. 14-16 all make excellent searching patterns on spring creeks. These sizes are well represented amongst the naturals.

Often, however, I've done well in timbered areas by searching with a No. 10 black carpenter ant. These large ants are common in areas where conifers—especially lodgepole pine—dominate the river banks.

In virtually all cases, ants, beetles and other small terrestrials should be fished dead drift. A long leader, of course, will help battle the tricky current seams prevalent along the banks where terrestrial-feeding trout often hold.

Grasshopper patterns, conversely, often benefit from a few slight twitches during the drift. Using a well-greased line and leader, allow the hopper to land with a small "splat." Give the trout a couple drag-free drifts. If these fail, cast again and impart a few gentle twitches with the rod tip or with the line hand. You can closely mimic the actions of a struggling hopper by doing this and frequently draw ferocious strikes.

In addition, hopper imitations sometimes induce violent strikes from bank-hugging trout when cast onto the bank and then carefully pulled into the river just below. Such a presentation closely mimics the way hoppers make an errant leap from the shoreline vegetation, ending up as easy targets for trout hovering in the shadows of a steep bank. These bank-hugging fish see or hear the soft splat of the fly and instantly react; perhaps they even see the airborn fly as it "jumps" from the bank.

This method of casting a hopper onto the bank, then pulling it into the water has its liabilities. Often the fly snags in the grass or brush on the shore; other times the taught line required to "jump" the fly into the water results in immediate drag.

For these reasons, a straight-forward drag-free drift is usually the best initial presentation. If the fish refuses several such drifts, try dropping the fly on the water close to the trout's window (one to three feet upstream from the trout's holding position), enabling your intended target to detect the soft splat of the landing hopper. If this method also fails, try casting onto the bank just upstream from the trout, and hopping the fly off the grass and into the water. The fly will almost always land more softly with this presentation than when cast onto the water—perhaps that is why it triggers a response from a selective fish.

To eliminate drag when employing this "bank cast," try to position yourself across and slightly downstream from your quarry. From this position, you can expect the fly line to drift downriver at the same pace as the fly, thus eliminating drag in most circumstances. If you must attempt this presentation from upstream of the trout, do so by releasing line from the reel and reaching the rod as far upstream as possible to pull the fly into the water, and then instantly pointing the rod toward the fish. Doing so will allow a two- to four-foot drift before the fly drags.

This same presentation will work with other terrestrials—ants, beetles, inchworms, and others—but becomes more difficult due to the smaller size fly usually used to mimic these insects. Nevertheless, the tactic works with all terrestrials. The smaller patterns can be deadly when fished this way on small spring creeks where you can approach to within 20 feet or so of the trout.

Trout will sometimes "bulge" or flash under a hopper imitation, indicating a sudden change of mind just before slamming the fly. Should this happen, switch to a smaller, more sparse imitation and try again. Or switch to a drowned hopper pattern, which often fools even the most stubborn risers.

In fact, a hopper or other terrestrial fished wet—just under the surface—works wonders on spring creek trout. When land-dwelling insects are in abundance, trout probably encounter as many or more drowned specimens as floating specimens. Just squeeze the air out of a fly under water to assure it will sink

quickly, then cast in the typical dry fly style, ahead of the trout with no drag. Use a second imitation as a dropper, fished dry, to act as a strike indicator or keep a close eye on the leader to detect the take. In fact, the combination of one dry hopper (the dropper fly) and one wet hopper (the lead fly) can be nothing short of deadly.

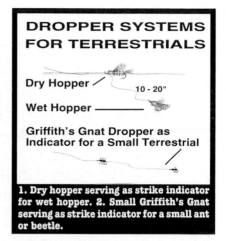

DROPPER SYSTEMS FOR TERRESTRIALS

Dry Hopper ⟋   10 - 20"

Wet Hopper ────

Griffith's Gnat Dropper as Indicator for a Small Terrestrial

1. Dry hopper serving as strike indicator for wet hopper. 2. Small Griffith's Gnat serving as strike indicator for a small ant or beetle.

Detecting a strike can prove difficult even when fishing terrestrials on top—primarily with ants, beetles and other small patterns. These imitations produce best when fished right in the surface film, where they are nearly impossible to see from any distance.

Two flies can solve this problem. When fishing small ants or beetles, try using a No. 16 Griffith's Gnat as a dropper. Unlike strike indicators made from foam or plastic, a small Griffith's Gnat never spooks trout. Yet even in a No. 16 this fly is easy to see on the water and thus helps in two ways: If you attach the dropper two feet above the lead fly, then you know where to look to locate the small terrestrial after you have cast. Should you be unable, still, to find the terrestrial pattern on the water, then at least you know to raise the rod tip at any rise within that two-foot radius of the Griffith's Gnat. Incidentally, sometimes the Gnat will rise a trout as well.

"Bank-bouncing" and two-fly tactics are easiest to perform when you are casting towards the bank, yet spring creeks frequently present opportunities to approach terrestrial-feeding trout from the shore below which they are holding. These fish can be tough, as they are easily spooked by too much noise on the ground above or by seeing the angler or the rod.

I used to fish a small spring creek in Montana where hoppers were abundant. The best section of stream flowed around a gravel-clad corner and collided with a steep, 30-foot-high embankment from which no approach was possible. The creek flowed along the base of this high bank for some 75 yards.

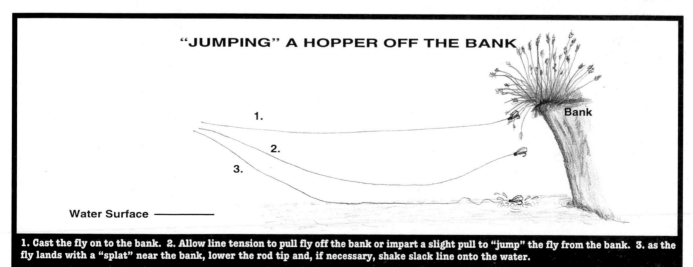

"JUMPING" A HOPPER OFF THE BANK

1.

2.

3.

Bank

Water Surface ────

1. Cast the fly on to the bank. 2. Allow line tension to pull fly off the bank or impart a slight pull to "jump" the fly from the bank. 3. as the fly lands with a "splat" near the bank, lower the rod tip and, if necessary, shake slack line onto the water.

The other side, which offered the only feasible approach, featured a cut bank rising some three feet above the water's surface and was covered with hip-high grass. A gentle riffle fed the pool from its top end. From there I would toss a live hopper or two into the pool and watch them drift along the bank until engulfed by a big cutthroat.

I could easily locate the feeding trout this way and then zero in on them one at a time. Approaching these fish, however, was more problematic than finding them. I had to drop to all fours and crawl toward the bank. Then I had to part the grass—ever so carefully—just enough to get my bearings.

Sometimes I would toss another live hopper in the creek to reorient myself. Using a long leader, I would then carefully flip a hopper pattern into the water, tight against the bank. Assuming I could make a decent presentation, with only the fly and a few feet of leader on the water, and keep myself and my rod as out-of-the-way as possible, I could usually count on two or three nice fish from that bank. One wrong move—stretch too high to peek over the grass, cast with my rod in the trout's view, move the grass too much, hang my leader in the grass so that the fly would drag—and I would have to rest the pool 20 minutes before the fish would resume feeding.

I took a friend there once. He performed the entire routine described above while I waited atop the high bluff on the other side of the river, intent on photographing the operation. Unfortunately, just as my friend threw a delicate cast above a huge trout, a gentle but untimely breeze blew his hopper into the streamside edge of the grass, where the fly held fast.

Now he was in a fix. I offered to meet him downriver with my rod as any further attempt to free the fly would surely spook the trout, which had risen noisily several more times. He declined my offer and instead clipped his leader off at the butt, dug into his vest for another and tied the new one on.

All the while he clenched the butt end of the snagged leader in his teeth to prevent it from dangling in the water below. He attached another hopper; made the cast; rose, hooked and landed a 22-inch cutthroat. Touche'. I gave him an A-plus for creativity.

The opposite side of that pool, below the 30-foot-high embankment, held terrestrial-feeding trout as well. They hovered tight against the steep bank, waiting for insects to fall from the grass and willows. The only possible approach was to cast across the pool from the bank where my friend hooked that big fish. If you could bounce a hopper off the bank, simultaneously employing a big upstream reach cast, you almost always rose a trout.

Sometimes a strong gust of wind would shoot dozens of hoppers airborn from atop the bluff. Those hopper clouds, desperately trying to fly to safety while descending toward the river, must have looked like Thanksgiving dinner to the trout waiting below. I'd swear the fish attacked some of those hoppers before they ever hit the water.

On those occasions when that cloud of wind-launched hoppers descended on the pool, I could tie an alder bud to my leader and expect to rise a trout—I know because I tried it.

Wind, in fact, plays a vital role in the general availability of terrestrials to spring-creek trout. Generally speaking, the best terrestrial fishing occurs below the windward bank, especially in the grassy meadow sections common to many of our spring creeks. Concentrate on the windward side (the side from which the wind blows), especially where steep, cut banks abound. Also look for swirling back-eddies where debris, terrestrial insects included, will accumulate.

Many such back eddies are characterized by a thin mat of off-white foam, which helps trap just about everything. Trout often cruise or hold in these eddies, just inches below the surface, sipping anything that looks edible—especially ants, beetles and other landborn insects.

Frequently, however, these trout are difficult to locate because their rises are subtle and are hidden by the swirling mat of foam. About all you can do is watch carefully and treat every back-eddy as if it were loaded with monster trout, all of them hungry, willing, and spooky.

Back eddies, incidentally, are great places to sample with a small insect or aquarium net to find out what trout foods are in the drift on a particular day. A careful examination of the contents of one of these eddies can tell you exactly what kind of insects you should be imitating. Sometimes you will find unusual items. I once discovered a number of tent caterpillars trapped in the foam of a back eddy. I clipped the hackle from a small wooly worm and caught several nice trout.

Tent caterpillars may not be the norm, but if you fish spring creeks, especially during the mid- and late summer, be prepared for just about anything. Spruce bud-worm moths are common on some streams, among them Oregon's Metolius River, where the small white moths become an important trout food at times.

Similarly, large nocturnal moths often attract spring creek trout at dusk and thereafter. Moth patterns can be fished dead-drift, but often perform better when twitched slightly during the drift and then allowed to swing across current on a taught line in the manner of a steelhead skating fly. The rises are always ferocious.

At times, where they occur in significant densities, inchworms and leafhoppers (like those commonly associated with Eastern limestone rivers) become significant to spring-creek trout. Crickets show up in trout stomachs fairly regularly also. Even mice, voles and shrews become trout food at times, large brown trout usually being the culprits.

Also, adult damselflies sometimes become available to spring-creek trout. Damsel nymphs, of course, live underwater, so the damselflies are not terrestrial in the sense of ants, beetles and hoppers. However, the nymphs live in weedy, non-moving water (such as sloughs and backwaters of the spring creeks) and are generally unavailable to trout in the streams. Thus only the adults merit our attention.

These adult damsels hunt smaller insects over the streams at times, with mayflies, midges and caddis all being fair game. Sometimes the delicate-looking, slender, blue damsels will end up on the water by way of a tricky breeze or some other mishap. Trout will eat them given such opportunity, so I always carry a few damsel patterns. If I see any number of these insects on the prowl over the water's surface, I keep my eyes peeled for loud, splashy rises that might indicate a trout preying on a damsel.

In any event, hoppers, ants and beetles are the important terrestrials on most of our spring creeks and anglers who learn to recognize terrestrial feeding and terrestrial water and who can fish imitations effectively can enjoy some of the season's best fishing. The streams harbor fewer anglers during late summer; big trout often hold in some peculiar places and act in an emboldened manner when pursuing land-dwelling insects.

Terrestrial Patterns

Some of the most productive terrestrial patterns are those that have been around for years, including Whitlock's

APPROACHES FOR BANK-HUGGING TROUT

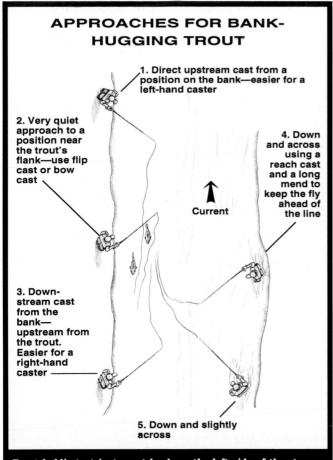

1. Direct upstream cast from a position on the bank—easier for a left-hand caster

2. Very quiet approach to a position near the trout's flank—use flip cast or bow cast

3. Down-stream cast from the bank—upstream from the trout. Easier for a right-hand caster

4. Down and across using a reach cast and a long mend to keep the fly ahead of the line

Current

5. Down and slightly across

Trout holding against a cut bank on the left side of the stream, looking downstream

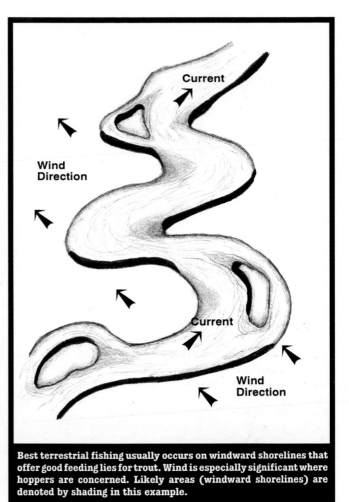

Current

Wind Direction

Current

Wind Direction

Best terrestrial fishing usually occurs on windward shorelines that offer good feeding lies for trout. Wind is especially significant where hoppers are concerned. Likely areas (windward shorelines) are denoted by shading in this example.

LARGE BACK-EDDIES

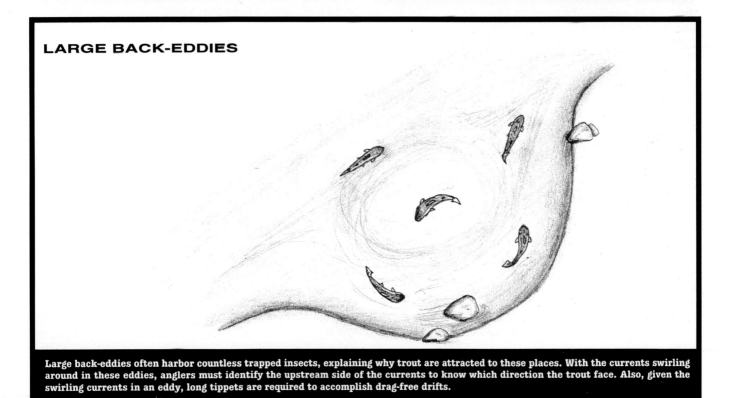

Large back-eddies often harbor countless trapped insects, explaining why trout are attracted to these places. With the currents swirling around in these eddies, anglers must identify the upstream side of the currents to know which direction the trout face. Also, given the swirling currents in an eddy, long tippets are required to accomplish drag-free drifts.

hopper, the fur ants and the peacock beetles. In addition, recent years have seen the development of some new and effective dressings, among them patterns incorporating closed cell foam and other synthetics.

Whatever terrestrial patterns you choose, remember that correct shape is often critical on spring creek trout: Ants should feature clearly segmented bodies; hoppers should be sparsely dressed.

The dressings suggested below are but a sampling of the numerous patterns around today. These, however, are dressings that have proven their worth on the flat waters of the spring creeks where selective trout abound. You needn't, of course, carry every pattern listed. Instead, choose two or three dressings for each terrestrial in a variety of sizes. Fish these diligently when the opportunity presents itself and choose your favorites from there.

In tying hoppers, crickets, and other large terrestrials, use a long-shank dry fly hook, usually 3X long and perhaps 1X fine. For ants and beetles, opt for a lightwire standard length dry fly hook (or a standard wire hook for small flies). Suggested sizes are given with each dressing.

*Letort Hopper (Ed Shenk)
body: yellow, cream or pale olive rabbit fur
wing: mottled turkey wing quill
collar: natural deer hair
head: deer hair, spun and clipped
sizes: 4-12

*Pheasant Leg Hopper
body: pale yellow or pale olive dubbing
rib: fine gold wire
underwing: yellow deer hair
wing: mottled turkey quill
legs: knotted pheasant tail fibers
collar: dark deer hair, sparse
head: deer hair, spun and clipped
sizes: 6-12 (not pictured)

*Henry's Fork Hopper (Mike Lawson)
body: cream, yellow or pale olive deer hair
rib: yellow thread
underwing: dyed yellow elk hair
wing: brown mottled hen saddle, laquered
head: elk hair, tied bullet style
legs: tan round rubber legs, knotted (optional)
sizes: 4-10

*High Desert Hopper (Shewey)
body: antelope or caribou, dyed pale yellow, cream or pale olive; tied toward rear and pulled forward
rib: thread to match body color
underwing: fine polar bear, dyed pale yellow or pale olive
wing: mottled oak turkey
collar: elk or deer hair, sparse
head: spun and clipped deer hair
sizes: 4-10

Dave's Hopper (Dave Whitlock)
tail: dyed red hackle fibers (optional)
body: pale yellow or pale olive yarn, including a loop extending over the tail
hackle: brown, palmered and clipped short
wing: yellow deer body hair, then a tent-style wing of mottled turkey
legs: mottled wing quill segments or trimmed grizzly hackle fibers, dyed yellow and knotted
head/collar: natural brown deer body hair (dyed yellow is optional) spun and trimmed.

Troth Cricket (Al Troth)
body: black elk, tied toward rear and pulled forward
rib: black thread
wing: black goose quill
collar: black elk hair with butt ends forming head
legs: black stripped goose
Note: For Troth Hopper, simply alter the colors of this pattern to match natural color of hoppers
sizes: 4-12

*Fur Ant
body: two distinct segments of rabbit, nutria or beaver dyed to match natural (dyed mole works well for very small sizes)
hackle: two turns of hackle to match natural
colors and sizes: black, No. 10-12 for carpenter ant, No. 14-20 for black ants; cinnamon, No. 14-18; fire (red butt, black head) No. 12-18

*Flying Fur Ant
body and hackle: Same as fur ant
wings: two sparse dun hackle tips, tied in below hackle to protrude at angles toward rear of fly, or a single duck quill section tied low over rear of body
Sizes and colors: black, No. 12-16; cinnamon or red, No. 12-18

*McMurray Ant (Ed Sutryn)
body: Pre-formed McMurray ant bodies (available at fly shops) to match naturals
hackle: two turns of hackle to match ant color
wings: (optional) hackle tips, Krystal Flash, polyethylene or similar synthetic material

*McMurray-Fur Ant
body: rear half, McMurray ant abdomen; front half, fur thorax
hackle: 2-3 turns to match body color
wings: (for flying ants)—a few strands of Z-lon tied spent
colors: black: No. 12-18; red: No. 14-18; fire (red butt, black head): No. 14-16

Parachute Flying Ant
abdomen: black or rust dubbed fur
post: polly yarn, gray or white
thorax: black or rust fur
hackle: dun, tied parachute style
sizes: 10-18
Note: this pattern will prove helpful to those who have difficulty seeing the typical low-profile ant patterns

*Foam Beetle
back: ethafoam or similar closed-cell foam, dyed black

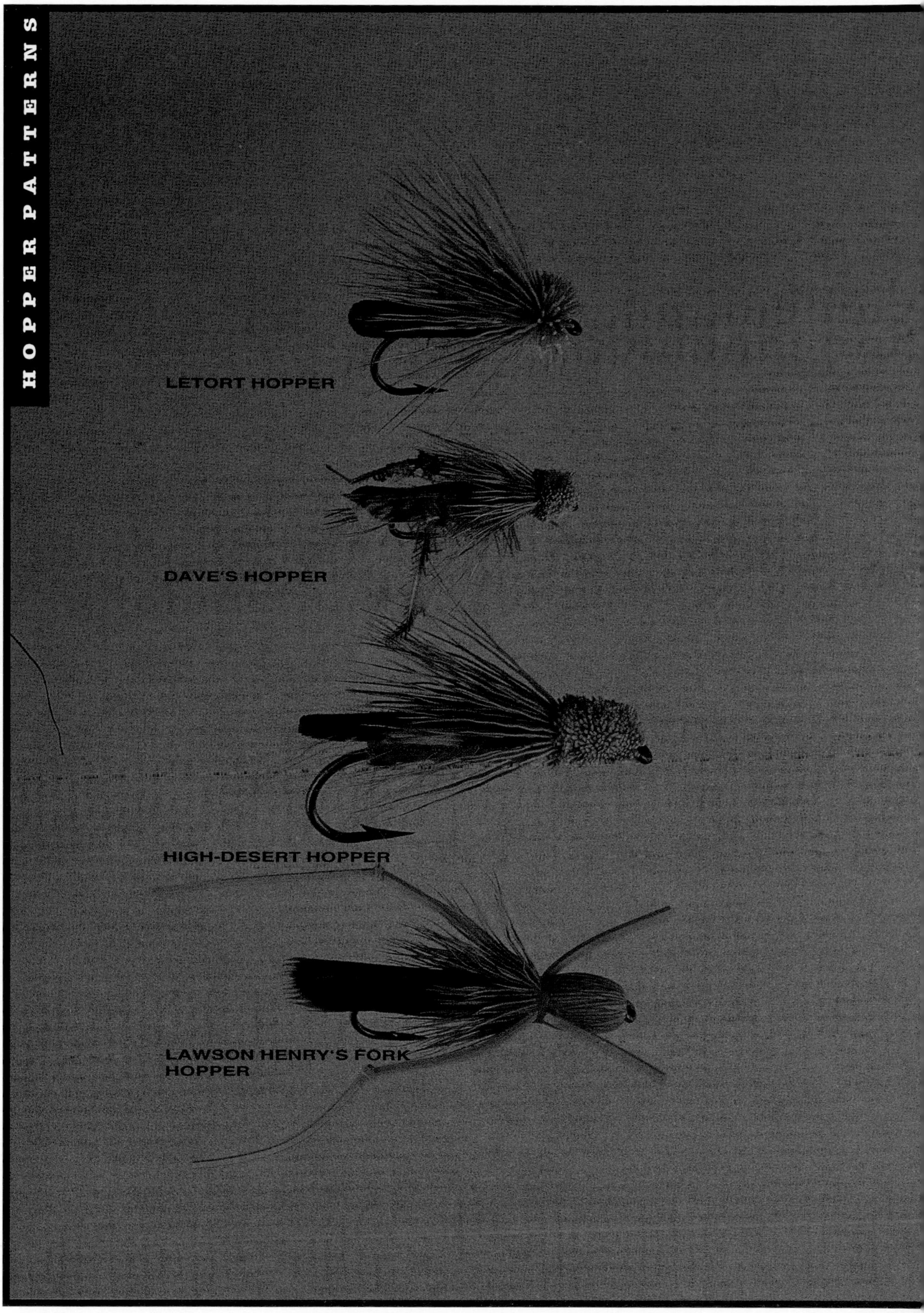

LETORT HOPPER

DAVE'S HOPPER

HIGH-DESERT HOPPER

LAWSON HENRY'S FORK
HOPPER

ANT PATTERNS

McMURRAY ANT

FLYING FUR ANT

PARACHUTE ANT

McMURRAY-FUR ANT

FUR ANT

CDC-FUR ANT

BEETLE PATTERNS

TIM'S PEACOCK BEETLE

HARROP PEACOCK BEETLE

FOAM BEETLE

DEER HAIR BEETLE

body: black dubbing or peacock herl
legs: two turns of black hackle, clipped flush below
head: continuation of foam used for back
Note: color can be varied to imitate specific beetles
sizes: 10-22

Deer Hair Beetle
back: black deer hair, tied in by tips
body: peacock herl, ostrich herl or dubbing to match natural
legs: butt ends of deer used for back; 3 or 4 per side
head: butt ends of deer hair used for back, flared slightly at collar and clipped
sizes: 10-18

*Pine Beetle (Shewey)
back: closed cell foam, colored dark gray
body: gray dubbing or gray ostrich herl
legs: two turns of slightly webby grizzly hackle, clipped below
head: continuation of foam used for back
antennae: fine grizzly hackle stems, clipped, tied about same length as body
sizes: 6-10

*Peacock Beetle
(Rene Harrop/ tied by McKenzie Flies)
back: peacock herl
body: peacock herl, countered with tying thread
legs: peacock herl stems
head: tying thread
sizes: 12-20

Waking Night Moth
body: white caribou or antelope, spun and trimmed to form robust, moth like body
wings: untrimmed tips of hair, tied spent
sizes: 4-10
NOTE: For the rare individual willing to explore the spring creeks at night (where legal), a big moth imitation and a big streamer pattern will prove very valuable. The moth should be allowed to skate gently across stream at the end of the drift in precisely the fashion of a waking steelhead fly.

*Spruce Budworm Moth (Tim Blount)
body: cream dubbing or foam
wing: white or tan deer hair
hackle: two turns of light ginger, clipped below
sizes: 10-12

Adult Damsel (Shewey)
hook: dry fly, No. 12
body: blue bucktail
wing: a few strands of pearl Krystal Flash, tied delta style
hackle: grizzly or dun, parachute style

PINE BEETLE

WAKING MOTH

TROTH CRICKET

ADULT DAMSEL

SPRUCE BUDWORM MOTH

MISCELLANEOUS TERRESTRIAL PATTERNS

SPRING CREEK DIARY

August, 1985; Henry's Fork

A fly angler could go years without ever experiencing a nuptial flight of ants blown of course and into the water. Or, as was the case that week on the Henry's Fork, the phenomenon could be a daily occurrence for a full week. Predictability is never the strong suit of the flying ants, but when mishap does befall them and they end up in the water, trout go nuts.

I'm not sure why trout like them; it's enough for me that indeed the fish seem to relish ants, especially when said ants arrive suddenly in hordes. These ants don't do well on the wing. They can fly all right, but in the face of any slight breeze their single pair of wings, grown and retained only long enough to get them through a mating dispersal flight, prove rather inadequate. I've heard it theorized that flying ants might mistakenly orient to the surface of the water rather than to some other landscape feature that would normally steer their movements.

Whatever the case, all the factors that make for outstanding ant fishing had assembled that week on the Railroad Ranch and each afternoon provided two or three hours of fishing so good that Timmy and I had to pinch ourselves occasionally to make sure we weren't dreaming. We left for home on a Sunday, just after fishing the ants again. I'd like to think we fished the last day of the good ant flights that week, but who knows, the way it had gone for us I wouldn't be surprised if the insanity lasted another week.

The next August we packed our gear and drove all night to get there. Same week, same weather, same enthusiasm. No ants. They can make for a rather fleeting affair.

Chapter 6

Spring Creek Caddisflies

By the thousands, Pale morning duns paraded down the river like so many tiny sailboats in a full-blown regatta. I singled out a decent trout holding several feet from a steep bank and I watched him for a few minutes: Rhythmic rises, one after another, all spaced by the same three-second interval. Mayfly duns floated over the fish unscathed, thus I determined he was taking emergers in the film.

I gave him both barrels. Again and again I presented a PMD emerger pattern with well-timed casts and considerable accuracy and yet I could not touch that trout. Still he fed ravenously. I inched closer, hoping for a better look. Maybe a hidden current was dragging my fly ever so slightly. I tried again with a similar maddening lack of results.

To hell with him. I marched right over there and took a good look. I sampled the surface drift with my aquarium net. Caddis pupa clogged the fine white mesh: Tiny caddis—the kind that make anglers cringe at the very size of the insects and cringe even more at the realization that the bugs now require imitation.

I had some No. 20 chironomid pupa and eventually I managed to fool perhaps the dumbest trout in the river. Other than that, the day was a bust.

Caddis can do that to you. A number of caddis are abundant on our spring creeks, some offering predictable and straightforward fishing, others sneaking up on you just in time to ruin a good mayfly hatch. Moreover, any attempt to conquer the spring creek caddisflies requires that you know enough about caddis life cycles and how fish react to them to determine what stage the trout are taking.

I'm not overly fond of the Latinization of fly fishing that has pre-occupied the minds of some anglers and writers over the last couple decades. Yet spring creek caddisflies only occasionally carry common names like green sedge or October caddis. And because different caddis offer different feeding opportunities to trout and thus require different angling tactics, some ability to identify the more common caddis will almost certainly improve success with these bugs.

Certain caddis emergences bring trout to the surface en masse; other emergences are insignificant. Yet these same caddisflies whose emergence is unimportant to the trout may return to the river to lay eggs in a manner that produces excellent fishing. Still other caddisflies produce reliable surface feeding during both the emergence and ovipositing. Finally, some caddis species will gather over the stream in huge numbers during mating flights, yet never touch the water and thus never attract trout.

If you know which caddisflies are important and when, you eliminate a lot of frustration sometimes inherent to spring-creek caddis fishing. More basic still is the need to recognize when trout are feeding on caddis.

Much of the available fly fishing literature tells us that caddisflies elicit wild, splashy rises from trout. This may be the case on freestone rivers where currents carry emerging caddis quickly downriver, but when caddisflies emerge on the slow, smooth water of a spring creek, trout can hover inches below the surface and devour the pupa as they pause in the surface film.

On slow spring creeks, then, a trout's riseform is rarely a reliable indicator of what that fish is eating. No doubt riseforms can provide clues, but they can often be deceptive instead.

Still, one characteristic of riseforms can reveal a caddis emergence quite predictably, that being the absolute absence of any visible insects on the water despite countless rises all around you. Most caddisflies escape their pupal shucks immediately upon breaking through the surface film and fly away instantly without drifting on the water. The small caddis, being especially hard for anglers to see, are notorious for causing these mystery rises.

Spend any amount of time on the spring creeks and you will eventually encounter such a situation. Trout boil and sip everywhere but you see not a single insect drifting on the surface. Even chironomids are evident when they cause trout to feed on top; mayfly spinners sometimes less so, but even they are more easily discovered than many emerging caddis flies. So when trout go crazy and you can't see a single bug on the water, think caddis and get out your bug net to sample the drift.

If indeed caddis flies are the culprit, you need only choose a pupa or stillborn imitation of the correct size and shade. Only on a few caddis emergences are adults of any significance to trout. Most often, stillborns and pupae fished in the film will prove far more productive than an adult caddis pattern.

Over the years, many anglers have advocated the use of various "lift" methods when imitating emerging caddis, but I've never found these techniques to be very successful on spring creeks. The reason, I imagine, is that during even a marginally heavy caddis emergence, spring-creek trout will hold just inches below the surface where they can intercept caddis pupa without having to chase them. In fact, during his research for the book *Caddisflies*, Gary Lafontaine learned that trout, even when holding deep, will follow an emerging caddis pupa to the surface before eating the bug, thereby taking advantage of the insect's most vulnerable stage rather than expending energy chasing the rising insect.

Sometimes, when I know of an immanent caddis emergence and arrive well ahead of its onset, I've been able to take fish by drifting caddis pupae near the bottom of fairly deep flows. Effective as it can be at times, this method leaves a lot to be desired when compared with the type of success possible fishing pupa in the film during the actual emergence.

As with any dense insect drift, heavy caddis hatches prompt trout to patrol narrow feeding lanes. Therefore, precise placement of the fly is critical, as is timing the rise so your offering arrives when the fish is ready to feed. On large spring creeks—the Harriman section of the Henry's Fork being the ultimate example—pods of large trout will move around even during a heavy hatch. Just as you creep within range and are about to cast, the trout move upstream or over to one side and you must begin your approach anew. No doubt some of these wandering fish have learned that feeding while roving about protects them from anglers: They detect the presence of an angler and, as Nelson Ishiyama says, "they revert to a craftier method of feeding."

Still, I have sat on the bank, with no other anglers

This pretty Wyoming brown trout rose for a spent caddis pattern.

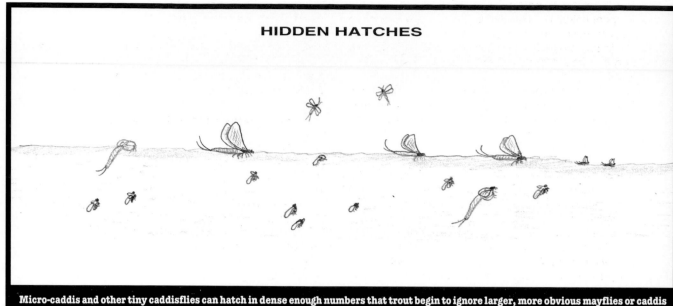

Micro-caddis and other tiny caddisflies can hatch in dense enough numbers that trout begin to ignore larger, more obvious mayflies or caddis and instead turn selective to the smaller insects.

about, and watched trout wander while feeding when they could have easily consumed ample food while holding in one place. I used to think that competition between individuals in a pod of fish, whether real or simply perceived on an innate level by the trout, causes the entire group to feed in a state of flux, constantly shifting positions. This may hold some validity, but it fails to explain why some individual trout, not associated with a pod of fish, will habitually wander during heavy hatches.

Perseverance coupled with continued stealth is the only way to combat these roving pods of trout. Luckily, this is less of a problem on small spring creeks and never a constant, even on the Henry's Fork. If at times such fish get too troublesome, you can always find a solitary feeder nearby.

In any case, the pupa imitations that prove so deadly during caddis hatches are, naturally, largely ineffective when trout key on egglaying caddisflies. Therefore you must first determine which caddisflies—emerging individuals or those returning to lay eggs—are being eaten by the trout. Sometimes this is easy, such as when countless thousands of caddis are crawling all over you—in your ears, under your glasses, all over your face—as you stand in the river and when trout bring the river to a boil that looks like a hatchery pond at feeding time. Such are the signs of some of the heaviest emergences. Other times, however, when activity is not so frantic, a sampling net proves invaluable.

Sometimes huge swarms of caddis hover over the water, but these are usually large flights of males intent on seeking mates. Trout have little or no opportunity to feed on these swarms, yet anglers often mistake this activity for a hatch or ovipositing flight.

Most actual egg-laying flights are more subdued, meaning you usually have to look pretty close to recognize that this ovipositing activity is responsible for the rising trout. Watch for caddis bouncing and skittering over the surface: Many species lay their eggs simply by depositing them in the surface film. Other species dive underwater, sometimes jigging up and down above the surface a few times as if to get their nerve up. Still others crawl underwater by way of shoreline rocks and vegetation. Some caddisflies, in fact, employ any or all of these

methods to lay eggs.

If you suspect ovipositing caddis are responsible for trout rising near shore, check overhanging plants, fallen timber protruding into the river, or partially submerged rocks. Those species of caddis that crawl underwater to lay eggs will often gather on and around objects from which they can access the river.

Traditional dry patterns can effectively mimic ovipositing caddis, but I've had much more consistent luck with downwing patterns dressed to imitate spent caddis floating flush on the water. Carl Richard's quad-wing caddis, originally designed to imitate caddis found on Midwest streams, long ago became the model for my favorite spent caddis patterns. (Incidentally, Richard's "half-hatch caddis" is one of my favorites for fishing hatches of small caddis on the spring creeks.) John Juracek and Craig Mathews, similarly, offer a down-wing caddis utilizing partridge or other soft-hackle material, wound in the wet fly style, to simulate spent wings awash in the surface film. Only recently have I employed these patterns and, as is typical with patterns originated by those two noted Yellowstone-area anglers, the flies have proven highly effective (not to mention easy to tie).

The spent caddis patterns should be fished dead drift and cast downstream to the trout, especially during heavy feeding activity. These flies are difficult to see on the water, especially in small sizes. A higher-floating dropper can help you keep track of your downwing fly. I use a sparsely dressed, hackleless elkhair or quillwing pattern (the same size as the naturals) as this second pattern. Sometimes trout will grab this indicator fly. Remember, however, that this second fly effectively doubles the opportunity for drag to impede the progress of the fly's drift, so use the dropper judiciously.

Caddis that dive underwater to lay eggs soon return to the surface to drift away spent and dying (or, in some cases, to fly away). I have often read about the promising opportunities to fish diving caddis below the surface, imparting some kind of action on the fly. I've never found such tactics to bring overwhelming success on the spring creeks, although I probably haven't given these methods a fair shake either.

I will, however, sometimes employ a dead-drift wet fly below my spent imitation. Results have been mixed, but I've taken enough trout on the wet-fly end of the tandem to justify this technique. In any event, a spent pattern or sparsely dressed standard dry pattern will produce the best results when trout key in on ovipositing caddis.

By now it should be obvious that doing your homework ahead of time will help considerably when you encounter caddis activity. Before going afield, familiarize yourself with caddisflies you might encounter on a particular stream. Carry imitations to match the important stages of any caddis you might find. When I travel for extended periods in the West, expecting to fish a number of streams, I carry enough caddis imitations—some general, some specific to certain hatches—to handle nearly any situation. Common body colors among caddis include olive, green, tan, brown and dark gray. I carry pupa and spent-wing adults (along with a few standard adults) in each of these colors and in sizes 14 through 20 with a few 22's to boot.

Trout often key on the size of caddisflies regardless of color. This behavior works to your advantage simply because, when two or three varieties of tiny caddis are adrift simultaneously, you need only match the naturals in size and not color.

In addition to the aforementioned Carl Richards' half-hatch caddis, which represents stillborn or cripple caddis emergers, I tie several types of similar emerger patterns, including the Juracek and Mathews antron caddis emerger and X-caddis. Sometimes one style of fly will produce when another fails, despite both being identical in size and color. Larvae imitations seem less useful on the smooth flows of spring creeks than on freestone rivers, but at times they will work. A few basic patterns in a variety of colors and sizes will cover you.

Spring creeks deserve dry flies and spring creek anglers fish these waters primarily because of the dry-fly opportunities. But on those occasions when nothing is going on, a caddis larvae can take trout (although in some cases I wouldn't want to have to prove that the trout see them as caddis larvae.)

At this juncture, a look at some of the caddis genera found on Western spring creeks might prove useful. Due to the lack of common names and the confusion among many of the common names (i.e. one common name, such as green sedge, might be used by anglers to describe any of several different genera of caddisflies), I have little choice but to offer the Latin names of the common spring-creek caddis genera. By and large, identification on the species level is unnecessary, although listed below are a few anecdotal examples of individual species of significance to spring-creek anglers.

In any event, the opportunity to fish caddis imitations on the spring creeks can be summarized very simply: Carry with you a general idea of what caddis activity might occur on a given stream and carry a selection of caddis pupae (designed to be fished at the surface) and adults (often spent-wing styles) to mimic the common colors and sizes. Remember also that mayflies and terrestrials still rule on the spring creek, but having that box of caddis patterns in your vest will keep you in the game on those occasions when the trout turn selective to significant flat-water caddis activity.

Listed below are the basic dressings for top-producing caddis patterns. Then, following the brief descriptions of various caddis genera, you will find listed the colors and sizes needed to mimic the respective insects. Where appropriate, dressings for patterns intended for use on specific caddis species (or genera) are given in full.

Quad-wing Caddis (Swisher/Richards)
hook: fine-wire dry fly; size to match natural
thread: black
wings: small body feather tips from bobwhite, hen pheasant, woodcock, snipe, or similar
body: fine dubbing to match color of natural
hackle: 2-3 turns of dun

Half-hatch Caddis (Swisher/Richards)
hook: dry fly
wing case: light gray hen hackle fibers
thorax: fine dubbing
shuck: bronze blue-dun cock hackle
Note: *shuck is a small hackle stem tied in with the fibers reversed in a 45-degree angle, covering the hook shank; Z-lon or similar can be substituted*

Hemmingway Caddis (Mike Lawson)
hook: dry fly
body: dubbing
rib: undersized hackle, palmered
wing: natural gray duck quill sections, rounded at end
thorax: peacock herl
hackle: a few turns of cock hackle wound through thorax

X-Caddis
(Craig Mathews/ tied by Umpqua Feather Merchants)
hook: dry fly
tail: Z-lon as trailing shuck
body: dubbing
wing: natural deer hair with butts left to form head (sparse)

Antron Caddis Pupa (Juracek/Mathews)
hook: dry fly
shuck: Z-lon, tied short
body: antron dubbing, loop dubbed
legs: brown partridge hackle fibers
head: dark grey dubbing

Iris Caddis (Juracek/Mathews)
hook: dry fly
shuck: Z-lon
body: dubbed (loop dubbed)
wing: gray or white Z-lon, looped and tied low over the body
head: tan dubbing

Spent Caddis (Juracek/Mathews)
hook: dry fly
body: dubbed
wing: natural elk, tied sparse, and followed by brown partridge hackle, which is swept back to simulate spent wings

Delta-wing Caddis (Larry Solomon)
hook: dry fly
body: dubbed
wing: dun hackle tips, tied delta style
collar: a few turns of dun hackle, clipped below

Lawson Spent Partridge Caddis
(Sheralee Lawson/tied by Umpqua Feather Merchants)
hook: dry fly, size to match natural

SPENT CADDIS

CDC ADULT CADDIS

DELTA-WING CADDIS

QUAD-WING CADDIS

X-CADDIS

SLOW-WATER CADDIS

HEMMINGWAY CADDIS

SPENT PARTRIDGE CADDIS

body: dubbing
wing: brown partridge flank, spent
hackle: grizzly-brown mixed, clipped flush top and bottom

Slow-Water Caddis
(Rene' Harrop/tied by Umpqua Feather Merchants)
hook: dry fly, No. 12-18
body: dubbed
hackle: cock hackle wrapped through thorax region and clipped below
wings: laquered hen hackle feathers, tent style

CDC Caddis Adult *(tied by Umpqua Feather Merchants)*
hook: dry fly
body: dubbing
underwing: few strands of Z-lon or similar
wing: CDC feather to match natural
legs: short CDC feathers, tied to the sides or two turns of hackle, clipped
thorax: dubbing as per body

LaFontaine Sparkle Pupa
(Gary LaFontaine/ tied by Umpqua Feather Merchants)
hook: dry fly or wet fly
tail: trailing shuck of fine antron sparkle yarn
body: dubbed and then fine antron sparkle yarn is pulled over top and under bottom
wing: elk or deer hair extending back over body, sparse
head: dark dubbing

Lawson Caddis Emerger
(Mike Lawson/tied by Umpqua Feather Merchants)
hook: wet fly or dry fly
tail: antron or Z-lon, tan or to match body color, tied as trailing shuck and extending over back of body, where it is held in place by a rib of fine wire
body: dubbed to match natural
wing: antron or Z-lon under partridge fibers
thorax/head: peacock herl

Soft-hackle Caddis Emerger
hook: wet fly
body: dubbed
wing: antron tied over back, sparse
hackle: partridge
thorax: same as body

Quill-wing Caddis
hook: dry fly
body: dubbed
wings: mallard quill segment, notched at rear, or two segments tied tent style
hackle: 2-4 turns dry fly hackle *(not pictured)*

Hydropsyche
Hafele and Hughes *(Western Hatches)* note that some 25 species represent the genus *Hydropsyche* in the West. Some of these species are common and important inhabitants of the spring creeks. The adults of these caddis frequently feature light brown or tan wings (often mottled) and bodies ranging from gray-brown to green. The antennae are the length of the body. No. 14 and 16 imitations match most *Hydropsyche* caddis found on the Western spring creeks.

Hydropsyche

Spotted sedge emergences can trigger heavy (and selective) feeding. These hatches begin during late afternoon or evening and like many other caddis emergences, last until after dark. Pupal patterns, fished in the film or just below the surface, produce best.

Prior to the actual emergence, female spotted sedges deposit their eggs on the water, sometimes triggering splashy rises by opportunistic trout. Trout feeding on the emerging caddis, in contrast, exhibit a classic methodical rise with nose, fins or tail breaking the water's surface. If a particular trout proves uncooperative despite persistent feeding, be sure to note whether her nose is breaking the water: During the spotted sedge hatch, some trout will concentrate solely on pupae just below the surface—their dorsal fin and tail may break the film, but their snouts remain submerged. Many trout, however, are content to take cripples and stillborns on top along with pupae just below the surface.

Gary Lafontaine *(Caddisflies)*, in fact, points out that *Hydropsyche* pupae "require a notoriously long time to shed their skin and fly away."

"The pupa take from minutes to hours to escape the water," Lafontaine continues, "most of this time spent drifting helplessly just under the surface film. It is not only their overwhelming numbers that make *Hydropsyche* pupae so important: it is this complete availability to the trout."

Lafontaine, incidentally, concludes that the *Hydropsyche* caddis may well be the "most important trout-stream caddis in America."

Antron Caddis Pupa: No. 14-16 with brownish yellow body
Lafontaine Sparkle Pupa: tan, No. 14-16
X-Caddis: pale green or tan, No. 14-16
Delta-wing Caddis: pale green or tan with gray wings, No. 14-16
Iris Caddis: No. 14-16; schuck: amber; body: pale green or tan; wing: gray or white; head: tan
Quad-wing Caddis: No. 14-16; gray wings, pale green or tan body
Lawson Spent Partridge Caddis: No. 14-16, olive body, grayish wings
Quill-Wing Caddis: No. 14-16, olive or tan body, watery dun-grizzly hackle

Cheumatopsyche ("little olive sedge")

Closely related to the larger *Hydropsyche*, the little olive sedge of the genus *Cheumatopsyche* looks similar with its brown wings and olive body. They are common on many Western spring creeks and although they rarely hatch in voluminous numbers, their emergence can stimulate good feeding activity.

The most fishable little olive sedge hatches often occur on cloudy days or during early morning (sometimes evening). Trout feed on the emerging pupae and on the adults, the latter of which ride the surface for a considerable distance upon hatching. Juracek and Mathews *(Fishing Yellowstone Waters)* say that seeing the newly emerged *Cheumatopsyche* adults riding the water is the primary indication that trout may be feeding on them.

The little olive sedge emergence spans the summer months, occuring anytime between mid-May and late August, depending on specific location. A No. 18-20 pupa (the same dressings used to imitate the larger *Hydropsyche*) works for the little olive sedge hatch and trout can be tempted to eat adult imitations as well. Some species of *Cheumatopsyche* feature olive-tan or tan bodies, so a few basic adult patterns dressed in various colors can come in handy.

Delta-wing Caddis or Quad-wing Caddis: No. 18-20
CDC Caddis Adult: olive body, gray wings
Hemmingway Caddis: olive body, dun hackle & wings
Lawson Spent Partridge Caddis: olive body, grayish wings
Quill-Wing Caddis: No. 18-20, olive body, brown hackle
Half-hatch Caddis: olive body

Lepidostoma ("Little brown sedge," "grannom")

The *Lepidostoma* caddis emergence occurs during mid-summer on many Western spring creeks and offers, at times, good fishing during the evenings and sometimes at other times of day. This emergence can be heavy and, as spring creek hatches go, the *Lepidostoma* offers straight-forward fishing: The adults ride the water for a time upon emergence, so both pupa and adult patterns will fool trout.

Named for its wing color, the little brown sedge features light brown wings, sometimes with grayish markings. Males display a distinctive grayish recurve to their wings. Body color ranges from olive to light brown, depending on species. Most *Lepidostoma* can be matched with a No. 16-18 pattern, although some go as small as a No. 20.

During late afternoon and evening egg-laying flights, little brown sedges will ride the water for some time. Because of their timing, these egg-laying flights can be confused with the actual emergence. Juracek and Mathews point out that "a seine will tell you right away whether pupae are present, indicating an emergence."

Antron Caddis Pupa: No. 18, olive-brown body
X-Caddis: No. 18, olive-brown to gray-brown body
Half-hatch Caddis: No. 18, brownish body
Quad-wing or Delta-wing Caddis: No. 16-20, olive-brown or gray-brown body
No-hackle Elkhair Caddis: No. 18, brown or olive-brown body
Spent Caddis: No. 18, olive-brown to gray-brown body
Lawson Spent Partridge Caddis: No. 16-20, brownish body

Quill-Wing Caddis: No. 16-18, brown body, grizzly-watery dun mixed hackle
Soft-hackle Caddis Emerger: No. 16, brown body

Brachycentrus/Amiocentrus

Depending on the particular stream or region, hatches of these important caddis can occur any time between early spring and mid autumn. May through August emergences tend to be most significant to anglers. The emergence and the egg-laying flights are both important to trout.

Brachycentrus occidentalis emerges in late May and June on several Rocky Mountain spring creeks. Rather robust for their size, the adults sport grayish bodies with clearly veiniated wings. Emergence and ovipositing occur during the late afternoon and evening. Other *Brachycentrus* and *Amiocentrus* caddis emerge during the morning and in many cases the ovipositing activity can be as or more important than the actual emergence. Thus, spent adult patterns often prove useful. Pupa patterns, fished in the film, produce well during the hatch.

Amiocentrus aspilus, listed by Lafontaine as the "little western weedy water sedge," emerges during the summer on many Western spring creeks. Pupae patterns (typically a No. 18), fished in the surface film, produce the best results.

Antron Caddis Pupa: No. 14-18; olive body, dark grey head
X-Caddis: No. 14-18; olive body; natural deer hair wing
Hemmingway Caddis: olive body, No. 14-18
Delta-wing or Quad-wing Caddis: olive body, No. 14-18
Spent Caddis: olive body, No. 14-18
Lawson Spent Partridge Caddis: No. 14-18, olive body
Quill-Wing Caddis: No. 14-18, olive body, watery dun hackle

Oecetis ("longhorn sedge")

Several Western spring creeks host substantial populations of a graceful-looking little caddis of the genus *Oecetis*. Between late May and September, egg-laying flights of *Oecetis* (sometimes called "longhorn sedge") may trigger selective evening feeding binges by the resident trout.

These caddis feature characteristically long antennae, two to three times the length of their wings, which in turn are rather long in comparison to the body. The wings are ashy gray; the body color ranges from greenish- or reddish-brown (males) to yellowish or tannish-brown (females).

A spent caddis pattern mimics the dying adults perfectly, although trout can be lured to a standard dry caddis pattern as well. As noted by Juracek and Mathews in *Fishing Yellowstone Hatches*, *Oecetis* caddis "may ride the water in a perfectly normal resting position, they may be found sprawled awash with wings fully spread, or in any position in between."

Quad-wing Caddis: No. 16-18, yellow-tan or yellow-green body
Lawson Spent Partridge Caddis: No. 16-18, yellow-green or yellow-tan body
Hemmingway Caddis: No. 16-18, yellow-green or tan body; ginger hackle, quill wings
Slow-water or CDC Caddis: tannish body, gray wing
Spent Caddis: No. 16-18, golden yellow or bright green body, woodcock or brown partridge wings
Quill-Wing Caddis: No. 16-18, bright green or gold body, ginger or watery dun hackle

SOFT-HACKLE CADDIS EMERGER

ANTRON CADDIS PUPA

IRIS CADDIS

HALF-HATCH CADDIS

LAWSON CADDIS EMERGER

LAFONTAINE SPARKLE PUPA

Helicopsyche

Between early May and mid August (depending on location), the *Helicopsyche* caddis hatches on many spring creeks. When present in large numbers, either at emergence or during egg-laying flights, these caddis can trigger good rises (although very close observation is required to tell whether trout are feeding on *Helicopsyche* or on one of several other caddis genera that invariably seem to be present at the same times.)

Helicopsyche borealis, found on the Henry's Fork and other spring creeks in that region, features dark grey-brown wings that hide an amber- or tan-colored body. A No. 20 or 22 pupa (for the evening emergence) or a dry spent pattern (for the ovipositing female) is required to mimic these small caddis. Again, however, the importance of close observation cannot be overstated when dealing with the myriad small caddis, *Helicopsyche* among them, since several may be active during any given rise (which does not always mean that trout will be keying on just one type: Sometimes they seem to key on size instead of any other factor, making any small imitation adequate).

Antron Caddis Emerger: No. 20-22; amber or tan body; dark grey head

Delta-wing or Quad-wing Caddis: No. 20-22, amber or tan body, gray-brown wings

Half-hatch Caddis: No. 20-22, tan body

CDC Caddis Adult: No. 20-22, tannish body, gray wing

Quill-wing Caddis: No. 20-22, tan or gold body, watery dun hackle (2 turns, clipped below)

Micro-Caddis (Family: *Hydroptilidae*; Genera: *Agraylea* and *Hydroptila*)

Micro-caddis are well-named: Their imitations must be tied on hooks ranging from No. 20-24. Hafele and Hughes tell us that at least 17 species of micro-caddis inhabit Western waters. Representatives of these tiny insects are abundant in most spring creeks.

Micro-caddis hatch during the summer months and at times the trout will feed heavily on them. *Agraylea* and *Hydroptila* range from tan to gray-brown to olive-gray in color with wings that lay rather flat over the back. Heavy emergences, which can occur during morning or evening, can trigger selective feeding. Pupae patterns, fished in the film, generally outperform adult imitations.

Gary Lafontaine (*Caddisflies*) explains that one common spring-creek micro-caddis (*Agraylea multipunctata*) is readily available during the early morning hours. Lafontaine writes, "...the crippled adults and pupae from the nighttime activity, plus a few fresh stragglers, are nearly always on the water at dawn during June and July. The trout lay at the edges of the weeds and sip these caddisflies steadily and quite selectively for the first hour of daylight."

Since few mayflies hatch at dawn, anglers should be on the lookout for micro-caddis activity during the early morning. In fact, during most of the season, spring-creek trout rising at dawn frequently signal caddis activity.

Micro-caddis that hatch during mid or late morning, or in the evening, despite their abundance in spring creeks, are frequently overshadowed by more significant hatches of mayflies or other caddisflies. However, often enough these caddis are present in adequate proportions relative to other insects to cause trout to ignore larger, more obvious bugs and concentrate on the tiny micro-caddis. At such times, anglers who pay close attention and sample the drift with a seine are likely to figure out why the trout are ignoring the larger insects.

Lafontaine Sparkle Pupa: No. 20-24

Delta-wing or Quad-wing Caddis: No. 20-22

Antron Caddis Pupa: No. 20-24

Half-hatch Caddis: No. 20-24, gray body

CDC Adult Caddis: No. 20-24, gray body, gray wing (omit legs)

Chimarra ("little black sedge," "little black caddis")

The little *Chimarra* caddis emerges on many spring creeks during evening or on overcast mornings or afternoons. As suggested by their common names, the "little black sedge" features a black body and deep gray or black wings.

A No. 18 or 20 fly mimics the pupa, on which the trout generally feed. As with many other caddis, the newly emerged adults escape their shucks and take flight all in virtually the same instant. Thus the adult caddis don't ride the surface for any distance and are largely unavailable to the trout.

Antron Caddis Pupa: No. 18-20, black body, starling hackle for legs

Half-hatch Caddis: No. 18-20, black body

Lafontaine Sparkle Pupa: dark grey, No. 18-20

Mystacides ("little black caddis," "black caddis")

On many spring creeks, this small, dark caddis (usually imitated with a No. 16 or 18 hook) hatches during the morning between mid July and early September. *Mystacides* caddis, unlike *Chimarra* caddis, typically ride the water for a considerable distance upon emergence, so trout have ample opportunity to eat adults along with pupae.

Mystacides feature extra-long antennae, blackish wings, and a dark gray-black body. A No 16 or 18 hackleless elkhair or quill-wing caddis will fool trout that are taking adults, but the pupae imitations, fished in the surface film, often prove more reliable.

Antron Caddis Pupa: No. 16-18, black body

Lafontaine Sparkle Pupa: No. 16-18, dark gray

Quad-wing or Delta-wing Caddis: No. 16-18, black body, dark dun wings

X-Caddis: No. 16-18, dark gray body

Hemmingway Caddis or Quill-wing Caddis: No. 16-18, dark gray body, dark wings

CDC Caddis Adult: No. 16-18, gray body, gray wing

Slow-water Caddis: No. 16-18, gray body, dark gray wings

Quill-Wing Caddis: No. 18, dark gray or black body, dark wings, black hackle

October Caddis ("Fall Caddis") (*Dicosmoecus*)

The September and October hatches of these huge caddis traditionally draw anglers to California's Hat Creek and Fall River. The pupae become active during the late afternoon, with the bulk of the emergence occuring around dusk and after dark. The adults are unmistakeable: They

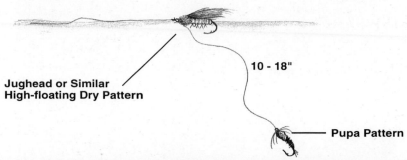

TWO-FLY SET-UP FOR OCTOBER CADDIS

10 - 18"

**Jughead or Similar
High-floating Dry Pattern**

Pupa Pattern

1. Use a jughead or similar high-floating dry pattern for a dropper. The jughead, tied to imitate the giant October caddis adult, features a spun deer-hair head that is bouyant enough to keep the fly from being pulled under by the lead fly. 2. 10 to 20 inches below the dropper, attach a pupa pattern, dressed to penetrate the surface quickly. As the flies drift downstream, impart short twitches with the rod tip or by tugging lightly on the line.

are an inch or more in length and feature a rusty-orange to pale tan-orange body of considerable bulk. The wings are a medium gray-brown and rather heavily veined.

Pupae of the Fall Caddis emerge by swimming to the surface in slow water, or by crawling or swimming to the shallows and then emerging. When available, the pupae are heavily preyed upon by Trout, often making wet flies very effective during the Fall Caddis hatch. These pupae patterns can be fished dead drift or with a lift technique—either method works. Also, since the females oviposit at dusk and after dark, a high-floating dry pattern, fished with slight twitches and skating movements, can draw explosive rises, even though you may not be able to see the fly by that time of night.

Incidentally, I have done well at times fishing a fall caddis pupa below a jughead or bucktail caddis on the same leader. If you employ this method, grease the dry and the leader above and attach a pupa pattern (designed to sink a few inches below the film) some 18 inches below. Then twitch the dry fly continuosly during the drift, an action that will also enliven the pupa hanging below. During a heavy fall caddis hatch, this two-fly assault usually proves deadly when presented down and across to trout. (See diagram above).

Fall Caddis Antron Pupa: No. 6 wet fly hook, orange body (optional: 3-5 turns of #.010 or .015 lead wire at rear of shank)

Shewey Fall Caddis Pupa
hook: wet fly, No. 6, slightly weighted
thread: black 8/0
body: pale tan-orange antron or seal dubbing, loop dubbed with Krystal Flash to form segmented look
wings: brown partridge hackle tips
collar: brown partridge over a few strands of orange antron sparkle yarn
head: gray or black ostrich herl

Jughead Caddis
hook: dry fly, 2XL, No. 6
tail: stacked deer hair or elk hair tips
body: orange yarn
rib: clipped brown saddle hackle
wing: deer hair
head: clipped deer hair

McNeese Orange Caddis Pupa *(Dave McNeese)*
hook: wet fly, No. 6-8
body: orange/light brown dubbing mixed
thorax: dark brown fur
wing case: dark gray duck quill segments
legs: brown partridge

Drowned October Caddis *(Shewey)*
hook: dry fly, No. 6-8
body: orange seal or imitation seal, loop dubbed to form segmented body
wings: tan Z-lon, antron yarn, or similar, tied spent and fanned
hackle: watery dun or medium brown, 2-3 turns behind wings, 2-3 turns in front of wings, clipped below

Orange Dry Muddler
hook: No. 8, 2XL dry fly
body: burnt orange
wing: dark deer hair
collar: dark deer hair
head: spun deer hair to form muddler-style head (*not pictured*)

Bear in mind that the above is a listing of most of the significant caddis flies found on our spring creeks, but does not attempt to cover every caddis you might encounter. Certain other caddis can be nothing short of abundant on certain water types, most notably in the riffle sections of some of our spring creeks. *Rhyacophila*, for example, is one of the more dominant members of some freestone environments and patterns to imitate their free-living larvae can make exceptional searching patterns on freestone waters.

At the risk of being redundant, I will again point out that the most important aspect in fishing over caddis activity is to first recognize whether emerging insects or ovipositing insects are responsible for the rise. Actual identification of the respective caddis genera and species is unnecessary if you have determined on which stage the fish are feeding and can then choose an appropriate pattern. And, assuming you are carrying a box of pupae and spent adults to mimic any color and size of caddis you are likely to encounter, fly choice will prove a simple task.

OCTOBER CADDIS PATTERNS

SHEWEY'S FALL CADDIS PUPA
McNEESE ORANGE CADDIS PUPA
SPENT OCTOBER CADDIS
JUGHEAD CADDIS

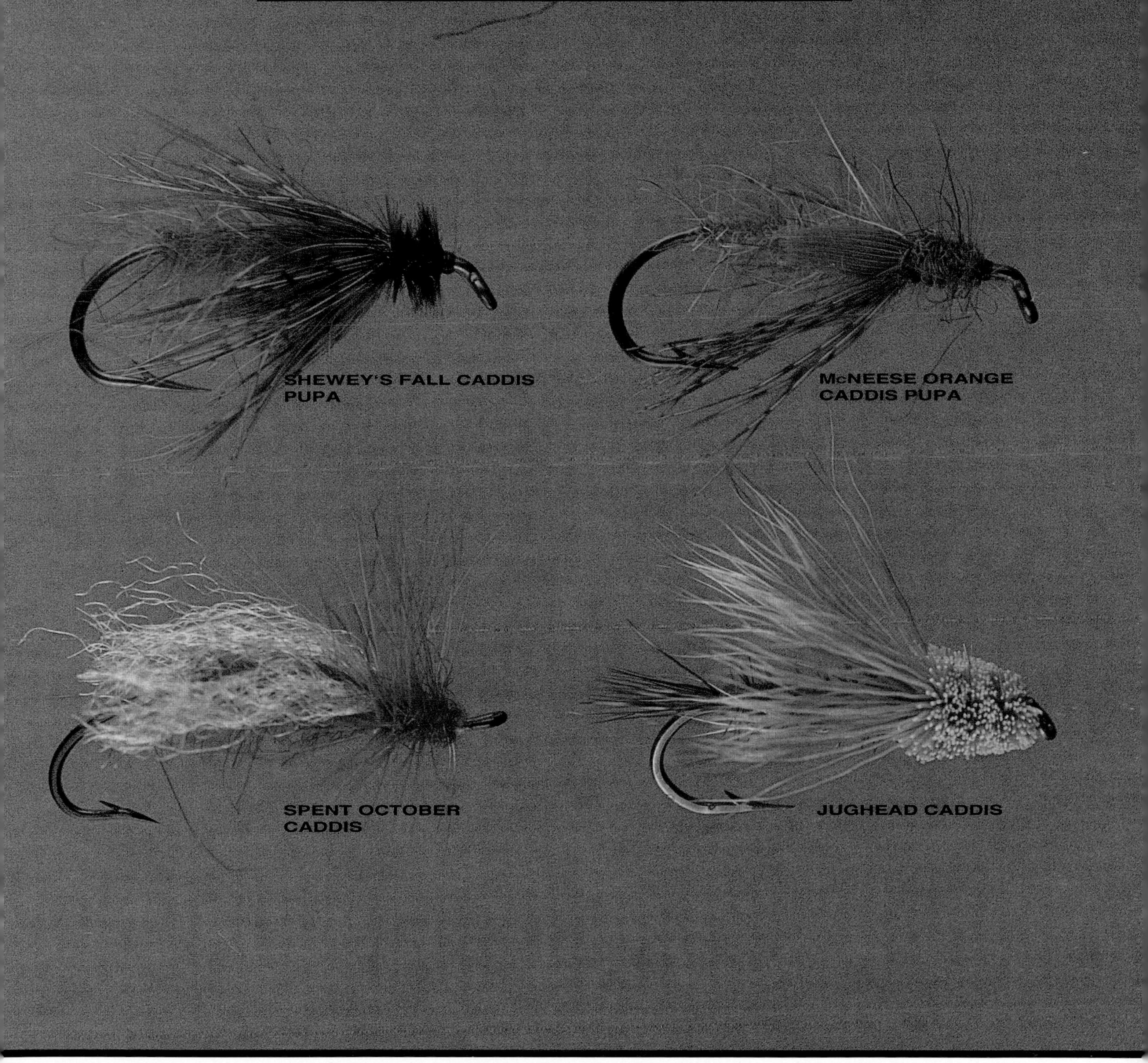

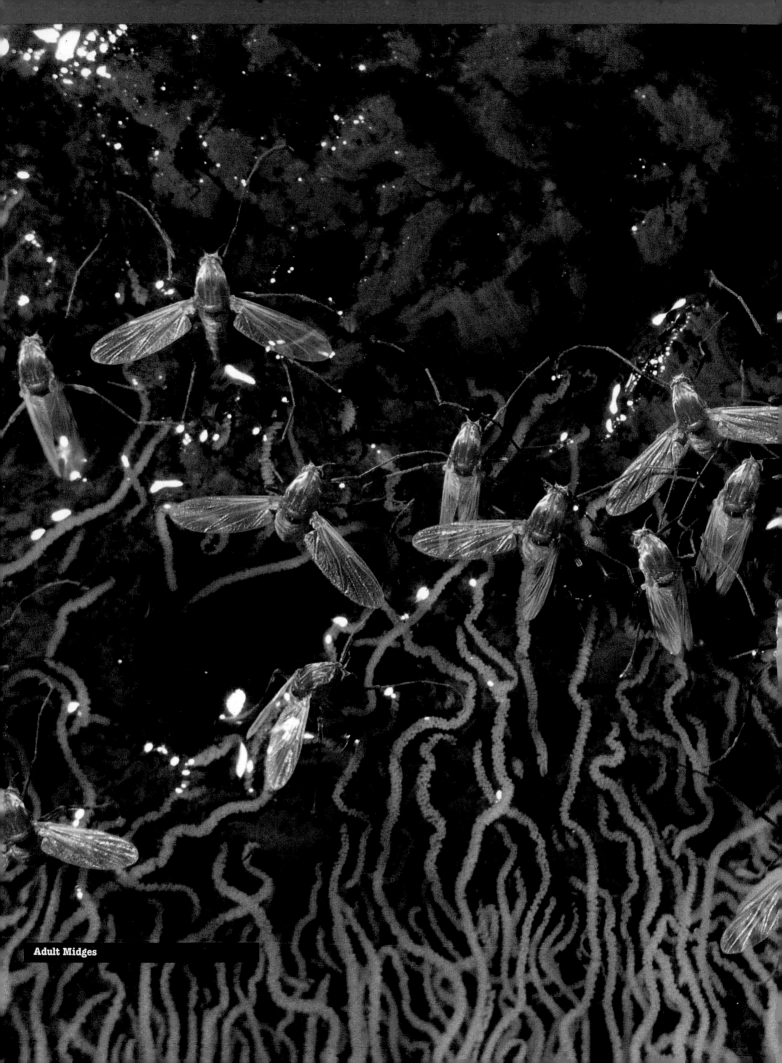

Adult Midges

SPRING CREEK DIARY

June, 1986; Take-it-Easy Ranch, Oregon

Okay, I'll be the first to admit that the pond-raised trout dumped into the spring creek on Take-it-Easy Ranch were not exactly brain surgeons. But I wasn't the one paying to fish for them. In fact, I was being paid to show other people how to fish for them.

One night during a tying demo, I tied up an adult damsel imitation and a three-inch long monstrosity that mimicked quite well the big green, blue and black dragonflies that were constantly hovering over the stream. The next afternoon I demonstrated the effectiveness of the damsel patterns, the lesson for the day being, "always be prepared for the unusual."

Although I hadn't really intended on fishing the adult dragonfly pattern, several of the students insisted that I terminate the lesson with a demonstration of that hulking monstrosity I had tied the previous evening. We picked out a big rainbow holding in about 16 inches of water. Laboriously, I cast the fly well ahead of the trout. It landed with a plop reminiscent of a big bass popper.

The trout didn't take the fly, but what really turned on the students was watching that rainbow back downstream with its nose just inches away from the fake dragonfly floating above. I paid out some line to extend the drift and the trout paced the fly, backing downstream some 12 feet before the fly started to drag. We got a bonus lesson about spring creek trout: they have every opportunity to inspect a fly and will at times go to great lengths to do so.

Chapter 7

Spring Creek Chironomids

They are so tiny and unobtrusive that they escape the angler's notice while he grows increasingly frustrated with the failure of each fly pattern that moves not a single trout amongst the multitudes that are quietly dimpling the surface. These are the midges; more precisely, the chironomids.

Chironomids are insects of the order *Diptera*, the true flies. They experience a complete life cycle, going from egg to larvae to pupa to adult. Further taxonomy on the chironomids is unnecessary from an angler's perspective. Art Lee once wrote in Fly Fisherman Magazine that the entomology of *Diptera* "is so complex that I gave up trying to fathom it long ago, at the loss of not a single fish."

Understanding how and when midges are available to spring-creek trout is far more important than memorizing the inconsequential differences between genera of chironomids. And combining this knowledge with the skills required to effectively fish a midge emergence will allow you the opportunity to take fish under the most rewarding of circumstances: Other anglers have departed in frustration, eager to seek easier hatches on easier water; you have the trout to yourself, along with the opportunity to rise them to the tiniest of flies. This is fly angling at its aesthetic best.

Moreover, chironomids emerge throughout the year on most streams, sometimes even on cold winter days. During the warmer months, chironomids are nothing short of abundant and trout, even large ones, will occasionally feed selectively on midges during hatches of much larger mayflies.

Yet despite their significance to spring-creek trout, chironomid emergences can indeed prove difficult to master. In fact I wonder if anyone has or ever really will master the midges. Part of the difficulty certainly lies in the average size of spring-creek midges. They are tiny, usually requiring an imitation tied on No. 20 through 28 hooks. No. 22's and 24's are common, although sometimes big chironomids, mimicked by No. 14 and 16 hooks, make an appearance.

Just seeing the tiny imitations on the water poses a major problem and one that is bolstered by the fact that you will generally be fishing surface-film emerger patterns. With practice (in fact, just by fishing streams on a frequent basis) you can learn to follow the drift without actually seeing the fly. This skill is derived from an ability to relate current speed and direction to the position and orientation of the fly during and after the cast and mends.

Midge fishing is synonymous with not seeing your fly, primarily because the pupae are by far the most significant chironomid stage to the trout. Bouyed by trapped gases, midge pupae ascend from the bottom somewhat leisurely. At the surface, the pupa hangs vertically in the film and the adult emerges, flying away instantly.

Because the adult midges escape so quickly, they are rarely of any consequence to the trout, the exception being on cold, blustery winter days when balls of adult midges, all clustered together, may ride the surface for a considerable distance. In any case, the pupae are greedily devoured by trout during a heavy emergence or, at times, even during a sparse hatch. As with any emergence, many individual chironomids will fail to escape their pupal shucks and will thus become what we call stillborns—always an easy meal for the fish.

Midging trout will generally patrol very narrow feeding lanes, so precise fly placement is critical. Also, as with dense emergences of other insects, trout will frequently settle into a feeding rhythm where they rise at regular, predictable intervals. You must time your cast so that the fly arrives at the trout's position just as she is ready to rise again.

During the early 1980's, I began fishing two or three flies at a time in many situations. Chironomid emergences are perfectly suited to this tactic. Frequently I will opt for one or two pupa imitations accompanied by a Griffith's Gnat, the latter mimicking a cluster of adult midges, but serving the more important function of helping me to track the drift of my flies.

Attach the droppers by adding eight- to 12-inch pieces of 6X or 7X monofilament to your tippet, joining them with blood knots and leaving a tag end (on each knot) on which you will attach a dropper fly. I prefer the blood knot for droppers because, unlike the increasingly popular surgeon's knot, the tag ends extend at right angles from the knot. This arrangement aids in preventing the droppers from wrapping around the main leader.

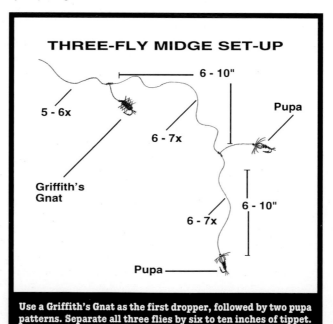

THREE-FLY MIDGE SET-UP

5 - 6x

6 - 10"

Pupa

Griffith's Gnat

6 - 7x

6 - 10"

6 - 7x

Pupa

Use a Griffith's Gnat as the first dropper, followed by two pupa patterns. Separate all three flies by six to ten inches of tippet.

Whenever possible, try to position yourself for a downstream presentation. Then drop the lead fly within two feet of a steadily feeding trout. With midges, you can often place the fly a foot in front of the trout without spooking him. You may have to offer numerous drifts before getting the fly in precisely the right place at exactly the right time.

Sometimes trout take chironomid pupae just below the surface, often leaving a telltale "bulge" on the water or sometimes breaking the water with their dorsal fin or tail. These trout often fall for an imitation fished just a few inches below the surface. Dead-drift will usually suffice for wet pupa patterns, but at times a slight lifting motion, imparted on the fly with the rod tip, can prove more effective on finicky trout.

For this latter technique, use a pattern that is either weighted slightly or is dressed on heavy-wire wet fly hook. Sink the fly on a dead-drift presentation and then lift the fly slowly through the upper foot or so of the water column, mimicking the natural's ascent from the bottom. From an upstream position, you can accomplish this lift by gently raising the rod tip while simultaneously extending your casting arm toward the target. If the first presentation fails, slide the leader to the side, pick up and try again.

Although midges come in many

Chironomids emerge throughout the year, even during the middle of winter, giving spring-creek anglers an opportunity to fish dry flies on those streams open year-around.

watch the trout. The inside of its mouth, gleaming white, will flash as the fish takes the fly or a natural. You won't be able to see your tiny flies, but if the trout opens its mouth to feed and you know your flies are in the vicinity, raise the rod tip very smoothly, only enough to detect any resistance. If in fact the trout took a natural, lower the rod tip and continue the drift, as you don't want to begin another cast until the flies have passed beyond the fish.

This fishing is probably more difficult than fishing midge pupae. But to actually watch a trout open its mouth to feed on unseen mor-

colors, precise shade is far less important in an imitation than is size. If possible, capture a few specimens to determine the right size fly to use. Trout sometimes see a lot of difference between a No. 22 and a No. 24. Incidentally, I always carry a few No. 14, 16 and 18 pupa patterns to match the occasional hatch of large chironomids.

Despite being secondary in importance, the color of the artificial should match that of the natural as closely as possible. Midges occur in virtually every color, but common shades include olives, browns, gray, tans, and black.

Midge larvae are of some importance to spring-creek trout, but larvae patterns are not nearly so useful to anglers as are the pupa imitations. At times trout feed heavily on midge larvae, but such fish seem uninclined to move very far to take such a tiny morsel drifting along the bottom. So unless you can actually watch a trout that is feeding near the bottom, midge larvae patterns won't prove particularly useful.

At times on our spring creeks, you do have the chance to sight fish to a nymphing trout. In these situations, a midge larvae pattern might be the ticket. I must admit, however, that I'll usually try a tiny pheasant tail nymph or scud in such situations. If these patterns fail to move a visibly nymphing trout, I might switch to a simple dubbed-fur larvae imitation, although I'll admit not an ounce of confidence in being certain that the fish see such flies specifically as midge larvae.

A long, light tippet is required to enable the tiny nymphs (No. 18-22 usually) to penetrate the surface film and descend to the trout's level. Much like they do when feeding at the surface, these deep-holding trout, in the presence of dense insect drifts, will patrol narrow feeding lanes. So you must get the fly close to the fish.

Cast well ahead of the trout and allow the flies to sink. Meanwhile, watch your slack leader to track their drift. Now

sels, knowing your fly could be the one, lends this tactic a certain exhilaration.

I often employ a small Griffith's Gnat (No. 18 or 20) as a strike indicator when fishing midge larvae or any other tiny nymphs. Attach this indicator fly as a dropper. If my target trout is holding under three feet of slow-moving water, I will attach the Griffith's Gnat some four feet above the nymphs. Also, when I fish two nymphs or larvae patterns simultaneously, I attach the dropper only six to ten inches above the lead fly. This assures that both will get down to the trout's level. I've often fished three tiny nymphs at once, all spaced by only a few inches.

A single fly, however, is a wise choice when fishing over the weedbeds because multiple-fly setups are that many times more likely to hang up. In sparsely vegetated stretches, however, two or three flies can double or triple your chances at drawing a trout's attention.

As a general statement, I think that midge larvae imitations are ineffective as searching patterns in comparison with small pheasant tails or imitations of the predominant mayfly nymphs. And when these midge flies do take trout, you can never be sure that the fish identified the pattern as such.

Patterns to match midge adults are somewhat more useful than larvae patterns, but even they pale in importance when compared to the pupal imitations. Still, once in a while trout will eat adult midges, assuming that the tiny insects remain on the water for any length of time. The best opportunity for adult midge fishing occurs on cold days between late fall and early spring when the chilled air prevents the bugs from taking flight immediately. Under these conditions, adult chironomids will sometimes cling together as they float downriver. Thus, you can use a rather large fly to mimic these clusters, despite the tiny size of the individual midges. The Griffith's Gnat is especially well suited to this task and a No. 16 or 18 pattern may well suffice when adults in the No. 28 range are clinging together to form little balls and flotillas.

Regardless of what chironomid stage you are imitating, long, light tippets are crucial. Instead of the usual three- to six-foot tippet, try an eight-foot tippet of soft 6X or 7X material. You may not land many big trout on 7X, but a No. 26 or 28 fly just doesn't seem to drift correctly with larger tippet

Designing The Midge Pupa

When chironomid pupae reach the surface of the stream during the emergence, they hang vertically with their fore-end penetrating the surface film. The remainder (and the majority) of their bodies remain vertically or angularly suspended below the surface. At times, spring-creek trout will key into this characteristic hanging position and steadfastly refuse any fly—real or imitation—that is not drifting in such a manner. During a heavy midge emergence, this moment of hesitation when the pupa reaches the surface offers trout their most energy-efficient opportunity to eat the tiny insects.

On a few occasions I've drifted pupa patterns over midge-feeding trout only to discover that the total failure of the fly was attributable to its failure to hang vertically in the surface film or to at least penetrate the film to some extent. Thus, on some occasions at least, an accurate imitation of the pupa's body position in the surface will spell the difference between hooking trout and spending the duration of the hatch scratching your head.

Suspending patterns, however, offer one serious drawback: The smaller the hook, the more difficult it is to make the fly drift the right way. A No. 18 or 20 suspending midge pupa can be tied to perform flawlessly; the same pattern dressed on a No. 24 simply floats like a cork regardless of design and if not, it generally sinks entirely. You can counteract this problem with tiny hooks simply by tying the pupa imitation very sparse. One such pattern that I am relying on more and more for tangling with ultra-puny-sized midges is a fly called Kimball's Diptera Emerger. A lightly dressed pattern, this fly allows for the hook alone to penetrate the surface film. I think the tiny hook bend, drifting below the surface, is probably taken by selective trout to be the tiny body of a miniature chironomid

Any number of effective patterns exist for mimicking the suspended midge pupa and that which you choose to fish is not so important, really, as testing the fly in the sink or bathtub to ensure that it performs properly. I've had especially good results with these flies when trying to match the larger (No. 16-18-20) chironomids. Much smaller than that and I fall back on the Kimball emerger

I might add that chironomid emergences that occur during the summer and early fall, bringing big trout to the surface, do not necessarily need to be fished with midge patterns. Sometimes these hatches seem to get big trout looking upward just enough that they will happily devour a well-placed ant or beetle, often with more sincerity than they seem to be showing toward the natural chironomids.

Midge Patterns

*Kimball's Diptera Emerger (Mike Kimball)
hook: fine wire dry fly, No. 18-28
tail: teal flank, tied long and splayed to represent pupa's trailing body shuck
thorax: dubbed fur or poly, color to match natural
abdomen: none

wingcase: small strand of white or light gray poly yarn, tied in to form exaggerated hump at the rear of the case and a gradual slope toward the eye of the hook.

*Suspender Midge Pupa
hook: fine wire dry fly, No.16-24
body: stripped herl
thorax: fine peacock herl or fine dubbing to match natural
head tuft: white foam or CDC feather

*CDC Transitional Midge
(Rene Harrop/tied by McKenzie Flies)
hook: dry fly, No. 16-22
tail: grizzly hackle tip or fibers
wingcase: dun CDC feather
body: fine dubbing to match natural
legs: fine dun CDC feathers

CDC Emerging Midge (Rene Harrop)
hook: dry fly, No. 16-24
tail: teal flank or grizzly hackle fibers
shellback: gray Evazote foam or similar
body: poly dubbing to match natural
legs: CDC fibers, gray-dun
head: extension of shellback

*Re-Vertical Midge Emerger (Shewey)
hook: dry fly, No. 16-24, upeye
tail: minute puff of white feather fluff (omit on smallest sizes)
body: fine peacock herl, stripped until final two turns
rib: fine gold wire (omit on tiniest sizes)
hackle: highest quality (very stiff) dry fly hackle to match hook size, 2-4 turns tied tight against the eye of the hook

Midge Larvae (Dave Whitlock)
thread: to match body color
rib: fine gold wire or thread
body: 50/50 blend of beaver belly and fine synthetic dubbing, color to match natural

*Stillborn Midge (Dave Whitlock)
hook: fine-wire dry fly, No. 18-28
pupal shuck: ostrich herl, length of hook
body: fine dubbing
wings: two dun or white hackle tips; CDC; or a few poly yarn strands
hackle: one or two turns of hackle, trimmed top and bottom

*Griffith's Gnat (George Griffith)
hook: dry fly, No. 14-22
body: peacock herl
rib: fine wire or tying thread
hackle: grizzly, reverse palmered

Adult Midge
hook: dry fly
body: fine dubbing
wings: grizzly or dun hackle tips, tied delta style
hackle: two turns dun or grizzly, clipped below

GRIFFITH'S GNAT

STILLBORN MIDGE

ADULT MIDGE

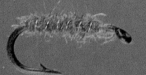

MIDGE LARVAE

RE-VERTICAL MIDGE EMERGER

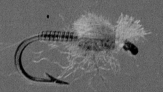

CDC SUSPENDER MIDGE PUPA

FOAM SUSPENDER MIDGE PUPA

KIMBALL'S DIPTERA EMERGER

CDC EMERGING MIDGE

CDC TRANSITIONAL MIDGE

The "salmon fly" or "giant stonefly" occurs on the riffle sections of some of our spring creeks, where the adults and nymphs alike can produce excellent fishing.

A golden stonefly clinging to an alder branch already occupied by a salmon fly.

SPRING CREEK DIARY

July, 1983; Silver Creek, Idaho

Late July is generally a comparatively quiet time on the Henry's Fork, so I was headed in that direction. I never got there, however, as Silver Creek got in the way.

Any fly fisher who could witness waves and waves of Trico's near the highway bridge on Silver Creek and then continue on without stopping would certainly have some explaining to do to the angling gods. That wasn't a problem with me. Within minutes I was parked at the conservancy water and stringing a rod.

Towards the lower end of the preserve, tight against the cattails, a trout rose rather inauspiciously. That *one* fish would occupy my entire stay at Silver Creek.

Throughout the Trico spinner fall this rainbow would gulp quietly, all alone, away from the hustle and bustle of the schooling trout nearby. He fed on the tiny spinners until the bitter end and then simply disappeared. Each day, after the trico's finished their waltz, I disappeared too, spending the afternoons up on the Big Wood River.

That same drill lasted four days, each morning finding me trying new approaches on that one big trout. I never hooked him. Rose him the second morning to an ant during the tail end of the spinner fall, but failed to hook up—either plain bad luck or he had realized and corrected his imminent mistake at the last possible moment and avoided the hook point.

It was a curious experience, fishing for that one trout for four days. Frustration was certainly part of it, but fascination, really, overwhelmed my frustration. I'm still not sure why I didn't pack my bags, tuck my tail, and whimper off to the Henry's Fork after a couple days trying for that fish.

I replay those four mornings on occasion, trying to figure out what else I might have tried. Perhaps I'm better off never figuring it out, as that trout makes a fine adversary from time to time, when I'm not actually fishing. We need a few trout like that; tough customers capable of occupying our imagination long after the actual encounter. They keep us coming back.

Chapter 8

Spring Creek Stoneflies

Stoneflies generally rank low in significance to anglers who fish the classic flat-water sections of the Western spring creeks: The stonefly hatches that do occur on these waters generally take place on the riffle sections, which resemble typical Western freestone streams both in character and in the techniques used to bring trout to the fly. Those that do hatch in and near the flat water are virtually always overshadowed by more abundant mayflies, terrestrials and caddis.

But where gravel- or stone-bottom riffle sections interrupt the smooth glassy waters owned by the mayflies, anglers can enjoy a temporary respite from those tough days when the flat water proves utterly frustrating. The stoneflies are common in these places and, in both their nymph and adult forms, these insects often prove irresistible to trout.

Some of these fast-water sections offer hatches of the famed Pteronarcys stonefly, commonly called "salmon fly" or "giant stone." These giant stones (usually an inch and a half or more in length) hatch between late May and early July (depending on specific location). As with other stoneflies, the nymphs migrate shoreward in search of rocks, limbs, logs, grass, reeds, bridge abutments or other structures on which the can crawl from the water. During the hatch period, when the nymphs are on the move, trout will move to areas where they can intercept those that tumble in the drift.

More common are hatches of the large golden stoneflies belonging to the genus *Acroneuria.* The *Acroneuria* stoneflies emerge from May through September, the precise timing depending again upon specific waters and locations. On some streams, *Acroneuria californica,* the inch-long, bright yellowish-orange stonefly, emerges in large numbers each day for one to three weeks and sporadically prior to and after this peak period.

In the Rockies and at high elevations elsewhere, *A. californica* emerges between mid June and mid July. At lower elevations, the hatch begins as early as the first or second week of May.

The other common golden stone *(A. pacifica),* also known as the "brown stone," "trout fly," "willow fly," or "brown willow fly," hatches over a longer period, beginning in May or June and lasting until August or September. Emergence is generally less concentrated and more sporadic than hatches of *A. californica.*

As with the salmon flies, golden stonefly nymphs are available to trout throughout the season and especially during the nymphal migrations. Between early and mid-morning look for newly emerged stoneflies on shoreline vegetation, rocks, bridge structures or other such places.

In fact, I make a regular habit of giving a good shake to a few streamside willows anytime I want to check for the presence of stoneflies: Grab a thick lower limb, shake hard, stand back and see what falls out. This trick works for any stoneflies (not just the aforementioned large species) because all will take shelter in the foliage of shoreline shrubbery. (Incidentally, by standing under the trees and shaking the branches, I've also managed to send an endless variety of spiders down my shirt, not to mention dislodging one green tree snake and a hornet nest, the occupants of which proved absolutely devoid of any sense of humor.)

Many stoneflies will return to the river in fairly dense numbers to deposit their eggs, such activity usually taking place between mid day and evening. On Oregon's Metolius River I've seen golden stoneflies engaged in ovipositing flights in such numbers that many of them mistook the road for the nearby river and tried to lay eggs on the pavement.

In addition to the large stoneflies, myriad smaller varieties live amongst the gravel and rocks of the riffle water. Among these are the little yellow stoneflies of the *Isoperla* and *Isogenus* genera, which thrive in cold, swift Western streams. Parts of spring creeks that fit that latter description often produce good hatches of these small (half to three quarters of an inch) bright yellow stoneflies. They frequently appear over the stream between early afternoon and mid evening when the females deposit their eggs in the water.

Typically these ovipositing flights of little yellow stones are rather sparse and are usually overshadowed by evening caddis or mayfly activity. Still, large concentrations do occur sometimes, rendering yellow stonefly patterns highly effective. Between May and August, in fact, imitations for these small stoneflies serve well as searching patterns for the riffle water of small spring creeks.

A few spring creeks, including Oregon's Metolius River and California's Hat Creek, host impressive populations of the little yellow stoneflies. They emerge late spring through mid-summer and can stimulate some good rises, with the best activity usually concentrated in and near the gentle riffles.

On several Western spring creeks I have encountered good numbers of other small stoneflies, primarily little green stones of the genus *Alloperla* and little brown stones (representing several genera). I have yet to see these small stoneflies cause selective feeding on the riffle sections of any spring creeks, but their imitations make excellent searching patterns and their presence in the riffles, along with other stoneflies, frequently inclines me to try flies that mimic stonefly nymphs.

One other small stonefly, the *Capnia* or winter stonefly, is definitely capable of causing selective surface feeding during its winter emergence. Where they occur, the *Capnia* stoneflies emerge from January to March (as well as November and December in a few places).

Black with brownish-colored wings, the winter stoneflies emerge around the warmest part of the day in the slower margins bordering riffle water. Look for them crawling on reeds, rocks and brush near back eddies, runs and gentle riffles. No. 14 and 16 patterns imitate these small insects.

Not all streams host sizeable hatches of the winter stonefly and many that do are not open to winter fishing. Still, when fishing a spring creek during the off-season, keep an eye peeled for the *Capnia* stoneflies. They provide one of the few opportunities in the West to fish dry flies during the dead of winter.

Imitations of winter stonefly nymphs generally prove marginally effective as the trout appear to feed actively only

An afternoon flight of little yellow stoneflies triggered a good rise on one stretch of this small, Rocky Mountain spring creek.

SMALL STONEFLY PATTERNS

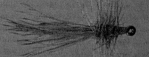

FLOATIN' FOOL

LITTLE YELLOW STONE

SPENT FLAT-WATER STONE

LAWSON'S YELLOW SALLY

LARGE STONEFLY PATTERNS

HENRY'S FORK GOLDEN STONE

HENRY'S FORK SALMONFLY

CLARK'S STONE

STIMULATOR

when fairly large numbers of the adults have emerged. Imitations for other stonefly nymphs, however, fish well on the fast-water sections of Western spring creeks even before and after the peak hatch period. A staple in my nymph arsenal, large hare's ear nymphs (No. 6-8) effectively mimic the common golden stonefly and are especially productive fished two at a time or in combination with one or two smaller nymphs.

Adult stoneflies, similarly, make effective searching patterns on the fast-water sections of the spring creeks, especially when the flies are cast under overhanging trees and shrubs. Sometimes a few slight twitches, imparted with the rod tip or by stripping line, will solicit smashing rises, even at mid-river. My favorite adult stonefly pattern, the jughead, floats exceptionally well and skates easily when dressed with floatant.

Small jugheads have proven so valuable on the riffle sections of several Western spring creeks that I would never venture astream without a few of these flies. In fact, spring creek anglers should always carry a few stonefly imitations for those times when the riffles look inviting (which is commonly the case after a day of frustration on the flat water.) The stoneflies may not hold a great deal of significance on the classically smooth waters characteristic of the spring creeks, but above or below these places, where boulder-strewn runs are broken by white water, the stoneflies comprise an important part of the trout's diet.

Stonefly Patterns

*Jughead
hook: 2XL or 3XL dry fly, No. 4-12
tail: deer or elk hair
body: wool to match color of natural (yellow, orange, olive, etc.)
hackle: brown, clipped short, then palmered through body
wing: deer hair
head: deer hair, clipped

*Henry's Fork Golden Stone
(Mike Lawson/tied by Umpqua F.M.)
hook: 3XL dry fly, No. 6-10
thread: yellow
tail: dyed yellow elk
body: yellow poly yarn, foam or dyed yellow elk
rib: trimmed brown hackle
wing: natural elk
head/collar: dyed yellow elk, tied bullet style and clipped below

Henry's Fork Salmon Fly
(Mike Lawson/tied by Umpqua F.M.)
hook: 3XL dry fly, No. 4-6
thread: orange
tail: black elk or moose
body: orange poly yarn
rib: clipped brown hackle
wing: natural elk or deer
head/collar: dark brown elk, tied bullet style and clipped below

Stimulator, yellow (Randall Kaufmann)
hook: 3XL dry fly, No. 6-12
tail: natural deer or elk
body: bright yellow dubbing
body hackle: grizzly
rib: fine gold wire
thorax: orange dubbing
front hackle: grizzly, wrapped through thorax

*Lawson's Yellow Sally (Mike Lawson)
hook: dry fly, No. 12-16
thread: yellow
abdomen: sulphur-colored dubbing
wing: fine, light deer body hair
thorax: sulphur-colored dubbing
hackle: 3 or 4 turns of light dun, trimmed top and bottom

Floatin' Fool
hook: dry fly, No. 12-18
tail: white poly yarn or calftail, clipped short
post: same as tail
body: fine peacock herl
hackle: black, tied parachute

*Little Yellow Stone
(Bob Quigley/ tied by Umpqua F.M.)
hook: 3XL dry fly, No. 4-10
thread: yellow
tail: dyed yellow deer hair
butt: fine red wool
rib: cream hackle, palmered
body: yellow dubbing
wing: yellow deer hair, butt ends extending beyond tie-down point to form head
collar: cream hackle
Note: substitute black or pale green body, deer hair and hackle for little black and little green stoneflies

Clark's Stone (Lee Clark)
hook: 2- or 3XL, No. 10-14
thread: to match underwing
body: gold flat tinsel covering hook shank
underwing: combed and stretched macreme' yarn, sparse, tied slightly past hook bend
wing: fine deer hair, sparse, unstacked
collar: a few turns of hackle, clipped top and bottom
colors: yellow yarn and cream hackle for little yellow stone; bright green yarn and dyed green hackle for little green stone; can also be tied in large sizes and colors to match the large stoneflies

Spent Flat-water Stone (Shewey)
hook: dry fly, No. 12-18
body: bright yellow or bright green biot, wrapped on shank
wings: pale yellow or pale olive sparkle yarn, tied flush and angling back to both sides of the body (sparse)
hackle: yellow or chartreuse, undersized; 3-5 turns, clipped top and bottom
NOTE: use dark brown-gray body, smoke-colored wings and black hackle for little black and little brown stones

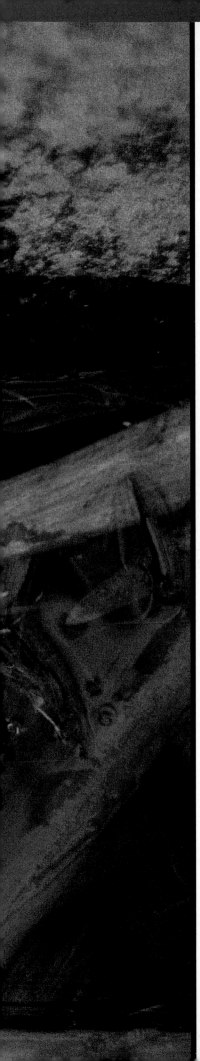

SPRING CREEK DIARY

July, 1983; Wyoming

Any little spring creek that looked like that just begged to be fished: meandering in exaggerated S-curves through a small valley and teeming with watercress, algae, moss and every other conceivable form of aquatic vegetation. A perusal of the fishing regs indicated public access.

Lot's of dimpling fish. They responded readily to a small Griffith's Gnat, but they were all mountain whitefish. I'm not knocking whitefish, but I don't hold a lot of regard for them when I'm bent on brown trout or rainbows.

I went in search of "trout-ier" water and soon found a deep channel, some five or six feet wide and surrounded by waving masses of aquatic weeds. Although whitefish continued to rise on the flats below, nothing stirred the smooth surface of this promising channel. Nonetheless I cast the Griffith's Gnat several times before convincing myself that nothing was coming to the surface.

I switched to a tandem of little pheasant tail nymphs, fished under a small indicator. Casting upstream and allowing the flies to drift through the channel from top to bottom, I soon discovered that Indeed there were brown trout in that stream. Lots of them. Little ones—eight to 12 inches—but each one as handsome a brown trout as I could hope to find anywhere. And aggressive. They couldn't resist those nymphs; I stood in one spot and caught 10 trout.

Pretty soon I got carried away catching small brown trout and whitefish. What was supposed to be an hour or two of exploration became an all-day affair. It reminded me of my childhood in eastern Idaho, fishing those little mountain streams and always wondering how a summer day, not to mention a summer, could disappear so quickly. The trout were bigger then; my world was smaller, less complicated. But for a day I was back in time, thanks to one small stream and a few small trout: If I could do for them what they, over the years, have done for me.

C h a p t e r   9

Spring Creek Nymphing

Most spring-creek anglers ply their craft on these exquisite waters for the opportunity to enjoy dry fly fishing at its finest. Indeed, the Western spring creeks deserve surface patterns, at least when the fish are rising. But what about those times when either no surface activity is forthcoming or when the surface activity that is in progress indicates that the trout are eating nymphs just below the surface? These are the times when a knowledge of nymph-fishing tactics for spring creeks will keep you in the game.

Let's tackle the latter phenomenon first: those times when trout concentrate on eating nymphs just below the surface, usually during a hatch of mayflies or caddis. During most spring-creek mayfly and caddis emergences, trout will eat nymphs greedily in the surface film and just below the film. This upper few inches of the water column provides easy pickings for trout. They need only hover just below the surface and gobble the nymphs as they concentrate at the surface.

Many times during these situations, floating nymphs, fished in the surface film, will work as well or better than patterns fished sub surface; other times, nymphs fished a few inches down will outperform those drifted on top. Recognizing when to employ either tactic is paramount to consistent success during many hatches. By watching individual trout you can usually tell where they are feeding.

A fish whose upper jaw is clearly visible during each rise is obviously feeding on insects in the film or on top. Conversely, a trout whose tail and/or back continually breaks the surface while its head remains submerged is certainly feeding on nymphs just before they reach the surface. Remember, however, that observing the feeding pattern of trout is best done one fish at a time because different trout will feed in different ways during the same hatch.

Other more subtle signs also indicate trout eating nymphs just below the surface: a slight "bulging" of the water caused by a trout working just under the surface, but not quite close enough for its fins to penetrate or nervous water caused by a pod of trout feeding in this manner; the flash of a trout's flanks as the sun glitters off his sides when he turns slightly to catch a nymph.

The tactics we employ to take nymphing trout at the surface revolve around one very simple fact: Spring creek trout, unlike trout in many free-stone, fast-water environments, can hold at the surface eating the nymphs as they arrive instead of chasing them as the ascend from the depths. Spring creek trout prefer this mode of feeding as it consumes little energy and requires less effort than chasing nymphs. Therefore, once a hatch has begun and is in full strength, virtually all large trout intent on eating the bugs in question will abandon deep lies and hold at the surface, taking their choice of nymphs, emergers, cripples and adults.

This feeding strategy employed by spring-creek trout during a decent hatch is good news for the angler as we need not worry too much about "lift" techniques designed to bring the nymph from bottom to top. Instead, if we determine that sub-surface nymphs are the key to taking a particular trout, we can simply fish a fly dead-drift and just inches below the surface or, if that fails, use a simple "mini-lift."

In reality, the mini-lift is as much a fly positioning trick as an actual attempt to imitate an ascending aquatic insect. Cast downstream and slightly across to your target trout, placing the fly about four feet upstream of the fish's position. Allow the nymph to dead-drift toward the fish, sinking along the way. About a foot short of the trout, raise the rod tip (or simply stop following the fly downstream with the rod tip) to bring the fly gently to the surface. You will see a subtle wake appear as the fly gains the surface. Immediately lower the rod tip to impart a drag-free drift. Your initial cast ideally allows the fly to pass into the trout's visual range at some depth before the fly is suddenly lifted toward the surface, where it dead drifts, mimicking the natural pause of any insect while it struggles to escape the surface tension.

DETERMINING FEEDING PATTERNS

"Bulging"—Sub-surface Feeding

Dorsal Fin, Back and/or Tail Penetrating the Surface, But Not the Head or Snout: Sub-surface Feeding

Snout Above Water— Surface Feeding

1. "Bulging" is caused by a trout feeding just below the surface; since the fish does not actually break the surface, you can safely assume that nymphs or emergers fished just under the surface will prove effective. 2. If dorsal fins, backs and/or tails penetrate the surface, but the trout's head or snout is never visible, you can again determine that the fish is eating insects just below the surface. 3. Seeing snouts above the water is a sure sign of trout feeding on insects in the film or on top.

A Henry's Fork Rainbow that took a pheasant tail nymph fished through the channel between two weedbeds.

The mini-lift is most effective during caddis emergences. Caddis tend to escape the surface tension and fly away much faster than mayflies and chironomids, allowing trout less time to capture emerging pupa just below the surface. Because of this, fish tend to feed more freely throughout the upper foot of water during a caddis hatch than during a mayfly emergence, wherein the nymphs take considerably longer to emerge into adults. During heavy mayfly hatches, trout can hold just below the surface, eating only those nymphs drifting in the upper one to three inches of the water column.

Naturally, the mini-lift is much easier to use if you can stalk to within 15-25 feet of the trout. The same is true for any kind of nymph fishing. In fact, positioning for surface-nymph tactics follows the same guidelines as for dry flies, with a down-and-across approach often proving easiest.

For most surface-zone nymphing, use a nymph dressed to sink just below the film (and, of course, one that will closely match the naturals, especially in size and form). If you do not intend to employ a mini-lift (which is rarely necessary during mayfly hatches) cast two to four feet above the trout, allowing the nymph just enough time to penetrate the surface and sink one-to four inches. A short, quick tug on the fly line after the cast has landed will help pull the fly under water.

Then watch the leader where it enters the water. If this proves difficult, use a strike indicator 12 to 36 inches above the fly. This strike indicator can take the form of a piece of yarn, a hollowed-out inch-long piece of bright fly line slid over the leader, a small cork or foam float, or a dry fly. If you see any slight hesitation or sudden movement of the indicator, gently raise the rod tip. My preference in strike indicators is a small dry fly attached as a dropper (or tied into the tippet) just a foot or so above the nymph. The only prerequisite for the dry fly is that it be buoyant enough to remain afloat rather than being pulled under by the nymph hanging below. (Incidentally, some spring-creek trout will shy away from hot orange, pink or chartruese indicators: The fish have seen too many of the bright indicators and are wise to them, so you might choose cream or white if you decide to employ yarn, corkies, or foam.)

During a heavy hatch, rules applied to dry-fly fishing also apply to fishing a nymph near the surface: Pick out one fish at a time, try to determine its feeding rhythm and time your cast accordingly, make a drag-free presentation, and slide the fly away and to the side before picking up for the next cast.

Unfortunately, timing the feeding rhythm can be more difficult with nymphing trout because some of their efforts to inhale the insects do not leave an impression on the water's surface. Some nymphing trout will hold right at the surface, with a fin or tail virtually always out of the water throughout the duration of the rise; others, however, hold a little deeper and might break the surface on every third or fourth feeding attempt. Still other trout, of course, will alternate from surface food to sub-surface food, inexplicably plucking an adult or emerger from the surface for every six or eight nymphs consumed.

In any case, timing the rise is really secondary to recognizing that a particular trout is indeed eating nymphs just below the surface. Make enough good casts and you're likely to time at least a few of them properly.

When necessary, surface-nymphing trout can be fooled by a straight upstream presentation (see chapter 2) wherein the fly and leader are cast directly over the trout's back. Remember, though, that this approach is best reserved for solitary feeders—try it on a pod of trout and you may well spook every fish.

Trout that are feeding near the bottom frequently leave themselves open to a wider array of approaches than those eating nymphs at the surface (holding below several feet of water, they cannot easily detect the presence of a leader or line drifting on top). First, however, you must identify likely holding areas where trout can feed readily on drifting insects. During those times when nothing is happening on the surface and I can't find a bank-feeder, I'll switch to a tandem of nymphs and probe the riffles, deep chutes, ledges, channels between weed columns and other likely looking places. In some places, especially on small spring creeks, trout may be visibly pursuing nymphs in shallow water.

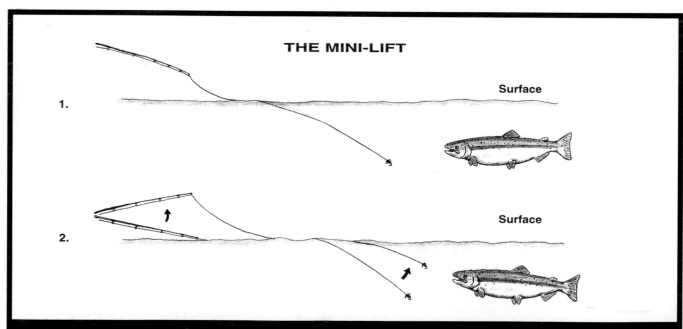

THE MINI-LIFT

1.

Surface

2.

Surface

1. Cast downstream and across, placing the fly several feet above the trout and then allow the fly to dead-drift, sinking along the way. 2. About a foot short of the trout, raise the rod tip or simply stop following the fly downstream with the rod-tip to bring the fly gently to the surface. You will see a subtle wake as the fly gains the surface. Immediately lower the rod tip to provide a drag-free drift.

UPSTREAM NYMPHING

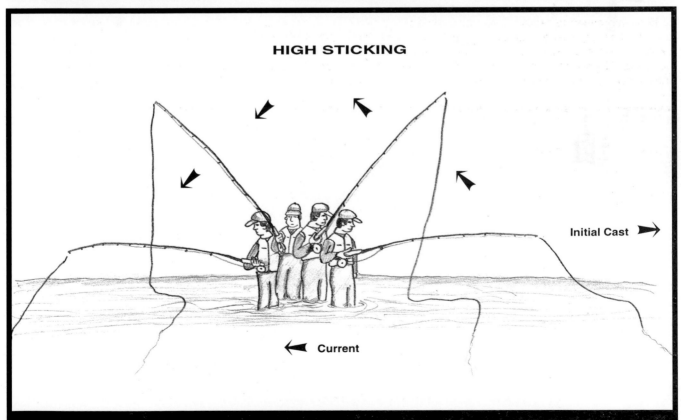

Surface

Current

Direction of Pull When Hooked

The upstream cast allows for solid hook-ups with nymphs because the leader helps pull the hook into the trout's mouth on the take. Conversely, the downstream cast can result in missed strikes because the fly is being pulled away from the trout when the angler raises the rod tip to set the hook.

HIGH STICKING

Initial Cast

Current

When casting up and across with nymphs, you will hook more fish if you maintain fairly direct contact with the fly. Thus, as the fly drifts downstream across from your position, raise the tip high to keep loose coils of line off the water. Then lower the tip again and point downstream to extend the drift.

The latter scenario—trout holding in shallow water and foraging on nymphs—requires as much stealth as any dry fly fishing. Sneak up behind the fish, preferably from on shore, and just watch for a time. Pick out an individual trout to pursue rather than simply flock-shooting. Is that fish feeding side to side as nymphing trout are prone to do? If so, does the fish seem to prefer one side over the other? How fast and how deep is the water and how far ahead of the trout will you need to cast in order to sink your fly or flies to its level?

Only after you have studied the trout for a time should you actually cast. A single trout or a pod of two or three trout, so long as they are holding under two or more feet of water, can usually be fished directly upstream. Using a long leader, cast over the trout's back so the fly lands far enough upstream to sink to the bottom. Then watch the leader where it enters the water or watch your strike indicator, which if used in shallow water should be small and unobtrusive. Assuming you can get close to the trout, a strike indicator, which can spook the fish, usually is not necessary in shallow water.

Cross-stream presentations work well on nymphing trout as well, especially those holding in deeper water. Using a strike indicator, cast far enough above the likely looking areas to assure the flies will reach the bottom. Then follow with the rod tip as the flies drift downstream. Raise the tip as the nymphs drift past your position, keeping as much slack line off the water as possible and therefore maintaining as direct a connection with the nymphs as possible. If the indicator hesitates or twitches, raise the tip with a smooth, quick motion.

You can fish deeply sunken nymphs downstream as well, although good hook-ups are never assured. To do this, cast well short of the target area and then flip or shake slack-line out the rod tip as the indicator drifts downstream. Ideally, you will pay out just enough slack line to keep the nymphs drifting freely. Any excess line beyond what is necessary will simply hinder your efforts to hook a trout.

Beyond any given presentation angle or technique for deep-fished nymphs lies the need to recognize ideal nymph water and ideal nymph times—those places and occasions where and when trout can most easily feed on insects drifting near the streambed.

Naturally, nymphs of a given species (or pupae in the case of caddis and chironomids) tend to be most active in the hour or so prior to actual emergence. Thus, if you know the approximate time schedule for the expected hatches of the day, you can begin fishing nymphs before the rise actually begins. In other words, if you expect the pale morning dun hatch to begin at 11 a.m., then you can be reasonably certain that PMD nymphs will be effective prior to that time. In

fact, you might very well decide to fish deep with nymphs up until the fish start showing themselves at the surface during the beginning of the hatch, then you can switch to nymphs fished just under the surface before ultimately switching to an emerger or dun pattern, depending on the observed preferences of individual trout.

Additionally, aquatic insects regularly partake in what entomologists term "behavioral drift." This means simply that certain insects will leave their lairs en masse at certain times to disperse downstream to new locations. Studies on some streams have concluded that major behavioral drifts occur at different times throughout the season and throughout the day, with night-time drifts being rather prevelant. For anglers, this

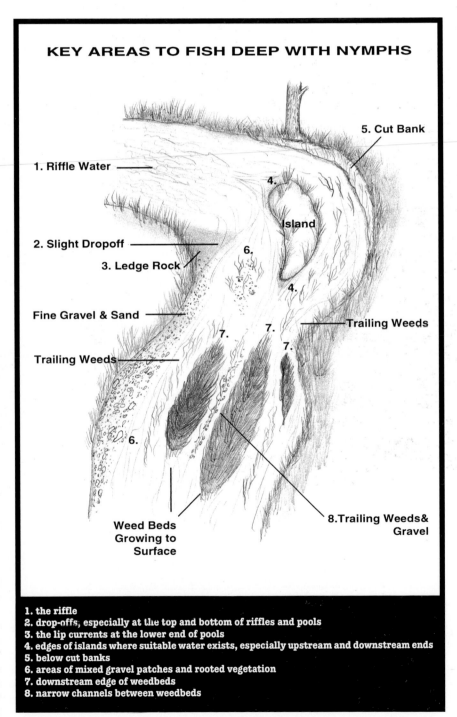

KEY AREAS TO FISH DEEP WITH NYMPHS

5. Cut Bank
1. Riffle Water
Island
2. Slight Dropoff
3. Ledge Rock
Fine Gravel & Sand
Trailing Weeds
Trailing Weeds
Weed Beds Growing to Surface
8. Trailing Weeds & Gravel

1. the riffle
2. drop-offs, especially at the top and bottom of riffles and pools
3. the lip currents at the lower end of pools
4. edges of islands where suitable water exists, especially upstream and downstream ends
5. below cut banks
6. areas of mixed gravel patches and rooted vegetation
7. downstream edge of weedbeds
8. narrow channels between weedbeds

translates to opportunity: During those early morning hours when no rise is in progress, nymphs can be very productive.

Knowing when to fish nymphs, then, is part of the equation. Deciding where to fish nymphs is another critical consideration. Trout can find an abundant supply of food around the large aquatic weedbeds that grow in the spring creeks. Fishing nymphs on the downstream end of weedbeds, especially those accompanied by fairly deep water and a bit of current, can prove exceptionally productive. In addition, look for any channels or runs fed by slightly faster water at the top. Such places often act like natural funnels for drifting nymphs. Similarly, the downstream edge of gravel bars, where they slope into deeper water, make excellent feeding grounds for nymphing trout.

Also cast to steep banks, especially those that are undercut. A nymph drifting along the bottom might tempt a trout hanging beneath an undercut bank; the same fish might never be in a position to see your dry-fly offering.

Lastly, the riffle-water sections of spring creeks provide abundant cover and opportunity for nymph-eating trout. In fact, these riffle sections can provide a welcome break from those days when the flat waters prove unproductive. A pair of nymphs fished under an indicator can work wonders when fished through good holding water in the riffles: channels, ledges, dropoffs at the head and throat of riffles, the lip-currents at the bottom of the riffles and any area scattered with sizeable rocks where trout can find cover.

Spring Creek Nymph Patterns

Spring creek nymph patterns fall into one of two categories: Those designed to suggest any number of natural insects and those meant to imitate one insect in particular. An example of the former, and truly one of the most effective spring-creek nymph patterns, is the pheasant tail nymph. These can be tied in a full range of sizes and in several shades. The traditional pattern calls for a body and shellback of natural ringneck pheasant tail fibers. You can add to your arsenal of pheasant tail nymphs by tying some with dyed olive and dyed gold pheasant tail fibers.

Given the fact that trout take nymphs in two different zones (along the bottom and just below the surface), carry both weighted and unweighted patterns. Those designed to be fished just under the surface should sink as a result of the weight of the hook and the style of the dressing. Any additional weight on these patterns, although necessary at times, will hinder their performance.

Listed below are dressing for suggestive nymph patterns, including imitations for scuds and cressbugs that are common in some spring creeks. Dressings to imitate specific mayfly nymphs, caddis larvae, midge larvae and stonefly nymphs are listed in their respective chapters.

Pheasant Tail Nymph (Frank Sawyer)
hook: wet fly, 2XL-3XL, No. 10-22
tail: a few pheasant tail fibers
body: pheasant tail fibers, wrapped up shank
rib: fine wire
thorax: fine peacock herl
shellback: pheasant tail fibers
legs: pheasant tail fibers (tips from shellback folded back and tied down)

Gold-ribbed Hare's Ear Nymph
hook: nymph or wet fly, 2XL, No. 10-20
tail: partridge fibers
body: dubbed natural tan rabbit fur
rib: fine gold oval or wire
thorax: same as body
wingcase: turkey quill segment, partridge, or Krystal Flash

Seal Fur Cressbug
hook: wet fly, No. 14-20
body: sparsely dubbed seal to match natural (various shades of olive, gray and cream are common)
rib: fine wire or thread (optional, especially on small sizes)

Shewey's Super Scud
hook: wet fly, No. 14-20
tail: woodduck fibers, short and sparse
body: rabbit/antron dubbing loop dubbed on Krystal Flash
back: woodduck fibers
rib: fine wire
colors: to match naturals—frequently shades of tan, gray and olive

Brassie (Gene Lynch)
hook: wet fly or dry fly, No. 14-24
body: copper wire
thorax: muskrat fur or similar

Zug Bug (Cliff Zug)
hook: wet fly or nymph, 2XL, No. 10-18
tail: peacock sword fibers
body: peacock herl
rib: fine wire
wingcase: woodduck breast, clipped short
beard: brown hackle or partridge fibers

Caddis Midge Nymph (Ed Koch)
hook: dry fly or wet fly, No. 16-24
body: rabbit fur dubbing, olive or brown
head: peacock herl

Peeking Caddis
(George Anderson/Umpqua F.M.)
hook: nymph, 2XL, No. 12-18
body: natural dark rabbit fur dubbing
rib: fine gold oval or wire
thorax: two turns of green or cream rabbit fur
throat: dark brown partridge
head: black ostrich

Partridge & Orange
(Sylvester Nemes)
hook: wet fly, No. 12-18
body: orange silk
thorax: two turns of natural hare's ear dubbing
hackle: partridge
Note: other body colors, including yellow, olive and amber, can be equally effective

ZUGBUG

BRASSIE

PHEASANT TAIL NYMPH

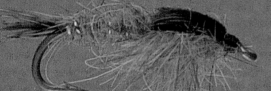

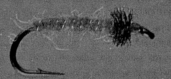

GOLD-RIBBED HARE'S EAR

CADDIS MIDGE-NYMPH

PEEKING CADDIS

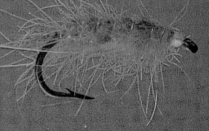

PARTRIDGE & ORANGE

SEAL FUR CRESS BUG

SUPER SCUD

What follows is a general guide to the most famous spring creeks in the West: The Henry's Fork of the Snake and Silver Creek in Idaho, Hat Creek and Fall River in California, the private spring creeks of Montana's Paradise Valley (Armstrong, Nelson's and DePuy's Spring Creeks), Oregon's Williamson and Metolius Rivers and Washington's Rocky Ford Creek. Included is information on the seasonal progression of hatches. Except for the private streams, where anglers pay a fee to be one of a restricted number of people allowed on the stream each day, the famous Western spring creeks can get crowded. Don't let that fact deter you. The presence of other anglers is a foregone conclusion during much of the year.

If you prefer solitude, fish early and late in the year and fish mid-week. Or, simply search out the myriad lesser known springs creeks: Flat Creek in Wyoming, Big Spring Creek in Montana, the Sprague or Wood River in Oregon, and countless others, large and small, that grace the Western landscape.

In addition, remember that many rivers in the West offer spring-creek characteristics even though they may not truly be spring creeks. Some, like a few of Montana's better-known (and lesser known) rivers, are fertile tail-water fisheries while others are simply meadow or valley sections of freestone rivers. On these tailwater and flat-land streams, the hatches can be virtually identical to those found on the spring creeks, with *Baetis*, PMD's, green drakes, Trico's and other important mayflies putting in their seasonal appearances. The techniques outlined in this book will prove equally effective on any flat-water stream—spring creek, tailwater or otherwise.

SECTION III

Chapter 10

The Famous Western Spring Creeks:
An Angler's Guide

The Henry's Fork:

Harriman State Park ("Railroad Ranch")

The Henry's Fork. If you have not fished here, do so: 200 feet wide in many places; dense aquatic weed growth; tremendous mayfly hatches; big rainbows; sometimes huge rainbows, which boast a higher 4-year average size than any of the other famous Western spring creeks. The Henry's Fork is an awe-inspiring river capable of producing some of the West's most incredible flat-water fishing.

But it can be tough on newcomers. It can be downright intimidating, not so much for its selective trout and dense hatches as for reasons such as those I've heard from first-timers: "I wasn't prepared for fish THAT BIG," and "I had no idea the river was SO HUGE." Yes it is a huge spring creek, the label "creek" really not at all fitting and no the fish are not always huge. Still, I've taken more 20-inch and over trout from the Henry's Fork than from any other river I regularly visit—when the Henry's Fork is "on," it is truly an amazing river.

But like any spring creek, you doom yourself to failure by defining success as any trip in which you catch 20 or more trout per day. Instead, count success as the opportunity to fish this phenomenal river, to cast over big wild rainbows, to hook a few, to land a few less; to watch the eagles soar high overhead, the swans and pelicans dine on the wide, glassy flats; to stand aside as mother moose leads her new calf astream, to watch the afternoon thunderheads descend on the Tetons and on Sawtell Peak.

The "Ranch" waters (Harriman State Park) open on June 15, by which time the pale morning dun hatch is typically under way. The "bird sanctuary," from Osborn Bridge on Hwy. 20 upstream to the ranch bridge, remains open until the end of September. The remainder of Harriman Park, including East Harriman (below Osborn Bridge) remains open until the end of November. The river, despite its size, can get crowded, especially during the early part of the season (June-July) when the green drake hatch draws a lot of attention.

Later, during August, the Tricos draw anglers from afar, but the river is rarely as crowded as it is during green-drake time. By mid-September, when *Baetis* and mahogany duns hatch, the crowds are gone. In short, time your trip according to the hatches you want to fish: The Henry's Fork is big enough that you can always find a fish to yourself somewhere along the 6-1/2-odd miles encompassed by Harriman Park. Moreover, some exceptional flat-water fishing can be had downstream from the park and above the Railroad Ranch, Box Canyon annually yields some of the river's largest trout to those fishing big nymphs and streamers.

For up-to-date information about the Henry's Fork and to hire guides, contact:

Henry's Fork Anglers Inc. Summer: HC 66 Box 491 Island Park, ID 83429 208-558-7525	Henry's Fork Anglers Inc. Winter: P.O. Box 487 St. Anthony, ID 83445 208-624-3590	Blue Ribbon Fly Shop P.O. Box 1037 West Yellowstone, MT 83201 406-646-9365	Jimmy's All Season Angler 275 A Street Idaho Falls, 83402 208-524-7160

Henry's Fork Hatch Chart

MONTHS	HATCHES	NOTES
June	Pale Morning Dun (*E. inermis*)	hatches at mid-day; spinner falls mid to late morning; both can be very heavy No. 14-16
	Baetis	late afternoon hatches; can be heavy, especially during inclement weather No. 20 is typical
	Green Drake (*Drunella grandis*)	Generally begins about mid-June; late morning to mid-afternoon; best on cloudy days. No. 10-12
	Brown Drake (*Ephemera simulans*)	Localized—mostly occurs on lower end of Railroad Ranch; hatches evening, often as late as dusk or thereafter; No. 8-10
	Brachycentrus caddis	Important throughout the Yellowstone area during June; emergences heavy
	Hydropsyche Caddis	Can produce dense hatches during late June-early July, generally late afternoon; Pupa most effective (No. 14)
	Micro-Caddis	Late June through July; usually evenings; No. 20-22 spent caddis works well.

	Oecetis caddis	evenings; oviposlting most significant, although emergence can trigger rises as well
	Various Caddis	Any number of other caddis can show up on the Railroad Ranch during June, though such activity is highly localized; carry a variety of downing adults and pupa
July	Small Green Drake *(D. flavilinea)* "slate-winged olive"	Can begin late June, but best hatches during July; can last until end of month; hatches late afternoon through evening; No. 14.
	Baetis	activity continues through at least mid July, with best activity on foul-weather days generally not as important as the early summer and fall emergences
	Brown Drake	hatch peaks in late June; lasts into July below Osborn Bridge. See notes above
	Green Drake	lasts through the first week of July, often ending by the 4th; best on cloudy days
	PMD *(E. inermis)*	continues during July; Spinner falls mid-morning; hatches late morning through mid-afternoon; No. 16-18.
	Various Caddis	Any number of caddis may be encountered, including micro-caddis, *Oecetus, Hydropsyche,* et al.; carry appropriate patterns; activity can be highly localized
	Terrestrials	can be very productive during July, especially late July—small ants, beetles, carpenter ants, hoppers; watch especially for bank feeders
August	PMD	often continues through first week of August
	Callibaetis	Can produce good rises during August, late morning-mid afternoon; No. 14-16
	Trico's	mid- to late morning spinner falls can produce excellent fishing; stay out of water until fish are rising steadily and confidently; No. 18-22
	Terrestrials	flying ant swarms can produce some of the season's best rises for anglers lucky enough to be in the right place at the right time—No. 12-16 winged patterns; also red ants and black ants, No. 14-18; smallbeetles and small hoppers (on windy days near grassy banks) can be very effective; big black carpenter ants (No. 10-12) can be highly productive fished to bank-hugging trout in vicinity of timber stands
	Mahogany Dun *(Paraleptophlebia)*	hatch usually begins by late August; more important during September; sporadic—late morning through mid afternoon; No. 16
	Baetis sp. (incl. tiny Western olive)	Hatches can occur mid- to late August, generally late afternoons, especially during foul weather. No. 20-24.
	Brachycentrus caddis	Usually provides excellent fishing during late August/early September
	Caddis	Carry a variety of caddis imitations to match localized hatches and egg-laying flights
September	*Baetis* (3 species, including tiny Western olive, formerlly *Pseudocleon* sp.)	Strong hatches of blue-winged olives, usually 1-4p.m. and usually followed by tiny western olive (No. 22) from about 4p.m.- 6p.m.: both hatches can be extemely dense, especially during inclement weather (which can also cause morning *Baetis* hatches); good *Baetis* hatches through mid-August
	Trico's	Trico hatch/spinner fall usually lasts until early Sept. mid-morning.
	Mahogany Dun *(Paraleptophlebia)*	increasingly important during Sept. mid-day hatches, 11 a.m. - 3 p.m. is typical; usually sparse, but their comparatively large size draws the interest of trout (No. 16)
	Callibaetis	*Callibaetis* activity can continue well into September, although hatches are sparse, large size makes them of interest to trout. No. 14-18
	Terrestrials	ants and beetles still very effective; grass hoppers effective during warm, windy weather along grassy banks
	Caddis	see notes for August

Silver Creek

Silver Creek, south of Sun Valley, Idaho, may be the country's richest trout stream in terms of the total mass of aquatic insects produced per unit of water. The Silver Creek Preserve, owned and managed by the Nature Conservancy, is the crown jewel of this magnificent spring creek.

The Conservancy water, along with most of the lower creek north of Hwy. 20, is largely wadeable. At its lower end, however, the preserve water flows through an impoundment where float tubes are by and large the rule. This tubeable water extends past Kilpatrick Bridge (the lower border of the Conservancy property) and through Purdy Ranch. Purdy Ranch is private property, but the stream itself is in public hands, so anglers can float the entire section (a feat which can take from half a day to a full day depending on how good the fishing is).

All of the Conservancy water and the remainder of the stream down to the Highway bridge at milepost 187.2 on Hwy. 20 west of Picabo is fly-fishing only, catch-and-release water. The season runs from Memorial Day weekend through the last day of November. Silver Creek can be crowded through mid-September, after which most of the people disperse. By mid-October and through November, even the popular Conservancy water is largely devoid of anglers. Despite the typical cold weather, mid-day fishing can be very productive during late fall.

For up-to-date information or to locate guide services for Silver Creek, contact the following:

Silver Creek Outfitters	**Jimmy's All Season Angler**	**Streamside Adventures**
P.O. Box 418	275 A Street	6907 Overland Rd.
Ketchum, ID 83340	Idaho Falls, ID 83402	Boise, ID 83709

Hatch Chart Information compiled with the help of Peter Crow of Silver Creek Outfitters, Ketchum, Idaho.

Silver Creek Hatch Chart

MONTHS	HATCHES	NOTES
Late May/ early June	*Baetis*	*Baetis* hatches occur throughout the season
	Pale Morning Duns (*Ephemerella Infrequens & Inermis*)	PMD hatch tends to be sporadic early, but gains in momentum through June; No. 16-18
	Brown Drake (*Ephemera simulans*)	traditionally runs for about the first two weeks in June, with the first few nights of the hatch being most consistent; best hatches on sections north of Hwy. 20; emergence generally more reliable than spinner fall, but still not as consistent as other mayflies with intensity and duration of hatch dependent on relative water levels and temperatures
	Callibaetis	may occur any time of the season, even during the first month, especially on some of the slough sections and slower reaches
July	Pale Morning Duns	good evening hatches; spinner falls A.M. Major hatch late June and July
	Trico's	begins mid-July (occasionally as early as the first week of July); good morning hatch and spinner fall, but spinner activity is most important
	Baetis	morning hatches that can occur before or during Trico activity; weather tends to dictate intensity and duration of hatch, with foul weather being best
	Callibaetis	consistent by July; occurs mid-morning to mid-afternoon
	Ants/beetles	a significant part of the drift by mid summer
	damsels	July hatches on slower reaches
	caddis, various	downwing, spent-style adults (partridge caddis) most effective; No. 16-20
August	Trico's	strong Trico activity in the mornings—a major attraction during August
	Baetis	common A.M. and during foul weather
	PMD's	remains a significant hatch until about mid-month
	Callibaetis	good hatches on sloughs and slower reaches
	Ants/beetles	significant throughout August
	hoppers	abundant during many years; imitations especially productive on windy days along grassy banks
	mahogany duns (*Paraleptophlebia*)	can begin during late August; important by September
	caddis, various	always carry a few downwing caddis patterns during summer, No. 16-20
September	*Baetis*	good hatches, especially A.M., but any time of day during cool, cloudy weather
	Mahogany duns (*Paraleptophlebia*)	consistent and important during Sept.
	Callibaetis	good hatches through much of Sept.
	Trico	hatches can continue into early Sept., but consistency wanes
	Baetis (Pseudocleon) "tiny Western olive"	late Sept.; hatches can be heavy
	caddis	carry spent patterns, including some large sizes (e.g. 10-14)
October/ November	*Baetis*	mid-day hatches
	chironomids	usually mid-day

Hat Creek

The meadow sections of lower Hat Creek, prior to 1968, had become infested with rough fish. But due to the tireless efforts of individuals from Cal-Trout and from several California state agencies, the Lower Hat Creek Wild Trout Project has transformed that section of stream into one of California's—and the West's—most impressive spring creeks. All this was accomplished by making Hat Creek the first fishery in the West to be managed specifically for wild trout.

This "trophy trout" section of Hat Creek flows from Hat Creek 2 Powerhouse to Lake Britton. The first half mile or so below the powerhouse is riffle water, complete with a large population of trout and replete with a dense allotment of caddis, stoneflies and other insects. Below that long riffle lies two contiguous miles of classic smooth, glassy spring creek.

Hat Creek fishes especially well during May and June and again during the fall. July and August hatches tend to be compressed toward morning and evening, but anglers willing to utilize a full spectrum of tactics can enjoy the less-crowded days of mid- to late summer.

As with all the top Western spring creeks, compound hatches, consisting of numerous species emerging simultaneously, are common. Nymphing during non-hatch periods can be very effective. Hat Creek is noted for its hatch of little yellow stoneflies: It is one of only a few rivers where this hatch is of major significance and is capable of causing selective feeding. Hat Creek is even more famous for its fall hatches of the giant orange caddis *(Dicosmoecus)*, which occur during October and November.

For more information and to arrange guide services, contact:

The Fly Shop • 4140 Churn Creek Road • Redding, CA 96002

Hat Creek Hatch Chart

MONTH	INSECT	NOTES
April/May/June	*Baetis* (several species, incl. tiny Western olive)	usually begins by late April or early May; morning through afternoon
	pale morning dun (*E. inermis*)	hatches mid morning through mid-afternoon; spinner falls mid to late morning; May to mid-June; also an evening emergence during June and July
	Green Drakes (*Drunella grandis* & *D. flavilinea*)	generally late morning to mid afternoon; May-early June
	Mahogany Dun	can occur afternoons during May, but late season hatch is more signifcant
	Trico	mornings; begins in June, lasts through Sept.
	Salmon Fly (*Pteronarcys*) and golden stone (*Acroneuria*)	near riffles and runs; begins in April, can last into mid-June
	Little Yellow Stone (*Isoperla*)	May-July; can cause significant feeding actvity afternoon/evening
	Hydropshyche Caddis	April-mid-June; afternoon/evening (No. 14-16)
	small caddis (*Amiocentrus, cheumatopsyche*, et al)	usually evenings; occasionally morning (No. 16-18)
	terrestrials	ants and beetles increase in importance as season progresses; ants can produce good rises during May-June
July/August	Tricos	good early morning activity; can be very heavy
	Baetis sp.	not as significant by mid-summer, but hatches can occur afternoon & evenings; sometimes mornings; overcast or foul-weather days, when they occur early-mid July, can produce good *Baetis* activity
	pale morning dun (*E. inermis*)	evening hatch can extend into July; spinner falls both early morning and evening
	caddis (various, incl. *Amiocentrus, Hydropsyche, Cheumatopsyche*)	generaly good through July; less so but available during August
	Little Yellow Stone	lasts through July, into early August
	terrestrials	ants and beetles; hoppers on windy days near vegetated banks
Sept/Oct/Nov	Tricos	usually lasts through Sept.; mornings
	Baetis sp.	good hatches October and November; early- to late afternoon; sometimes available by mid Sept.
	Giant Orange Caddis (*Dicosmoecus*)	a long-time favorite hatch on Hat Creek; October and November during late afternoon and evening (start as early as mid Sept, but October/November hatches more reliable)
	terrestrials	trout will feed oportunistically as long as terrestrials remain part of the drift; especially near shoreline vegetation
	Mahogany dun	less significant on Hat Creek than on other Western spring creeks, but can trigger some trout to feed selectively; afternoons during Oct./Nov.

Fall River

Fall River, California's famed blue-ribbon trout fishery, is unique among Western spring creeks in that very little wade fishing and shoreline access is available. This fact stems from the private ownership of both banks and the fact that the river is almost entirely too deep to wade. The stream itself, however, is a legally navigable waterway and as such is public property. Anglers on Fall River fish almost exclusively from prams and other small boats, usually powered by an electric motor.

Fall River is a classic spring creek, its flowage emanating from a place called Thousand Springs before meandering through Fall River Valley. The Fall is so rich that, on average, more than 3,000 rainbows inhabit a mile of stream in the prime sections.

All of the tactics for spring-creek angling apply to Fall River, but instead of wading, you'll be concentrating on positioning the boat in the ideal place for making a presentation—one reason why an experienced Fall River guide can be a big help. Anglers can launch at any of several access points: Cal-Trout established an access point at Island Road Bridge, but get there early as the site has parking space for some 10 vehicles; Rick's Lodge and The Fly Shop Outfitters run a fee access on the upper river on Metzger Road (they also offer guides and boat rentals); The California Dept. of Fish Game worked out a lease agreement to open a launch area at the PG&E site on Glenburn Road (the "Dredge Site").

Prime season on Fall River runs from April through October. Along with the typical spring creek hatches of *Ephemerella*, *Baetis* and Trico's, Fall River hosts a long-famous hatch of giant yellow mayflies *(Hexagenia limbata)* during late June and early July. In addition, the Fall offers exceptional evening caddis activity during July and August.

For up-to-date information about Fall River or to arrange guide service for the Fall, contact the following:

The Fly Shop	**Rick's Lodge**
4140 Churn Creek Rd.	Glenbourne Star Route
Redding, CA 96002	Fall River Mills, CA 96028
916-243-5317	916-336-5300 April-Nov
	916-336-6618 Dec-April

Fall River Hatch Chart

Months	Insects	Notes
April/May	pale morning dun	mid-morning- early afternoon spinner falls usually in mornings before emergence
	Baetis	localized hatches can occur just about any time, especially during wet or overcast weather; typical time frame would be from late morning to late afternoon
	Green Drake	not particularly dependable on Fall River, but overcast, cool weather during May can trigger decent hatches, primarily up stream from Spring Creek Bridge
	Caddis (Green Sedge)	evening activity becomes heavy during mid to late May , No. 10-12 pupa best
	ants	flying ants can occur during May
June/July	pale morning dun	excellent hatches and good spinner falls during June, slowing down during early July; hatch occurs mid morning to early afternoon; spinner fall earlier.
	Baetis	hatches about same time as PMD's; best during inclement weather
	Hexagenia limbata yellow may	the "Hex hatch" begins during mid-June and lasts through mid July; late evening hatch, usually continuing into night; best in lower sections
	Caddis	excellent evening activity during June and July, especially green caddis, No. 14-18
	terrestrials	can be of localized significance anywhere on the river, especially with bank-feeders
August	pale morning dun	hatches continue, although not always as strong as earlier emergences
	Trico's	can be prolific, especially in area around Island Road Bridge; hatch/spinner fall occurs between 8-10:30 a.m.
	Callibaetis "speckled dun"	hatches mid- to lower river, usually mid morning to early afternoon; No. 16-18
	caddis	good caddis hatches during evenings
	terrestrials	ants, beetles, hoppers productive on "smorgasboarding" trout and on bankfeeders, especially during windy days
Sept/Oct/Nov	pale morning dun	morning hatches intensify during September and lasts into October; daylight spinner falls return as well
	Trico's	hatch usually runs through September and well into October, with August/September activity being most consistent and heaviest
	Callibaetis	morning/early afternoon hatches continue through most of Sept.
	Baetis	good *Baetis* hatches occur afternoons during Sept and October, usually beginning with *B. parvus* (blue-winged olive) during early- to mid-afternoon and continuing with tiny western olive by late afternoon (the typical pattern on Western spring creeks); entire hatch is centered around mid-day by November; fall hatches are more consistent than early season hatches
	Giant Orange Caddis (*Dicosmoecus*)	hatches late afternoon/evening on upper river; tends toward the sporadic side, but at times can be heavy and very fishable
	Green Drake	green drakes hatch again, albeit sporadically, during fall, usually from late September through early to mid November
	Caddis (various, incl. micro-caddis & small olive caddis)	often good caddis activity during fall (generally same species as Hat Creek)
	terrestrials	can still produce good fishing; localized and most important to trout holding near overhead cover

Located in southern Oregon, near the town of Chiloquin, the Williamson River is well-known for its hatch of gray drakes *(Siphlonurus* mayflies) and giant yellow mayflies *(Hexagenia).* The Williamson is also renowned for its frustrating fishing.

What a newcomer to the Williamson should realize is that the increasingly popular lower river holds a comparatively small population of resident trout. Instead, the big rainbows that anglers pursue on the lower Williamson are lake-run fish: They ascend the Williamson from Klamath Lake. The spawning run brings trout out of the lake and into the river. In addition warm summer water temperatures in Klamath Lake will prompt many trout to enter the river and remain there for several months. At times, these migratory trout will prey on the Williamson's tremendous population of insects, sometimes hording surface foods and other times completely ignoring the hatches and instead feeding on nymphs near the bottom. Other times, the trout behave much like steelhead, feeding only infrequently (and progressively less frequently the longer they are in the river) and being more susceptible to steelhead fly fishing tactics than to typical spring-creek methods.

Unfortunately, much of the Williamson's shoreline is tied up in private hands, so bank access is limited for wading fishermen. One of the more popular access points is Collier Park where Spring Creek empties into the Williamson (most of the lake-run rainbows spawn in Spring Creek). A few other access points are available as well, although floating is usually the method of choice for the lower river. The first several miles above the lake are best suited to a small, motor-driven craft; at various points farther upstream, drift boats, canoes, rafts or other small craft are perfect. Several launch sites are available for drifters, but, like California's Fall River, a guide can be a big help the first time or two you fish the Williamson.

The good news is this: The trout are big. Three- to six-pound rainbows are the norm when the Klamath Lake trout are in the river and many fish from seven to 12 pounds are available as well. In addition, a good population of 12- to 15-inch yearling rainbows enter the Williamson and are more responsive to the river's hatches than are the big fish. These hatches can be phenomenal and on those occasions when the trout respond well to the surface, you stand a chance of taking truly huge rainbows on dry flies.

Moreover, if you prefer to fish smaller water with resident trout, the upper Williamson offers challenging, classic flat-water fishing complete with an exceptional "black drake" and *Hexagenia* emergence. Rainbows—including large ones—and brook trout inhabit the upper river, much of which runs through private property, including the Yamsi Ranch. Owned by the Hyde family, Yamsi Ranch offers, for a fee, access to several miles of river, lodging, meals and guide service. Part of the upper Williamson also runs through the Winema National Forest, which is public property.

In reality, then, the Williamson is two different rivers. When the big lake-run trout of the lower river ignore the hatches, anglers should be prepared to fish nymphs and streamers on a fairly long line, much in the way of steelhead angling. If doing so is not really your game, then plan your trip to include a visit to the upper river, preferably during one of the major hatches, such as the black drakes, *Hexagenia*, or Tricos.

For more information on the Williamson River, contact:

Williamson River Outfitters
P.O. Box 699
Junction of Hwy. 97 & Hwy. 62
Chiloquin, OR 97624
503-783-2677

Yamsi Ranch
P.O. Box 371
Chiloquin, OR 97624
503-783-2403

Bear in mind that, on the lower Williamson, even the most profuse of hatches may not elicit a response from the lake-run rainbows. These trout act more like steelhead and are more prone to respond to tactics used to take steelhead on a fly: down-and-across presentation with streamers and nymphs, using a sinking line in deeper water and a sink-tip or floating line in shallower water. Try wooly buggers, zonkers, marabou muddlers, stonefly nymphs, various large non-descript nymphs, or other favorite streamers. References for steelhead fishing tactics: *Northwest Fly Fishing: Trout & Beyond*, by John Shewey; *Advanced Steelhead Fly Fishing*, by Deke Meyer; *Steelhead Fly Fishing and Flies*, by Trey Combs (all published by Frank Amato Publications, Portland, Oregon). The rainbows and brook trout of the upper Williamson, however, act and react like the resident spring-creek trout that they are.

Williamson River Hatch Chart

MONTHS	INSECTS	NOTES
May 25-June	*Baetis*	hatches can be heavy, although trout don't always respond well
	Green Drake	#10-12, mid morning-afternoon; intensity varies, but can stimulate good rises
	pale morning dun	good hatches occur mid-day with inclement weather triggering the best hatches
	Callibaetis	emergence can occur almost anytime between late May and August, with better hatches during June and July
	salmon fly & golden stonefly	morning or evening emergence; mid-day to late afternoon ovipositing flights; riffle sections only, can produce good fishing
	various caddis, *Hydropsyche, Amiocentrus, cheumatopsyche, et al*	localized hatches can be very heavy during June; afternoon-evening June; afternoon-evening
	Giant Yellow May *(Hexagenia)*	begins during mid-June and lasts through early July; most intense activity occurs at dusk and thereafter; No. 8 paradrake or fish the nymphs (which are usually productive during the early stages of the hatch)
	Black Drake (Gray Drake) *(Siplonurus occidentalis)*	spinner fall is the important stage and it can be very heavy right at dusk and after dark on bright, sunny days, or anytime from mid-afternoon to evening during inclement weather; sometimes the spinners even appear during the morning on bad weather days; begins during late June, but July is better
July/August	Black Drake	excellent spinner activity during July; see notes above
	Hexagenia	hatch continues throught first week or two of July; see notes above
	Callibaetis	good hatches (and spinner falls) during July; best on slowest sections; No. 14-16; usually mid-day but will vary in timing and intensity with inclement weather
	Trico's	begins during July and lasts through August; mid-morning; sometimes trout respond very well, other times the mayflies escape unbothered by the rainbows; No. 20
	pale morning dun	hatches not as heavy as those during June, but can produce good rises at some locations; #18
	various caddis	a number of different caddis species are active during July and August, including an orange caddis (No. 12—14) that is similar to, but much smaller than the giant October Caddis that hatches later; also *Brachycentrus* and *Hydropsyche*, et al. Best caddis activity usually occurs afternoon and evening
	terrestrials:	ants & beetles; hoppers along grassy banks; from mid-summer to mid-autumn
	little yellow stonefly	riffle sections; sporadic; No. 14-16
September/ October	Trico's	good hatches through early September, sometimes longer; see notes above
	Baetis	heavy autumn hatches around mid-day; typically No. 20-22
	various caddis	sporadic late afternoon evening activity of small caddis
	October Caddis	strong evening hatches of these huge caddis trigger good rises; No. 8 adults & pupa
	terrestrials	can be important, especially during windy days (hoppers near grassy banks)
	chironomids	dense emergences during fall, but usually don't elicit much response from large trout

Oregon's Metolius River is unlike other spring creeks discussed in this section because the majority of the river exhibits the physical characteristics of a freestone stream: a continual series of riffles, pools and rapids; gravel and stone bottom; a fairly steep gradient. Nonetheless, the Metolius is a true spring creek, emanating from an underground source just a few miles above the tiny town of Camp Sherman (the only town on the river).

The Metolius, in reality, offers two distinct fisheries: First, the river is planted heavily with pan-sized, hatchery-reared rainbow trout. These trout, by and large, dominate in all of the easy-access, "trouty-looking" water of the upper river. These hatchery-reared trout, which keep the masses happy and assure that many will visit the Metolius River each year, constitute the first of the river's two fisheries. But they thrive at the expense of the river's wild trout, which constitute the river's more challenging and more rewarding fishery.

Wild rainbows, along with a few brown trout and a handful of brook trout, inhabit the river, but these fish are evident only to those who know where to look. Tim Blount, who worked at the Camp Sherman fly shop for a time, puts it this way: "You've got to work to find the river's wild trout because they live in the more inaccessible places where the average angler either isn't willing to fish or simply can't fish effectively for lack of appropriate casting and line-control skills."

Indeed, those willing to work will find the wild trout of the Metolius, especially in the hard-to-fish lower river and in the less-crowded, more challenging parts of the upper river. What's more, despite its freestone appearance, the Metolius offers tremendous hatches of all those insects one would expect from a rich spring creek. A part of the upper river is even open during the winter, so anglers can at times fish over cold-weather hatches of *Baetis* mayflies, winter stoneflies and chironomids.

Incidentally, the Metolius harbors one of the West's healthiest populations of bull trout (actually a char and sometimes mistakenly called dolly varden). These fish, which reside primarily in the deeper pools and chutes, will hit large saltwater-style streamers during the early morning and late evening. They commonly run four to eight pounds and a number of fish larger still are caught and released each year.

For More Information on the Metolius River, contact:

Creekside Fly Shop	**The Fly Box**	**The Valley Flyfisher**	**The Fly Fisher's Place**
345 High St. S	923 SE 3rd Street	153 Alice Avenue S.	P.O. Box 1179
Salem, OR 97302	Bend, OR 97702	Salem, OR 97302	Sisters, OR 97759

Metolius River Hatch Chart

MONTHS	INSECTS	NOTES
December-March	chironomids	good hatches can occur any time of year, but off-season hatches more important because they are not overshadowed by mayflies, stoneflies, and caddis; even the heaviest winter hatches do not necessarily draw trout to the surface, but it pays to carry imitations
	Baetis	hatches of blue-winged olives can occur during any month on the Metolius; winter hatches are usually at warmest part of mid-day; typically No. 20
	little brown stonefly (*Capnidae*)	emergence generally begins late January; generally lasts for an hour or two between noon and 3 p.m.; No. 14-18
	Western March Brown (*Rithrogenia*)	hatch can start as early as mid-March; typically warmest part of day (e.g. mid afternoon). No. 14
April-May-June	*Baetis*	mid-day (see notes above)
	Western March Brown	good hatches can occur around mid-day
	pale morning dun	mid-day, can be heavy in places and can elicit good rises; No. 16-18
	Green Drake	mid-day hatches can be fairly dense; No. 12
	brown willow fly (early golden stonefly) golden stonefly	sporadic emergences around mid-day during April (sometimes as early as late February); No. 6-8; Later emergences during morning and evening. some heavy ovipositing flights occur during afternoons; the golden stones remain active through out the summer, although best activity is May-July; No. 6-8

	ants/beetles	terrestrials become productive by May, with some heavy (although brief and localized) flights of fairly large dark brown ants (No. 14) during May and through the summer; beetles can be productive any time May-October
	various caddis	the river produces good hatches of numerous caddis; carry upwing patterns (e.g. elkhair caddis) for riffles and downwing patterns for flat water, along with pupa patterns for *Hydropsyche, Cheumatopsyche, Brachycentrus, Oecetis, Rhyacophila*; also, a large *Dicosmoecus* caddis with a tan-orange body emerges sporadically during late spring (No. 8-10).
July-August	*Baetis*	see notes above; typically No. 20; warm, sunny weather constricts hatches and pushes them toward morning and evening; sometimes a larger *Baetis* (No. 16) hatches during afternoon
	pale morning dun	hatches continue through most of summer, although late summer hatches shorter and less intense
	green drake	typically has peaked by early July
	golden stone	see notes above
	little yellow stone *(Isoperla)*	sporadic and rarely heavy, but taken by opportunistic trout
	various caddis	see notes above; afternoon/evening emergences and ovipositing activity
	ants/beetles	can be very productive and important during summer
	spruce budworm moth	active afternoons during July and August; can cause selective feeding; use white, poly-wing dry caddis, No. 14
Sept./Oct./ Nov.	*Baetis*	good hatches into early to mid-fall; afternoons
	Green Drake	another large *Drunella* species begins emerging by early to mid September
	pale morning dun	hatches can occur during September and October; No. 18
	terrestrials	important through September and into October
	October Caddis *(Dicosmoecus)*	large orange caddis hatches can be heavy; late afternoon/evening emergence and ovipositing; mid Sept-early Nov. No. 6-8
	various caddis	not as significant as earlier, but good afternoon/evening caddis activity can bring trout to surface through mid-autumn
	chironomids	good hatches can stimulate rises throughout autumn
	little brown stonefly	sporadic hatches can occur nearly any time No. 16-18

Rocky Ford Creek

In the heart of Washington's "seep lakes" region lies a lovely little spring creek known as Rocky Ford Creek. Unique among Western Spring Creeks because wading is not allowed, Rocky Ford offers challenging fishing for some fairly large rainbows amidst a rather stark and seemingly barren landscape.

Rocky Ford creek, seven miles total in length, is replete with algae growth, cattails and other tell-tale signs of a slow-moving, fertile spring creek. Moreover, it contains a healthy population of scuds, a protein-rich food on which trout can grow quickly. Rocky Ford also harbors a tremendous chironomid population and its trout often feed selectively on the small midge pupa.

In addition to the abundant chironomids, Rocky Ford offers a dense Trico emergence, strong populations of *Baetis* and *Callibaetis* mayflies, pale morning duns, and various caddis. Despite all of this, anglers should carry a few streamers (wooly buggers being popular) to fish during non-hatch periods. Cast across or down and across and then worked with a stripping motion, wooly buggers and other streamers can draw ferocious takes from 14- to 24-inch rainbows.

The only real downfall to Rocky Ford Creek is its relative proximity to the Seattle and Tacoma metropolitan areas. A four-hour drive puts anglers from those heavily populated areas onto some of the state's best trout fishing and at times the stream can be crowded. Those willing to walk a mile or more downstream, however, can avoid much of the crowd on days when the parking lot is full of cars.

For more information on Rocky Ford Creek, Contact:

Gary's Fly Shop • 1210 W. Lincoln Ave. • Yakima, WA 98902 • 206 457-3437

Rocky Ford Creek Hatch Chart

MONTHS	INSECTS	NOTES
December–March	chironomids	dark—usually black or dark gray, No. 22-24; best hatches occur mid-day; pupae most effective, although cold weather that keeps the adults from flying away immediately equates to good fishing with a Griffith's Gnat or other adult pattern
April-May	chironomids	see notes above
	Baetis	strong hatches, typically late morning or afternoon; No. 20
	scuds	small olive and gray scuds can be productive any time of year; a simple seal fur cressbug or hare's ear (No. 16-18) will suffice
	streamers	can be productive during non-hatch periods; try black wooly bugger or similar
June-July-August	Trico's	mornings, No. 18-20 (2X short)
	Baetis	see notes above, No. 18-20
	pale morning dun	mid morning to mid afternoon, depending on weather; No. 16-18; good hatches can occur through mid July, decreasing thereafter
	Callibaetis	excellent hatches can occur late morning to mid afternoon; No. 14-16
	mahogany dun (*Paraleptophlebia*)	not as dependable as on Rocky Mt. spring creeks, but can stimulate good rises late July through early Sept. (mid-day); No. 16-18. Best hatches on cool, overcast days
	various caddis	afternoon & evening activity; No. 16-18 with olive-tan body; No. 18 with grayish body
	terrestrials	ants/hoppers can be very effective, especially on windy days; hopper densities vary from year to year, but when abundant, trout relish them; occasional nuptial flights of flying ants will stimulate rises
	scuds	see notes above
	streamers	see notes above
Sept-October	Trico's	can last into early September
	Baetis	good hatches can occur just about any time during the fall, with best activity on overcast days; No. 20-22
	Mahogany Dun	see notes above
	terrestrials	good hopper fishing on warm, windy days; ants can produce any time, especially with bank-hugging trout and during occasional ant flights
	chironomids	abundant and important during autumn; see notes above
	scuds	see notes above
	streamers	see notes above
	various caddis	less abundant by autumn, but afternoon/evening activity can cause selective feeding at times; little olive sedge, No. 18-20; micro-caddis, No. 20-22; et al

In assembling this section of the book, I hesitated to include these three Montana spring creeks for one simple reason: All are pay-to-play streams running through private ranches. In other words, anglers must reserve time on the creeks by paying, as of this writing, $50 per person per day. For that $50 bucks you share the stream with a limited number of anglers (Armstrong: 10 rods per day, DePuy's: 15 rods per day, Nelson's: 6 rods per day).

But there is no escaping the fact that a lot of anglers pay the money and fish these spring creeks—so many, in fact, that these three waters are amongst the most widely known of Western Spring Creeks. Virtually every angler familiar with the names Henry's Fork and Hat Creek has also heard and read about Nelson's and Armstrong. So, no matter what my or your feelings are about pay-to-play fisheries, I've included these streams simply because they are quality spring-creek fisheries and because they have earned fame amongst fly anglers.

The following information is excerpted from an information sheet compiled by and available from George Anderson at the Yellowstone Angler in Livingston, Montana:

"**Armstrong Spring Creek** is perhaps the easiest to fish because of its wide, shallow riffles and pools. Most of the fish caught are rainbows with many in the 14-18-inch class. Some rainbows are larger, and a few good-sized browns are present but not often caught. There is about 1-1/2 miles of fishable water on Armstrong, and the scenery, with the Absaroka Mountains as a backdrop, is spectacular. All the spring creeks share this magnificent scenery."

"**DePuy's Spring Creek** is actually the lower portion of Armstrong creek before it flows into the Yellowstone River. There is more water available than on the O'Hair Ranch (Armstrong Spring Creek), including a few ponds and sloughs that harbor some big trout. DePuy's recently embarked on a stream improvement program, lowering some ponds, increasing the length of stream sections, and adding more angler facilities. Some stream sections are easy to fish, while other are deep and narrow, and more difficult to fish. Most fish are rainbows in the 12-18 inch range, but in sections you will find more browns, with some over two pounds, and some cutthroats. There is about 3 miles of fishable water on DePuy's. You will see lots of waterfowl, including ducks, geese, and swans, along with white-tail deer, beaver and muskrat."

"**Nelson's Spring Creek** is a real classic, and favored by many of the best fly fishermen. There is about 3/4 of a mile of water available to fish, but an awful lot of good, big trout are packed into this stretch. The fishing is more difficult with flatter pools that demand the utmost in delicate presentation, fine tippets, and small flies. Lots of rainbows in the 16-18 inch class with some larger. There are always a few big fish around, and they are tough to catch. Browns and cutthroats are present in fair numbers and there is some influx of spawning cutthroats from the Yellowstone in July."

These three spring creeks require advance booking, often as much as a year ahead of time. You can contact George Anderson's Yellowstone Angler or you can make the bookings yourself by calling the ranches:

Armstrong Spring Creek: 406-222-2979 • **DePuy's Spring Creek:** 406-222-0221 • **Nelson's Spring Creek:** 406-222-2159

All three creeks are open year-round, with prime dry-fly fishing occuring between mid March and October. The summer months are booked well in advance, but anglers willing to fish early and late in the year might find themselves alone on one of the creeks (from November through March, incidentally, the streams charge half rate).

The hatches are essentially the same on all three creeks, although some variation in timing can be expected. The information for the hatch chart below was compiled by Brant Oswald and George Anderson. In addition to the hatches, anglers should note that the typical array of spring-creek nymphs will work, especially during non-hatch periods. Small- and medium-sized streamers can be productive during evening and during windy, stormy days. For more information about the Paradise Valley spring creeks or to secure a guide, contact:

Brant K. Oswald Fly Fishing Services
117 South 9th Street
Livingston, MT 59047
406-222-8312

George Anderson's Yellowstone Angler
P.O. Box 660
Livingston, MT 59047
406-222-7130

Armstrong, Depuy's, Nelson's Spring Creeks Hatch Chart

MONTHS	INSECTS	NOTES
March-April	*Baetis*	typically begins mid-March, with best hatches from late March through April; No. 18-20; as is typical for *Baetis*, best hatches during bad weather
	Midges	can be important any time during season with strongest hatches during spring and in September
May	*Baetis*	hatches last into May, although peak is in late March and April; No. 18-20
	Midges	see notes above
June/July	Pale Morning dun	hatches usually begin between the June 10 and 15 (sometimes earlier on Nelson's); strong hatches through July, but tapers off quickly around the second week of August. No. 14-16 early; No. 18 later
	Centroptilum "Sulphur" or "Sulphur dun" "pale watery dun"	begins around first week of July and peaks mid July through mid-August; late after noon emergence; trout key on emergers, but duns can be important late in the hatch when clusters of adults, cripples and stillborns start to stack up against weed lines and logs). Parachute Emerger and Swimming Sulphur patterns recommended. (see chapter 4) No. 20-22
	Midges	hatches occur throughout season; can be significant-mornings and evenings
	Baetis	Afternoon hatches; sometimes inconsistent, but can stimulate good rises
	Terrestrials	beetles and ants can be very productive throughout the summer. Hoppers can take trout along grassy banks (best on very windy days)
	Caddis	brown, No. 16-18. Can cause good rises during early- to mid-June
August	*Centroptilum*	strong hatches until mid-August (see notes above)
	Pale Morning dun	hatches generally last into mid-August with less dependable hatches through late August; No. 18.
	Terrestrials	ants and beetles important and productive through summer; hoppers near grassy banks on windy days
	Midges	see notes above
	Tricos	mostly insignificant on the creeks except for parts of DePuy's, where the spinner fall can at times be fishable.
September/ October	*Baetis*	strong hatches begin when fall weather patterns move in: as early as Labor Day or as late as mid-October. Strong hatches can be expected when autumn begins in earnest; hatches continue into November and sometimes into December.
	Midges	reliable morning hatches during September, although bright weather equates to difficult fishing
	Terrestrials	ants and beetles important as long as warm weather lasts

(Hatch Chart information provided by Brant Oswald and George Anderson.)

Epilogy:
Another Day On a Spring Creek

It was tough. I hadn't seen a fish rise in hours, not even a bank feeder or whitefish for that matter.

Far upriver I could see Tim. We had separated during late morning in hopes that at least one of us would find something worth casting to. Since then it had been a dreary game of watching and waiting; sneaking and stalking; wading with purpose when a single trout rose once but wading aimlessly most of the time, hoping that a feeding fish would feel compelled to take pity on us.

Like Tim, I was now sitting on the bank just watching, hoping, almost willing even a single trout to rise.

And it was hot. Damn hot. A relentless August sun had made waders unbearable so I'd shed them some time back. After that I reverted to just watching again, scanning the river's flat surface for any sign of a feeding trout. Nothing.

Three turkey vultures circled high overhead. Not once did I see even one of them flap its wings. They just circled and soared, rocking back and forth on those long black wings, looking for their next easy meal or maybe just circling and soaring and rocking because that's what buzzards are supposed to do on hot summer days.

When I next glanced upriver, Timmy was in the water. "The lucky son-of-a-bitch found a rising trout," I thought.

He hadn't, though. He was just fording the river.

Again I scanned the wide flats. Perhaps I could fish nymphs, if not here then maybe down below in the riffles. To hell with it. I'd wait right here until the rise started, which it was bound to do sooner or later.

So I waited and watched. Still nothing. Somewhere under that quiet surface teemed dozens of fat rainbows, but they wanted nothing to do with us that hot afternoon.

"Maybe I ought to go find Tim and then go find a cold beer, or at least a wet one," I thought. We could return later when the cool of evening would overwhelm this sweltering August afternoon.

I stayed, though, not really watching the wa-

ter so carefully now. To move would have been utterly laborious at that point. A small lodgepole pine offered what little shade it could muster and I sat there, propped against that little tree flicking away an occasional ant and wondering for the umtieth time whether, given the choice, I would take a brutally hot day like this one or a bone-chilling afternoon during January—a pointless debate really, since I'll take whatever kind of day gets me outdoors.

Twigs snapped to my right and I looked over my shoulder to see Tim, shoulders slumped, trudging through the tall grass.

He didn't see me until I mumbled, "God damn hot."

Wiping beads of sweat off his brow with a bare arm, Timmy just sighed, the long, hot walk down the bank obviously having taken its toll on him. "Too hot," he finally agreed.

"You got that right," I replied, "seen any fish moving?"

He'd seen about as many as me, meaning none. He pulled up a nearby rock and just sat their for a time, watching the river meander by ever so silently. Those buzzards still circled high overhead. I offered Tim the last drop of water from my canteen. "We could go fish the lake," Tim suggested half-heartedly.

"Yeah, or maybe we could go drag nymphs through the riffles."

We did neither. Instead we just sat their, watching the river and sweating. Nothing stirred and the day just kept getting hotter. What little shade we found proved no match for a cloudless blast-furnace of a day. With every drop of sweat we lost a little of our usually abundant enthusiasm.

"How about a beer," Tim offered after a while, "We can come back later."

Sounded reasonable to me. Laboriously we shouldered our gear and lumbered over to the trail that ran along the river's bank just in time to see a single, gulping rise at mid-river. Another rise followed, teasing us; tempting us. Neither of us said a word. None needed saying.

"I'll buy the first round," I said finally, as we turned our backs and shuffled through the unwavering grass towards the cars.

Appendix:
Notes On Tying and Buying Flies

Sooner or later, most serious spring-creek anglers begin tying their own flies. We used to do so out of necessity as the flies we relied on most were never readily available anywhere except in a handful of destination fly shops. Things have changed in that regard. With the success of large commercial tying companies like Umpqua Feather Merchants and McKenzie Flies (whom import most of their flies) and the growth of domestic commercial tying, virtually every fly shop is well stocked with high quality, effective trout patterns, including spring-creek flies.

When you peruse the fly bins in search of spring-creek flies for that upcoming trip, pay close attention to the relative sparseness with which each fly is dressed. Sparse patterns generally outfish their over-dressed counterparts. For example, look through a bin of several dozen PMD no-hackle duns. In many cases, you will notice a distinct range of body sizes per each hook size: Perhaps they are all No. 14's, but some have bodies fat enough for a No. 12 hook; others feature bodies thin enough to fit a No. 18 hook.

When in doubt, err on the side of sparsity. This is especially important where small flies are concerned: An over-dressed No. 20 blue-winged olive looks nothing at all like the real insect.

Many shops sell flies with the barbs already squeezed flat. If you find this not to be the case, you might ask an employee to pinch the barbs off your flies before you leave the store. Certainly you can handle this task yourself with a pair of needlenose pliers, but we all break a few hooks off accidentally in the process of de-barbing a batch of tiny flies and you might as well let the fly-shop employee bear the blame. During my fly shop days, I made a habit of offering to pinch barbs down for customers. If I made a mistake, I replaced the fly at our expense. If the customer breaks the hook off while astream, he or she has little recourse (and likely that will be the only fly that would have taken a trout.)

If and when you tie your own spring-creek flies, still bear in mind that sparsity is a virtue. So too is hook strength, which is why I prefer Partridge wet fly hooks (Code L2A) for No. 14 through 18 patterns. Partridge does not make these hooks smaller than No. 18, so for No. 20 and 22 patterns, I use the Partridge L3A (Captain Hamilton Dry Fly) and for No. 24-26 flies (on those rare and unfortunate occasions when such ridiculous sizes are appropriate), I use either Partridge's Vince Marinaro Midge Hook (Code K1A) or Mustad ring-eye dry fly hooks.

When I tie floating patterns, I treat the fly with floatant during the tying process by working Gink or a similar floatant into the dubbing. This procedure saves time on the stream, although I generally apply another coat if circumstances allow (e.g. if the hatch hasn't started yet or if darkness is not yet threatening).

Further Reading

Selective Trout, by Doug Swisher & Carl Richards; Nick Lyons Books, 1971

Fly Fishing Strategy, by Doug Swisher & Carl Richards; Nick Lyons Books, 1975

The Caddis and the Angler, by Larry Solomon and Eric Leiser; Stackpole Books, 1977

The Complete Book of Western Hatches, by Dave Hughes and Rick Hafele; Frank Amato Publications, 1981

Fishing Yellowstone Hatches, by John Juracek & Craig Mathews; Blue Ribbon Flies, 1992

Fly Patterns of Yellowstone, by John Juracek & Craig Mathews; Blue Ribbon Flies, 1987

Flies: The Best One Thousand, by Randle Scott Stetzer; Frank Amato Publications, 1992

Flies for Trout, by Dick Stewart & Farrow Allen; Mountain Pond Publishing, 1993

The Art of Tying the Nymph, by Skip Morris; Frank Amato Publications, 1993

Mayflies, the Angler and the Trout, by Fred Arbona; Winchester Press, 1980

Tying and Fishing Terrestrials, by Gerald Almy; Stackpole Books, 1978

Western Streamside Guide, by Dave Hughes; Frank Amato Publications, 1987

Fishing the Midge, by Ed Koch; Freshet Press, 1972

Caddisflies, by Gary LaFontaine; Nick Lyons Books, 1981

Tying the Swisher/Richards Flies, by Doug Swisher & Carl Richards; Stackpole Books, 1980

Emergers, by Doug Swisher & Carl Richards; Lyons & Burford, 1991

Index